BEFORE THE OIL RAN OUT

Britain 1977–86

Ian Jack

SECKER & WARBURG
LONDON

First published in England 1987 by
Martin Secker & Warburg Limited
54 Poland Street, London W1V 3DF

Copyright © 1987 by Ian Jack

The Author and Publisher are grateful to the following for
permission to reproduce material: *English Journey*, J. B. Priestley,
William Heinemann Ltd; *Collected Poems*, John Betjeman,
John Murray (Publishers) Ltd; *Brideshead Revisited*, Evelyn Waugh,
A. D. Peters & Co Ltd; *The Road to Wigan Pier*, George Orwell, the
Estate of the late Sonia Brownell Orwell; 'The Kingdom' from
Collected Poems, Louis MacNeice, Faber & Faber Ltd.

British Library Cataloguing in Publication Data

Jack, Ian
    Before the oil ran out: Britain 1977–86.
    1. Great Britain – Social conditions – 1945.
    I. Title
    941.085'8   HN385.5

ISBN 0–436–22020–2

Set in 11 on 13 pt Lasercomp Times by
Richard Clay Ltd, Bungay, Suffolk
Printed and bound in Great Britain by
Billing and Sons Ltd, Worcester

CONTENTS

Preface

My wife is Indian. Soon after we got married she moved from Delhi and we began to look for a house in London. Neither of us could drive; for several weeks we took buses and trains around the northern and eastern reaches of the city to look at undistinguished and therefore affordable property. The prices, even so, seemed steep – £35,000 for a spartan piece of Victorian terrace with dry rot in the beams and shilling-in-the-slot gas meters on every floor. I pined for a flat-fronted Georgian home – astragals and balustrades – until I finally realised that we would never afford one. My crude sense of domestic aesthetics was expanded and revised downwards to include Victorian bay windows and Edwardian red brick, and the 'original features' which the estate agents promised us lay inside. I gushed obediently over cornices and iron firegrates. But my wife had more basic criteria, unfettered by the cobwebs in the old curiosity shop of post-modernist British culture. 'The light's no good, far too gloomy . . . the street's too noisy . . . the garden faces north.' She paid no attention to the cornicing. 'Why is it,' she asked irritably one day, 'that you attach so much importance to the past?'

That was in the summer of 1979, shortly after Margaret Thatcher's government came to power. At the time I attempted to answer the question in generalities which hinged on a national loss of self-esteem and a lack of faith in the future. Only later did I see that this general nostalgia, the

.mmon currency of television commercials and every poli-
.ical party (bring back the family! bring back full employment!), was underpinned in my own case by a very personal
mourning which I have attempted to describe in the first part
of this book. Most people must have their different versions
of this underpinning. My only excuse for exploring it is that,
as a journalist, I have spent a great deal of the past twenty
years blundering into other people's lives and it seemed time
for me to blunder into my own.

Today, in 1987, that summer of eight years ago now seems
like a bend in the river of recent British history, when the
sluggish (and relatively comfortable) flow of British decline
turned suddenly into a spate of change. Who in 1979 could
have predicted that urban and sometimes lethal rioting would
become an intermittent feature of British life; that quayside
crowds would wave farewell to troopships bound for war in
the South Atlantic; that, on many housing estates, children
would freely barter for heroin? But such scenes are only the
rippling, wayward surface of the tide-rip. The fundamental
current beneath has attacked and refashioned the British
economy, with social and psychological repercussions which
have finally swept away the notion that we are a uniquely
cosy nation whose future can be constructed as a peaceful
continuum of the past. What is surprising now, perhaps, is
that my post-war generation grew up with this idea. An
American academic, M. J. Wiener, has written:* 'Until the
later 1960s the generally accepted frame for the history of
Britain over the previous century was that of a series of success
stories: the bloodless establishment of democracy, the evolu-
tion of the welfare state, triumph in two world wars, and the
enlightened relinquishment of empire.' As Wiener says, this
'happy frame' disguised and distracted us from a darker trend,
the long journey towards 'an economic Sargasso Sea'.

This is a frequently debated subject, and this book is not a
collection of economic journalism. But some statistics are in

* *English Culture and the Decline of the Industrial Spirit, 1850–1980*,
Cambridge University Press, 1981

order. Since the industrial revolution, Britain has paid its way in the world by making goods and selling them abroad. In 1983, for the first time in its peacetime history, the country actually imported more manufactured goods than it exported, to the tune of 2.5 billion pounds. In the period January to November last year that deficit rose to 5.4 billion pounds. Thanks partly to North Sea oil, we have become a nation of consumers rather than producers, de-industrialised but still eager for the fruits of industrialisation. The results include unemployment figures which hover above three million, and a sharp acceleration in the drift of wealth to the south. Money has always tended to move south in Britain, as though it were obeying some immutable Newtonian law, but now it is not just the cream off the top, a case of Bradford profit being spent in Bond Street. The actual generation of wealth has moved south, as well as the spending of it. Between December 1979 and September 1986 the number of people who worked in manufacturing industry declined by almost two million, from 7,053,000 to 5,128,000. Most of the jobs lost were in northern England, the West Midlands, Wales, Scotland and Northern Ireland; in fact ninety-four per cent of *all* jobs lost since 1979 were north of a line drawn between the Wash and the Bristol Channel. This is a new frontier, a successor to Hadrian's Wall and the Highland Line. Above it, wealth and the population dwindle; beneath it, both expand. Of course the division isn't absolute. Glasgow has Porsches and London poverty. Overall, however, it is difficult (I would say impossible) to avoid the conclusion that large parts of Britain and its population now serve no wider economic purpose than the service of themselves. For many people, their link with history – the functions and behaviour, morality and religion of their recent ancestors – has been snapped.

Another American academic, the historian Christopher Lasch, wrote of Reaganite conservatism in 1986:* 'In their implication and inner meaning, these (neo-conservative) individualist values are themselves profoundly anti-tradi-

* *New Statesman*, August 29, 1986

. They are the values of the man on the make, in flight
. his ancestors, from the family claim, from everything
. ties him down and limits his freedom of movement. What
is traditional about the rejection of tradition, continuity and
rootedness? A conservatism that sides with the forces of rest-
less mobility is a false conservatism. So is the conservatism
false that puts on a smiling face, denounces 'doomsayers' and
refuses to worry about the future. Conservatism appeals to a
pervasive and legitimate desire in contemporary society for
order, continuity, responsibility and discipline; but it contains
nothing with which to satisfy these desires. It pays lip-service
to 'traditional values', but the policies with which it is associated promise more change, more innovation, more growth,
more technology, more weapons, more addictive drugs.'

President Reagan appealed to the 'frontier spirit'. His ally
across the Atlantic summoned up 'Victorian values'; while her
popular champion, Britain's largest selling daily newspaper,
the *Sun*, mined a seam of xenophobia and ignorance (*Arab
pig*! *Arab rat*! *Lies Asians told at Heathrow*!) which would have
shamed Gordon of Khartoum and Roberts of Kandahar.

Cut off from history, we rub our noses against the glass of
the museum case. Britain has the largest and most zealous
community of railway hobbyists in the world – and Europe's
most neglected railway system (since 1979 it has lost twenty
per cent of its freight traffic and seventy per cent of its freight
wagons). Also, remembering our old role as the world's greatest trading nation, we love ships. We preserve them, collect
prints of them, elegise them as doughty British artefacts in the
Falklands War – and watch, apparently unconcerned, as our
share of the world's merchant fleet has declined by two thirds
over the past eight years (and may not exist at all by the
Nineties; the British Council of Shipping warns of a future
where ships are 'built abroad, registered abroad, crewed
abroad, managed abroad').

Do we need to destroy the past – to give it the sack, as it
were – before we can build a future? The pieces in this book,
apart from the first and last, were first published in the *Sunday
Times*, whose proprietor, Rupert Murdoch, certainly seems to

believe so. They were written in the nine years before tha newspaper broke sharply with its troubled industrial tradition and flitted one day early in 1986 to picket-proof offices in East London. They are journalism and contain all the scars of the trade; the marks of haste, quick and faulty judgment, jokes that seemed funny at the time. But I hope they give some sense of the decade we have been living through.

It is an oblique view; there are dispatches here from India and southern Africa, but nothing from the miners' strike. It is also a partial view; there is little here from the prospering environs of London's new orbital motorway or resurgent towns such as Cambridge and Winchester. But I am well aware that most people in Britain are better off than they have ever been. According to the Government's annual gazette of statistics, *Social Trends*, the total disposable incomes of British households rose by eleven per cent in real terms between 1980 and 1985. More people own more things than ever before. When Mrs Thatcher came to power, only eighteen per cent of households had tumble-dryers, only forty per cent deep-freezers, only fifty-five per cent central-heating. In 1985 those figures were respectively thirty-three, sixty-six and sixty-nine per cent.

However unequal their distribution, these are not despicable comforts; but are they securely based? In 1986 oil companies drew 2.6 million barrels of oil a day from the North Sea and Britain reached its peak as an oil producer. In the previous year oil taxes had supplied the Chancellor with ten per cent of his budget. Now oil production is moving down the graph. The forecast for this year is 2.4 million barrels a day, for 1990 1.9 million barrels, for 1995 1.1 million barrels. By the early years of the next century – less than twenty years from now – Britain will probably cease to be a significant producer of oil. Some sophisticated (or perhaps Sophistic) analysts argue that this won't be bad, that Britain will be wrenched back to commercial sanity when the value of its currency floats downwards, unsupported by oil. But given the lack of industrial investment during Britain's peak oil years, it is difficult to see what will provide our living.

We may look back then at the present time as the eye of a necessary hurricane which we did well to endure and survive. Or we may remember it fondly, amused by our shock at the trivial levels of urban violence and the small disparities in wealth; nostalgic then for these prelude days, our second Phoney War.

I am indebted to many of my former colleagues on the *Sunday Times* for their friendship, encouragement and ideas. In particular I should like to thank the paper's successive editors, Harold Evans, Frank Giles and Andrew Neil; the editors of its magazine, Hunter Davies, Ron Hall, Peter Jackson and Philip Clarke; and Don Berry, Bobby Campbell, Stephen Milligan and David Robson. I owe a similar debt to Donald Trelford, editor of the *Observer*; John Lloyd, editor of the *New Statesman*; to my agent and publisher, Gill Coleridge and David Godwin; and last and perhaps most to Aparna, my wife.

FINISHED WITH ENGINES

Under the surface of flux and fear there is an underground
movement,
Under the crust of bureaucracy, quiet behind the posters,
Unconscious but palpably there – the Kingdom of individuals.
                          The Kingdom, Louis MacNeice

My father wrote a kind of autobiography in the years before
he died. I have it now beside me in a big brown-paper envelope, a hundred and fifty pages of lined foolscap covered
with the careful handwriting – light on the upstroke and heavy
on the down – which he learned on a slate in a Scottish
schoolroom eighty years ago. He called these pages 'a mixture
of platitudes and personal nostalgia'. Is this mixture any good?
Would you want to read it? I don't know. My father's life
spanned eight decades of the twentieth century, but he met
nobody who mattered very much and lived far removed from
the centre of great events. He was born in the year the Boer
War ended, in a mill town in the Scottish lowlands. A co-
operative society hearse took him to a crematorium in the
same town six months before Britain fought what was
probably the last of its imperial wars, in the Falklands.

He was too young for the Somme and too old to be called
up for El Alamein. He never saw the inside of Auschwitz and
knew nobody who had. He neglects to tell us his role (if any)
in the General Strike. He worked for most of his life as a

I

steam mechanic, though he always used the word 'fitter'; a good one, so I have been told by the people who worked beside him (though that may just have been politeness; I have no real way to judge; naturally as a boy, I regarded him as a genius). Certainly, he was conscientious. He took the problems of work home with him. Drawings of faulty steam valves would be spread on the kitchen table and he would sometimes speak bitterly of his workmates, scowling into his food and exclaiming:

'I told old Tom Ramsden where to stick his overtime!'

'That damned Macdonald! Calls himself a fitter! Took half the morning to take three washers off!'

He did not prosper. He started work as a fourteen-year-old apprentice in a linen mill on five shillings a week and progressed variously through other textile factories in Scotland and Lancashire, into the engine-room of a cargo steamer, down a coal pit, through a lead works and a hosepipe factory. He loved applying for jobs – studying the advertisements, removing the cap from his fountain pen, resting the lined foolscap on a chessboard he had made for himself, writing steadily in an armchair near the fire – and only fate in the shape of unwelcoming managements prevented his moving to jute mills on the Hoogli or a colony of French progressive thinkers in the South Pacific. Instead he ended his working life only a few miles from where he had begun it, and in much the same way; in overalls and over a lathe and waiting for the dispensation of the evening hooter, when he would stick his leg over his bike and cycle home. He never owned a house and he never drove a car, and today there is very little public evidence that he ever lived. I mean by that those symbols of 'continuity' which the British make so much of, items such as tombstones, memorial benches, educational bequests, country property, private copses, ancient colleges, law firms or literary agencies that can be pointed out as 'father's' or 'the family's'. Few of his workplaces survive. The cargo steamer went to the scrapyard long ago, of course, but even the shipping line it belonged to has vanished. The coal pit is a field. Urban grasslands and carparks have buried the foundations of the mills. The house he grew up in has been demolished and replaced with a traffic island. The school which taught him the careful handwriting has made way for a supermarket. In this way, de-industrialisation has disinherited the sons and daughters of the manufacturing classes; a benign disinheritance in many respects, because many of the places my father worked were hell-holes, but also one so sudden and complete that it bewilders me.

Still, there is this 'mixture of platitudes and personal nostalgia' in the brown envelope. But I'm exaggerating the paucity of what he left behind. There was actually *much* more than the contents of the brown envelope. There were books, suits from Burtons, long underpants, cuff-links, shirt armbands, pipes which continued to smell of Walnut Plug, the polished black boots he always preferred to shoes, half-empty bottles of Bay Rum, tools in tool-boxes, shaving brushes, cigarette cards, photograph albums, photographs loose in suitcases, tram tickets, picture postcards sent from seaside resorts and inland spas, Rothesay and Llandudno, Matlock and Peebles. *Here for the week. Weather mixed. Lizzie and Jim.* What a man for collecting! He loved to preserve the moments of pleasure in his life. Even here, interleaved among the foolscap, I find stray pieces of the ephemera he was so reluctant to discard, as though his life and the words that described it required evidence and decoration. Here is a card from the Cyclists Touring Club for the Christmas of 1927, here a bill from the Spring Lodge Hotel (family and commercial) for sixteen shillings and fourpence, here a menu from the mess of the cargo steamer *Nuddea* dated October 12, 1928 (that day's lunch, somewhere in the Tropics, comprised pea soup, fried fish, roast sirloin of beef). And here, a smaller envelope inside the larger one, is a pamphlet on humanist funeral ceremonies; 'when it is desired that no reference should be made to theological beliefs but, rather, to the ethical and natural aspects of human life'. He left no explicit instructions, but the hint is clear enough. He wanted a humanist funeral ceremony, and we only half-obliged. How? Because, by eschewing clergymen we eschewed

3

the ceremony; because we did not stand at the lectern and read aloud from the scraps of card which tumble from this smaller envelope. We didn't, for example, stand up and say:

> I want no heaven for which I must give up my reason and no immortality that demands the surrender of my individuality.

Or:

> Forgive me Lord, my little joke on thee
> and,
> I'll forgive your one big joke on me.

Or even:

> *Out of the night that covers me*
> *Black as the pit from pole to pole*
> *I thank whatever Gods there be*
> *For my unconquerable soul . . .*
> *It matters not how strait the gate*
> *How charged with punishment the scroll*
> *I am the master of my fate*
> *I am the captain of my soul.*

The last is a once-popular poem by the Victorian writer, W.E. Henley. The first may be by Colonel Ingersoll, or Charles Bradlaugh, or J. B. S. Haldane, or any other of those Victorians and Edwardians who challenged Christian theology and whose work my father collected in the volumes of the *Thinker's Library*, little buff books which lined the top shelf of the bookcase, each with a silhouette of Rodin's Thinker on the spine. He had an aggressive belief in non-belief; combative doubt was his religion. So why, after the last smug notes of the electronic organ had died away, did we not stand up and oblige him? Perhaps we hadn't yet discovered the inner of the two brown envelopes, though I think we had. More likely, we felt uneasy about the effect such words would have on the aging people, some of them church-goers, who had gathered at the crematorium. It might have meant a 'fuss', and fusses at all costs were to be avoided. But can that really be the explanation? Did we really throw out W. E. Henley because later, in the privacy of their hallways, hanging up the coats and hats which had protected them from the chill of a Scottish December, some people might say: 'That was a queer thing to hear at a funeral'? No, it can't be. The truth is that a strident proclamation of my father's doubt would have sat strangely out of kilter with the last quarter of the twentieth century in Britain. Who, in this country of the don't-knows, now doubts doubt? It would have been like listening, that day in the crematorium, to the proposition by Copernicus that the earth moved round the sun. It was an oddity that we simply tidied away, in a performance as neat and short as the curtains which, operated by some electronic device, swing silently together and close the view of the coffin as it rolls smoothly towards the gas jets.

I was born in 1945 and grew up in the Scotland of the Fifties. There is a conventional shorthand picture of this decade. It includes Suez and Harold Macmillan saying that we had never had it so good; rock-and-roll and an emergent youth separatism; Richard Hoggart and belated celebrations of the working-class; and English films which, whenever they wanted to convey a sense of obscure lives lived in humble homes, tacked to their soundtrack the noise of distant goods trains. We ourselves lived close to a railway line and today I recognise the last as a crude attempt at social realism. As to the rest of the picture, it undoubtedly tells a story. The people of Britain move steadily from austerity towards affluence. Average Britons become better fed, better housed, better paid. The idea of empire gets a fatal knock. Mothers buy washing-machines. Youths inspect their pimples in the bathroom mirror and prepare themselves for the long Saturday afternoon of the next decade. I recognise the picture but I can't find myself in it. Some vital element is missing. It lacks a background of the past. Not the immediate past of ration books and swastikas, but something further away, some folk memory of a fall from grace.

In our house we lived with old times; concurrently in the

1910s and Twenties as well as the Fifties. The past sustained us in a physical as well as mental sense. It came home from work every evening in its flat cap and dirty hands and drew its weekly wages from industries which even then were sleep-walking their way towards extinction. As a child I lived with a man, my father, who embodied it and spoke of it continually; so much so that for me the past sometimes seemed inseparable from the present. Sometimes, however, it did not. From quite an early age I sensed that my father was at odds with his surroundings, that something had gone wrong with his life – and hence our lives – and that I had been born too late to share a golden age, when the steam engine drove us forward and a watchful God still held the helm. Scotland, land of the inventive engineer! Glasgow, the workshop of the world! I hoped the future would be like the past, for all our sakes. I day-dreamed. I drew plans for new railways powered by old breeds of steam locomotive; devised time-tables for Clyde ferries which would burn coal and resume their journeys to long-abandoned piers in remote sea-lochs. Paddle steamers would again slide down the slipways, designed by my Uncle Lindsay who worked in the drawing office of an engine works in Greenock. The people, meanwhile, would be filled with goodness. They would abandon Freemasonry and flee the public houses (both peculiarly Scottish evils, according to my father) and board tramcars for evenings organised by the Independent Labour Party. They would flood out of football grounds (the ruination of the working class, according to my father) and cycle off, with tents, to the Highlands. I imagined these new people in railway compartments, exchanging loco-motive numbers, identifying the seabirds that rose flapping from the fields, taking out their pocket volumes of the *Thinker's Library* and disproving the Biblical miracles we learned at school.

Like many of his generation who had believed and then dis-believed in a Christian God, my father was addicted to the notion of goodness. Its frequent non-appearance grieved him; people should be good. Here is a paragraph from the brown-paper envelope, written of himself and his young fellow tradesmen in the early Twenties:

> We turned to socialism and read voraciously Marx, Jack London, Upton Sinclair and Eugene Sue. We took a great interest in the achievements of Lenin and Trotsky. We intended, and may have succeeded just a wee bit, to make the world a better place to live in. But we expected too much to happen too soon, and we did not realise how heavily the dice was loaded against us.

This links goodness to other ideas – equality, social justice – but in fact I think he liked it equally in the abstract, as a moral force which might one day well up in human souls like water from a burst in an unsuspected mains pipe. He himself wanted to be good and largely succeeded, being kind, honest, hard-working and sober. Lust, avarice, envy – if they existed in him – must have been deeply repressed; though, perhaps the price of this repression, a cantankerous anger would often burst out. He was, I suppose, a model citizen and a model worker (the idea that the socialism of his generation stemmed from the 'politics of envy' is absurd; the politics of innocence, more like). And yet this desire 'to make the world a better place' had its annoying aspect. He could be perverse. He would feel sorry for people. He would frequent musty shops which more sensible customers avoided, because 'Och, I felt sorry for the chap, he's hardly any trade.' He would befriend smelly travellers on buses, because 'Poor Jimmy, he's no' quite right in the head.' He would stop for interminable conversations with sad people – a deformity here, a stammer there – in the High Street of our nearest town, because there was 'no harm in them'. I thought all this subtracted from his dignity and wished myself apart from him, staring sullenly into shop windows or adding up the numbers on the bus ticket.

He had an excellent nose for the forsaken. Suffer little sadnesses to come unto me. In 1956, the summer before Suez, he took us to Aberdeen. It was my first proper holiday and the first evidence, perhaps, of a slightly increased disposable income; all previous excursions had been to the homes of

7

aunts and grandparents. That spring we studied the brochures which declared Aberdeen 'the Silver City with the Golden Sand' and the words 'boarding house' became part of the evening vocabulary. My father chose a name and address and corresponded with the landlady. My mother didn't like the sound of it, she noticed that the address did not carry the distinguishing asterisk which marked the approval of Aberdeen's Town Hall. But my father tutted and persisted: it would be fine, the landlady sounded a nice wee woman. We went by train (an express; high tea in the dining car) and then by bus to a grey suburb in the lee of a headland where the North Sea sucked and boiled. It quickly became obvious that the house was 'off the beaten track', a phrase and a situation which always recommended themselves to my father. It lay a change of buses away from the beach but very close to a fishmeal factory. The smell of rotting fish hung over the street and crept into the house, to slide off the polished rexine of the sofa and chairs but lay permanent grip to the dead collie dog which the landlady had converted into a rug. The whiff of more marine life, cooking in pots, came from the kitchen. We ate boiled and fried haddock for a week and were reminded constantly that Aberdeen was then the premier fishing port of Europe. This was twenty years before the oil came in.

At night I shared a room with a young man who had an institutional haircut and dug for a living in a market garden. Other young men, equally shorn, emerged for the breakfast kippers. Mrs MacPhail, the widowed landlady, had claimed them after they had reached the age limit of the 'special schools' which contained them during adolescence. On the first morning we walked to the lighthouse and stared forlornly across the harbour mouth towards the inaccessible beach. My father said we would just have to make the best of it; the other lodgers were 'decent enough laddies . . . a wee bit simple but hardly proper dafties . . . there's no harm in them.' And there wasn't. On wet evenings the hardly-dafties took me to the cinema, and on the night before we left they gave us a kind of concert in the room with the dog rug. My room-mate, Johnny, sang *If I Were a Blackbird I'd Whistle and Sing*. Another hummed *A Gordon For Me* through a comb and paper. A third placed a favourite new record on the radiogram and again and again we heard: *Zambezi! Zambezi! Zambezi! Zam!* The next morning my father rose at an extraordinarily early hour to pay the bill – he had a terrible fear of missing trains – and surprised the landlady, naked and trying to cover herself with the remains of her pet collie. It was, as my father often remarked later, 'a sight for sore eyes'. He would mention the experience whenever the word Aberdeen looked likely to occur in a conversation, even if others of us, more than twenty years later, had been talking about the oil rigs which were now moored in the firth outside the house, or what would happen to the country when the oil ran out. A story had rescued an ill-fated experiment in holidays from deserved oblivion.

Stories: he was full of them. Eventually they became a family joke. We teased him about them and he laughed at himself. But that was later. In the Fifties he still commanded the family stage. I thought of myself then as the boy with his chin in his hands in Millais' picture, 'The Boyhood of Raleigh', a print of which hung in the front room (the family's reward from the *Daily Herald* for taking out a subscription to the paper in the circulation wars of the Thirties). Relatives and friends would visit on a Sunday afternoon and my mother would bake steak pie and juicy currant slices dusted with sugar. The talk would plunge backwards. The trouble with the past was that there was so much of it. People who had died in the Great War forty years before were discussed as though they lived around the corner. I had missed a great deal. Not only the splendid bright-blue locomotives of the Caledonian Railway and the open-topped trams which had scraped their way through the narrow streets of the nearest town, but also family saints such as Great Uncle Jack, who, despite a wound which would have given him a cosy instructor's job in a base camp, had insisted on returning to Flanders. In his own words, polished as a kind of memorial to him: 'I can't keep on preparing these young lads to be sent out to that Hell.' He was shot in the head by a sniper soon after. A dozen years later, when my father worked down the pit, he met a 'brusher' (an underground labourer) who had known his dead uncle. 'He was a guid lad,' said the brusher, in the West Fife dialect my father did not need to imitate. 'He wad hae geen awa' his ain erse an' shitten through his mooth.' It was an epitaph my father liked, though he always took care to modify the language in front of women and children; 'as thick as ess [ie shit] in the neck o' a bottle' was a peculiar simile it took me many years to untangle.

There were also family villains. Great Uncle Archie, for example, whom God had telephoned one Edwardian morning and sent off to South Africa as a Baptist preacher. His earlier work partly redeemed him in my eyes. He served his apprenticeship in John Brown's yard in Clydebank and there, so my father said, he had helped to build the *Lusitania*. I could never understand why a man should exchange such a fine career, building four-funnelled liners driven by turbines, for the dreary job of telling darkies about the loaves and fishes. But my father had an explanation: 'Preachers only work one day a week and never get their hands dirty.' He came to see us once, in a car, and lived up to all our expectations of him. He thanked the Lord before every filled dish and cup, not only the welcoming steak-pie but also the parting tumbler of cream soda. He showed me how the Bantu shook hands and spoke sonorously about the evils of the cinema; the 'biograph' as they still called it in South Africa, giving me my first clue that his adopted country was a backward place. We surrendered to laughter after his car puttered down the street, though my father instructed us to be kinder. He had a troubling inconsistency when he came face to face with the people we had thought of as his enemies. He said Great Uncle Archie was 'maybe not a bad sort of chap' and we should remember that he was old.

My father never extended such gentle revisionism to his uncle's elder brother, his own father. He flits briefly through the manuscript:

My father, then a comparatively young man of thirty-two or thirty-three years of age, spent quite a lot of time with his pals in the Cottage Inn, and to counteract this attraction my mother would sometimes persuade him to 'bide in the hoose and get the phonograph oot for the bairns.' We had two or three dozen wax barrel records and all of them started off by letting us know that 'this is the Edison Bell Recording Company with . . .' It might be Harry Lauder singing *Stop Yer Tickling Jock*, or it might be *Goodbye Dolly Grey* or *Two Little Girls in Blue*. But whatever it was, it was always a wonderful evening with my father not coming home drunk and sick.

That is his first and last appearance in the only written record of his only son. Even apart from his drinking he was, in my father's view, a sorry specimen of the weakness and ignorance which had stalled the forward march of the working classes. He attended Freemasonic 'smokers' and followed a most unsecular football team, the Glasgow Rangers, whose Protestant supporters upheld the union between Britain and Ireland and cried havoc on the Pope, the priesthood and the Irish Fenians. Also, by the standards of the time, he was lazy. He had given up his trade as a bleacher, but casual labouring jobs in the linen factories did not suit him. His wife, my grandmother, went out and found him irregular work as a caretaker of small Presbyterian churches and branches of Scottish banks. Their marriage had the black and white quality of a Victorian tract. My father worshipped his mother. This is not too strong a verb. My elder brother bought Penguin editions of D. H. Lawrence and once remarked that there was ' a touch of the Paul Morel' about my father's relationship with our grandparents. I didn't understand the reference at the time, but now, reading the manuscript, I think my brother rather understated the position. My father quotes Wordsworth in his mother's memory ('A perfect woman, nobly planned . . . and yet a spirit, still, and bright, with something of angelic light') and constructs an adoring picture of her Christian resolve and domestic diligence – St Joan with a scrubbing brush. She read tea-cups and wrote verse and took out membership of the British Women's Temperance League. Her father had also been a great drinker, first as a sergeant with the British army in India and later as an exciseman in a whisky warehouse in Leith. He died alone and befuddled in a common lodging house; 'acute alcohol poisoning,' said his death certificate. His widow, once a midwife in the army cantonments of the United Provinces, died soon after in a Fife lunatic asylum; 'chronic melancholia,' was the recorded verdict.

People on my father's side of the family seem to have been given an unfortunate option: they either bent too far backward or fell flat on their face. It was a common pattern that once echoed through generations of Scottish family life.

When my grandmother died, in 1955, the chastened victim of her reforming energy came to stay with us. My grandfather had long ago substituted nights in the Cottage Inn with afternoons spent in vegetable allotments, but now he had grown too old to delve. His only ally in life by this stage was pipe tobacco – 'thick black' – which was weighed from jars and brought home in paper bags. He wore a waistcoat with a watch chain and went for long walks in his best suit, smoking. His boots covered seven or eight miles a day and, like my father's, were polished every morning; the first sound of the day after the fire grate had been poked clear of ashes. It was a cramped time, five people and three generations in a small flat, and for a few weeks my grandfather and I slept in the same bed. He was eighty-one and I was ten. He had an odd growth, like a cartoon bump, high on his scalp and I watched it nestle into the pillow at night, after he had folded his suit and tapped out his pipe and climbed carefully under the blankets in his woollen underwear, a soft white body encased in faded cream. He still used the old Scots word 'semmit' for vest. As a boy, he once told me as we lay together on a windy night, he could remember the storm that blew down the Tay Bridge in the winter of 1879. 'It fairly rattled the slates in Glasgow.' But that was the only interesting information he ever divulged, and he left soon after. There had been rows. He was not an easy man to amuse and, games of draughts and dominoes apart, could not amuse himself. Books came with him from my grandmother's, but he had never opened them.

He didn't read. From an armchair he would stare straight ahead, with watery eyes which looked permanently grieved. Only walking seemed to stimulate him, and on country roads where other old folk still walked he would stop and talk intimately to strangers, to complain that his son treated him badly and that he'd be better off with his daughters. The gossip returned to us, as it was bound to do, and he left suddenly one afternoon with his cardboard suitcase. 'Aye, and never come back,' my mother shouted down the outside stair. He never did. He lived for another seven years, six miles away, but I never met him again. Once I spotted him from the top of a bus, walking and smoking through the edges of the town he had known as a young Victorian on the spree. He wore his usual air of remembered hurt. That day I bought my first gramophone record, the Everly Brothers singing *Wake Up Little Susie*, and imagined for a moment that the past was in retreat.

A bridgehead to the present had been established some years before when my brother, eleven years older than me, returned from two years in the RAF with a craze for jazz. He bought a small portable record-player called a 'Disc-Jockey' and played brash and rickety music in the front room. *Hold that Tiger! Oh Play that Thing!* Long-playing records in bright sleeves began to be scattered around the sofa: the Original Dixieland Jazz Band, King Oliver, Kid Ory, Ken Colyer. These were old sounds – my brother was a confirmed New Orleans revivalist who frowned at words such as 'bebop' and 'swing' – but even so my father heard them with alarm. 'Just a damn racket,' he said, 'noises from the jungle.' It was in fact the dance music of his twenties, but he had never frequented dancehalls. Soon arguments broke out and my brother retreated with his machine to the bedroom, where clarinets squeaked and trombones rasped behind a closed door, hushed in their banishment. My father could never be reconciled to music which suggested physical abandon or sex. Syncopation was an American product, like the motor car, and it offended him. He liked melodies with the serene motion of the reciprocating

13

steam engine, and when he counterattacked, and began to buy records of his own, he came home with Kathleen Ferrier and Paul Robeson and the Glasgow Orpheus Choir; songs about home, Heaven and lost love. *Blow the Wind Southerly, Water Boy, Oh Rowan Tree, All in an April Evening.* 'My, that's a bonny tune,' he would say. Sentiment moved him easily. He craved the contemplative melancholy of old Europe and struggled against rhythms which led to a loss of self in physical action – jigging bodies somewhere in Africa, fornication in the bordellos of Louisiana.

I was living with a Scottish Edwardian. My friends at school had different kinds of fathers who had worn uniform in the last war and hummed songs by Bing Crosby and Nat King Cole. They padded about in soft-soled shoes rather than nailed boots, smoked Capstan rather than Walnut Plug, drank beer and not cream soda (my father was not a complete teetotaller but a bottle of beer in the house was an event). On Sunday nights increasing numbers of them watched variety shows on television. Until I was seventeen we stayed loyal to the wireless, though even here I grew fretful in my father's cause and prayed that every edition of *Family Favourites* would contain melodies my father liked. Oh God, give us the *Barcarolle* from the *Tales of Hoffman, Nymphs and Shepherds* sung by the Manchester Girls Choir, or on the 'at stand in the 'all, *the Biggest Aspidistra in the World.* Please do not send too much Vera Lynn. The wailing of *The White Cliffs of Dover* would have him spitting in disgust.

It was around this time, thirty years ago, that I decided he was too good to live. The present was too inimical, he was beleaguered by too many enemies: the Wolseleys and Austins that sometimes threatened to crowd us off the road as we went off together into Fife on our bikes; my brother's unwavering commitment to Basin Street; a new kind of fitter on the shop-floor, 'you can scarcely trust them wi' a chisel ... thick as ess in the neck o' a bottle.' I became terrified that he would die, and every evening for a few weeks, or perhaps months, I would run down the hill and stand by the war memorial and wait for him to come freewheeling round the corner with his cycle-clips pinned over the trouser bottoms of his boilersuit. He was never late – he wasn't likely to be waylaid by pubs – but I was sometimes over-anxious and early, and would pass the time watching the trains which rattled overhead, across what had once been called 'the Eighth Wonder of the World'.

Our village lay at the northern end of the Forth Bridge, three large cantilevers which had been built with great technical ingenuity, and at some cost in human life, to carry the railway one and a half miles over the Firth of Forth. The village without the bridge was unimaginable. Its size reduced everything around it to the scale of models; trains, ships, the village houses, all of them looked as though they could be picked up and thrown into a toy-cupboard. The three towers rose even higher than our flat, which stood in a council estate 250 feet above the sea. On still summer mornings, when a fog lay banked across the water and the foghorns moaned below, we could still see the top of each cantilever poking up from the shrouds; three perfect metal alps which, when freshly painted, glistened in the sun. It was opened by Albert, Prince of Wales, in 1890. Postcards sold in the village post office still described it as the world's eighth wonder and went on in long captions to describe how it had been built. More than 5,000 men had 'laboured day and night for seven years' with ingredients which included 54,160 tons of steel, 740,000 cubic feet of granite, 64,300 cubic yards of concrete and 21,000 tons of cement. They had driven in 6,500,000 rivets. Sixty workers had been killed during those years, some blown by gales into the sea and drowned, others flattened by falling sheets of steel.

For several decades the bridge dazzled Scotland as the pinnacle of native enterprise, and then slowly declined to the status of an old ornament, like the tartan which surrounded its picture on tea towels and shortbread tins. People of my father's generation had been captured by its splendour and novelty. Pushing his bike as we walked together up the hill, he would sometimes say ruefully: 'I became an engineer because I wanted to build Forth Bridges.'

My father began his apprenticeship in 1916 in one of Dunfermline's many linen mills. The town was famous for the quality of its tablecloths and sheets – 'napery' used to be the generic word – and ran along a ridge with a skyline spiked by church steeples and factory chimneys. The gates of my father's first factory were only a few hundred yards from his home. He writes:

> The first year . . . I spent as the familiar of one Thomas Thomson, the oiler. Auld Tammy, he'd be about sixty, was a very conscientious workman, a dour Presbyterian, an elder of the church, and had such a determined nature that he sometimes bit through the stem of his clay pipes. I can see him now marching home from church on Communion Sunday all dressed up with his tile hat and claw-hammer coat, resembling, more than anything else that I know of, a black beetle just about to open its wing-cases.
>
> His antagonist in religious matters was Sam the watchman, also an elder of the church. We started work at seven o'clock and it was our custom every morning to spend ten or fifteen minutes before starting time in Sam the gatekeeper's lodge, where on Monday mornings a most edifying discussion would take place, usually on religious orthodoxy. If Sam liked the minister's 'subject maiter' (of the sermon of the day before) then Tam was bound to be 'mair takkin up wi' his deleevery'. And vice versa.

He describes the factory:

> There were over 700 looms weaving everything from narrow huck-a-back towels to very wide double-damask tablecloths, and, as the pattern of every cloth depended on the jacquard, each loom would be controlled by one to six machines. The jacquards were in three capacities, 'four-hundreds', 'six-hundreds', or 'nine hundreds', and could be single-lift single-cylinder, double-lift single-cylinder, or 24 and 32 row self-twilling machines. They were fixed on pine beams ten or twelve feet above floor level . . . and the 'iler laddie' [himself] was expected to jump from one beam to another, which could be four or five feet away.
>
> We oiled and greased and greased and oiled . . . pirn winding frames, bobbin winding frames, cop winding frames, overpick and underpick looms, dobbie machines, beetles, calendars and

shafting. There was never an end to shafting! A main shaft approximately 250 feet in length driving 32 wing shafts of an average length of 75 feet. This was all underfloor ... and eight of these wing shafts had to be oiled every day when the engine stopped for the mill dinner-hour.

Later he moved to the blacksmith's shop, where he made 'hoop iron box-corners' for the packing department and learned how to handle a hammer and chisel. 'Chap [chip] man, chap!' said the blacksmith. 'Ye couldnae chap shite aff an auld wife's erse.' Eventually, towards the end of his apprenticeship, he was transferred to the engine house:

> Sometimes I would be allowed to attend the mill engine for a week or a fortnight. It was a Watt type double-beam steam engine with two independent cylinders, 36-inch diameter pistons, a six-foot stroke and a speed of 85 revolutions per minute. After draining and regulating the supply of steam to each cylinder, what a satisfying feeling it was to watch the beams see-sawing and the cranks revolving to the rhythmic up-and-down stroke of the piston rods carrying the parallel motion. (The chief attraction of the steam engine seems to be the regular speed of the cranks' rotation in relation to the variable speed of the piston as it sweeps the cylinder.)
>
> Then, taking diagrams from each cylinder with an old Richards Indicator, and studying the cards, I felt just as a doctor must feel when sounding his patient's lungs with a stethoscope. If the cards were all right and the beat of 85 revs per minute had become automatic listening, then I could relax, and as smoking was just tolerated in the engine house, have a Woodbine. It is said that the ratio of the unpleasant to the pleasant experiences in life is as three to one. The engine tenting [tending] was one of those pleasant intermissions.

Reading this, I try to construct a picture of my father thirty years before I knew him. There he sits smoking a Woodbine next to the cascading, burnished cranks of the mill engine. I know from snapshots that he has curly black hair and a grave kind of smile. Perhaps he's reading something – H. G. Wells, a pamphlet from the Scottish Labour Party, *The Rubáiyát of Omar Khayyám* – and memorising passages for the commonplace book he has started to keep. *Tis all a chequer-board of nights and days / Where destiny with men for pieces plays.* The engine pushes on at eighty-five revolutions per minute. Shafting revolves in its tunnels. Cogs and belts drive looms. Shuttles flash from side to side to weave tablecloths patterned with the insignia of the Peninsular and Oriental Line and the Canadian Pacific Railway. Stokers crash coal into the furnaces – more heat, more steam, more tablecloths – and black clouds tumble from the fluted stone top of the factory chimney, to fly before the south-west wind and then to rise and join the smoke-stream from a thousand other workplaces in lowland Scotland; jute, cotton and thread mills, linoleum factories, shipyards, iron-smelters, locomotive works. Human and mechanical activity is eventually expressed as a great national movement of carbon particles, which float high across the North Sea and drop as blighting rain on the fjords and steppes of the underdeveloped peasant nations to the east. Great Uncle Jack has been in his grave for five years by this time. Thomson the oiler still wonders about the exact location of Hell, but my father has come to think of it as placed, quite precisely, as a series of hollows and escarpments in France. He is still a believer, but he has substituted cycling trips for Sunday church attendance. He is out in the morning early and wheeling carefully over the tram lines long before the church bells ring; and by the time they do he has traversed the Fife coalfield, stopped, and brewed tea beside a stream.

To spin past a hatted crowd on its way to church always gave him tremendous satisfaction. 'They'll be listening to the blethers of some minister,' he would say when we rode to-gether in the Fifties, 'while here we are halfway up Glenfarg and watching the sparrowhawks.' He stood apart from crowds – church crowds, football crowds, pub crowds – and watching the sparrowhawks I began to see his life, fancifully, as a long day's excursion on the bike. It would end where it began; a circular progression through fresh countryside towards the dead streets of a Scottish Sunday evening, after the last ice-cream van had gone home. Homework on the table, hymns and palm-court violins on the radio. In a strictly geographical sense this circularity is almost true. At the age of fifty he went back to work in the factory where he'd been apprenticed more than thirty years before. The years between had changed him into the man I grew up with; fattened by my mother's cooking, black hair reduced to strands of silver, an experienced but ill-rewarded maintainer of an old technology for parsimonious managements in bowler hats. The schoolroom notion of history as a series of battles always made sense to me because it replicated my father's own history as I heard (or overheard) it every evening, in the legends of his struggles on the shop-floor. The battle with X of the British India Steam Navigation Company, with Y of Cross's Ltd, cotton-spinners, with Z of the Fife Coal Company. Were these the normal grievances of a skilled man in a country which undervalued skill: or were they fissures to an unspoken core of grief? I was too young to know then, and his manuscript omits most of the anger I remember. It is written by a mellow old man. 'Looking back over my life,' he writes towards the end, 'I find that I cannot grumble.' He has shifted the balance from unpleasant to pleasant experience – to Woodbine time in the engine-house. He writes interestingly of his days at sea, sailing home from Queensland with a cargo of sugar, picking red ants out of his food, listening to the Hindustani of the engine-room las-cars as, two or three to each large spanner, they tighten nuts on leaking valves. Even his year down the pit – Lum-phinnans Number XI, popularly known as 'The Peeweep', the Scots word for the lapwing and its call – is remembered with humour and compassion. During one shift he is stand-ing with a young miner when news comes that the young miner's father has been killed by an underground train of runaway coal tubs; 'the memory of this has stayed with me for a long time.'

He could not stand the pit for long, but jobs became scarcer in Scotland as the Twenties wore on and the economic de-pression deepened. He began to look for work in England. A successful application to a newspaper box-number took him to a cotton mill in Lancashire. Here his memories take on shades of Jess Oakroyd and the Good Companions. He stayed for some months in a theatrical boarding house run by a Mrs Walker, who baked large potato-pies and kept a crowded home:

> We were so crammed up at one time that Mrs Walker slept on the kitchen couch; 'The Yellow Hand' had the parlour all to himself; Mack, Reid, Schofield and I were in the front bedroom; the snake-charmer was in the back; while Mrs Walker's sister had the screened-off bed in the bathroom and a comedian from Fiery Jack's circus slept in the bath.

Other lodgers included a dancing troupe called The Glen Louise Girls, of whom my father kept postcards, signed to him with their love. The Glen Louise Girls were flappers. They wore shingled hair and frou frou frocks and showed the camera a lot of teeth and leg. They were also my first idea of sex; I wished my father had married one. Instead he married a freckled girl from a mining village in Fife, who worked in a linen mill pulling cloth across a table and inspecting it for flaws. They had courted for years, through letters to and from his ship and over sweets shared from cone-shaped paper bags in cinema halls. He describes her lovingly. He came north for the wedding and together they went south, to two bare rooms above an off-licence which my father had improved for his bride with pre-Raphaelite prints – Dante and Beatrice, Ruth and Naomi – and hung above the fireplace a picture of a literary hero, Charles Dickens. Soon they had a son, who died; another, who lived; another, who died; and then, after fifteen years of marriage, a late replacement, me.

I find that I cannot grumble. And yet throughout the Fifties he could and did, without ever once complaining directly about the matter of his two dead children.

My father's return to his old factory in 1952 was a complete accident, the result of yet another letter to an anonymous box-number underneath the words 'Maintenance Engineer Wanted'. It was his tenth move and it brought the family home to Scotland from Lancashire. My mother had fretted to be home among her 'own folk' after twenty-two years among people who called her husband Jock (his name was Harry) and talked of grand weeks in Blackpool. My father hadn't minded Lancashire. He liked to imitate the dialect of the cotton weavers and spinners; it appealed to his sense of theatre, just as the modest beer-drinking and the potato-pie suppers of the Workers' Educational Association sustained his hope that the world might be improved, temperately. The terraced streets shut my mother in, but my father, making the best of it, found them full of 'character'; men in clogs with Biblical names – Abram, Eli – and shops that sold tripe and herbal drinks, sarsaparilla, Dandelion and Burdock. He bought the *Manchester Guardian* and talked of Lancashire people as more 'go-ahead' than the wry, cautious Scotsmen of his childhood. Lancastrians were sunnier people in a damper climate. They had an obvious folksiness, a completely realised industrial culture evolved in the dense streets and tall factories of large towns and cities. Lancashire meant Cottonopolis, the Hallé Orchestra playing Beethoven in the Free Trade Hall, knockers-up, comedians, thronged seaside resorts with ornamental piers. In Fife, pit waste encroached on fishing villages and mills grew up in old market towns, but industry had never completely conquered an older way of life based on the sea and the land.

Later he would talk of Bolton as though he had been to New York, as a place of opportunity, with witty citizens who called a spade a spade. A Lancashire accent, overheard on a Scottish street, would have him hurrying towards the speaker. Often he was disappointed:

'Do you mind me asking where you're from?'

'Rochdale.'

'Och I'm sorry, I thought it might be Bolton.'

Sometimes he was not. A meeting with a Bolton man might produce half an hour's conversation and a story to tell us at home: 'You'd never credit it. I met a chap up the town this morning whose sister used to serve in Openshaw's the butchers. You mind that girl wi' the cleft-palate who was always laughing?' But my mother winced at the thought of Lancashire drizzle and Lancashire butcher's trays filled with offal, and at the memory of two small bodies which had been buried in Lancashire soil.

We moved. The furniture went by van while we came north by train, behind a locomotive with a brass name-plate; *Prince Rupert*. I was seven. I held a jam-jar with two goldfish, whose bowl had been trusted to the removers, as *Prince Rupert* hauled us over the summits of Shap and Beattock. The peaks and troughs of telegraph wires jerked past like sagging skipping-ropes. Red-brick terraces with advertisements for brown bread and pale ale on their windowless ends gave way to austere villas made of stone. The wistfulness of home-coming overcame my parents as we crossed the border; Lancashire and Fife then seemed a subcontinental distance apart and not a few hours' drive and a cup of coffee on the motorway. Our carriage was shunted at Carstairs Junction and we changed stations as well as trains in Edinburgh. Here English history no longer provided locomotive names. We had moved to new railway territory with older and quainter steam engines named after glens, lochs, and characters from the novels of Sir Walter Scott. At dusk we sped across the Forth Bridge behind an Edwardian machine called *Jingling Geordie*, rushing past our new home and on towards the small shipbuilding town where my mother's father – the grandfather I always preferred – had settled.

He met us on the platform. Nobody kissed and nobody touched (we never did; did anybody there, then?), but my grandfather was pleased to see us. 'Come in, come in, you'll be hungry.' A refugee from the pits and now retired from his later work as a rivetter's labourer, he lived as widower at the top of an old house with crowstep gables and a pantile roof. Plates of chips and mutton-pies arrived at the table. The gas mantle was lit – plop! – while my mother took a torch and led me downstairs to the outside lavatory. Then I dozed on a makeshift bed as my parents talked about their journey, idly and endlessly as adults always did.

'Thon was a queer-like chap who got on at Preston. Him and his fancy socks and his meat-paste sandwiches.'

'Och but there was no harm in him. He was a cheery soul.'

'The English are great ones for their meat-paste, right enough.'

When I awoke the next morning rivetters were already drilling like noisy dentists in the local shipyard, and express trains drifted, whistling, along the embankment next to the sea. The smells of damp steam and salt, sweet and sharp, blew round the corner and met the scent of morning rolls from the bakery. Urban Lancashire could not compare with this and, like my mother, I never missed it. But what was linear progress for a seven-year-old may have been the staleness of a rounded circle for a man of fifty, and this little industrial utopia of my childish eye – rivets, trains, rolls, the passive geniality which once marked the people of northern Britain – had foundations which were already rotting. Two days later we moved a few miles down the coast and into our home beside the Forth Bridge, and my father went to work in his new-old factory. It was a shock:

The scrap merchants were at work; they had removed most of the looms and machinery from the old weaving shed, which made it a most cheerless place. The blackbirds were nesting in the old jacquard machines. All the beam engines had gone and the surface condenser on top of the engine house in the mill road was now standing dry and idle. The latest engine [installed in 1912] was a marine-type compound; it was also standing idle with the twelve ropes still on the flywheel. The engine packing and all the tools were still in the cupboard, the indicator, all cleaned, lay ready to take diagrams, there was even a tin of Brasso and cloths for polishing the handrails. It seemed as if everything was lying in readiness for an unearthly visitor to open the main steam valve. But there was no steam, everything was cold and silent . . .

The fitting shops had an unworkable steam hammer and an old-fashioned slotting machine, dated 1851. But one of the old beam engine houses contained a decent ten-inch centre lathe, a good little milling machine, welding equipment etc, which enabled us to cope with the breakdowns, which were varied and plentiful . . . The toughest job of all was adapting the old-fashioned single-lift jacquard to work *à la* Heath Robinson in combination with the modern Swiss looms. Notwithstanding the somewhat interesting work, the mill really had a very depressing effect on everyone. It always seemed to me like a locomotive lying on its side with the boiler burst but the wheels still turning.

The views from our new house were astounding. On the day we moved in, in October, 1952, I stood at the top of the outside stair and watched a procession of trains crossing the bridge and a tall-funnelled cargo steamer passing below. Unladen and high out of the water, its propeller flapped playfully with the river at the stern. The view south ended with the Pentland Hills, the view east with Berwick Law and the Bass Rock, two bumps on the horizon of the North Sea. Pressing my nose against the front-room window and squinting to the left I could see Edinburgh Castle and the gas-works at Granton. Straight ahead, a mile and a half across the Firth, stood the whitewashed inn where David Balfour had been kidnapped in Robert Louis Stevenson's *Kidnapped*. In Lancashire all we could see from our windows were back-gardens and washing and more houses like our own, with all the doors painted in council green. My parents' phrase, 'moving up home to Scotland', took on a literal meaning. It was as though we had been catapulted from a pit bottom into daylight.

But there were drawbacks. Our new house was a top flat in a small street which had been built as part of a slum-clearance project in the Twenties (slums are not just an urban phenomenon; the street's original tenants came from a tumble-down collection of buildings on the shore known as the Lazaretto, an old leper colony, long deprived of lepers). My father insisted that it hadn't been built well. Like all Scottish houses made of brick rather than the traditional stone – which by the late Fifties meant most Scottish houses – its walls had been rendered with sand and cement and then covered with pebble-dash, to conceal and make weatherproof the crumbling products of Scottish brickworks. This worked; the rain and wind were kept out. But a kind of internal weather roamed around the flats, through partition walls and floorboards and down chimneys. If a south-west breeze rose above moderate on the Beaufort Scale, smoke from our fire would billow back into the living-room. The smell of frying leaked through the chimney breast from the flat below. In the evening the sound of Scottish country dance music and the football results rang through the floorboards from the same source.

'Stenhousemuir Nil, Alloa Athletic Nil.'

'And now and for the next thirty minutes the music of Jimmy Shand and his band.'

Our own wireless, its dial unlit, stood silent and pious in the corner.

The Davidsons downstairs were naturally noisy. They smashed firewood and coal on the kitchen floor with an elderly axe-head, and roared at their pet mongrel, Rover. They spat great streaks of phlegm on our shared concrete path. They were not quite right in the head. One boy had been sent to an asylum – some in the village called it 'the laughing academy' – after he interfered with the railway line and nearly derailed a Sunday school excursion bound for Perth. Another learned cobbling in a special establishment. Their father and mother had separately run off. On Saturday nights their grandfather got drunk and was towed by Rover up the hill from the pub. Doors crashed shut, frying pans overturned. My father's patience with 'folk who were a wee bit simple' showed signs of exhaustion. He would invert a brush and thump the handle on the linoleum. 'Give us some peace for Heaven's sake.' And in the silence that followed, if it followed, he would recall our house in Lancashire, built of glistening Accrington brick, and our neighbours there; good quiet people whose only fault was their gullibility regarding Winston Churchill –'good old Winnie,' they said – whom my father loathed for all kinds of reasons, starting with the seige at Sidney Street, which only later became more widely fashionable.

I grew up too influenced by his capricious and sometimes heretical dualism. The universal battle – good versus evil, Christ versus anti-Christ – whick took up mornings in Sam the gatekeeper's lodge had been outflanked inside my father's head by the doubts contained in the *Thinker's Library*, but that manoeuvre had not removed the need for material certainties. Slipping from the Rock of Ages, he clung to a group of lesser boulders: a wide range of prejudices and mini-bigotries which included heroes from history, toilet articles and rival makes of bicycle. He could adopt a firm position on

25

the most trivial question. For headaches he swore by Anadin; for washing a strange blue soap, fiercely antiseptic, called Neko. He would trawl through chemists' shops in pursuit of once-popular patent medicines – Sanderson's Throat Specific was one – and sometimes return triumphant with two years' supply. For him, rarity equalled efficacy and value. Longevity of manufacture gave products an extra cachet. We stuck to pink toothpaste when white was in fashion, to tin Hornby trains when they looked endangered by the cheaper plastic models of Triang. The advertising line 'accept no substitute' was invented for him. He accepted no substitute for Duncan's chocolate gingers, Bassett's liquorice-allsorts, Mitchell's 'American' cream soda, Ogden's Walnut Plug tobacco. Every Christ had an anti-Christ in this world of consuming passions. I thought then – perhaps still think – of the world as easily divisible into eclectic lists of good and bad.

Good	Bad
Robert Burns, ploughman poet, believer in universal brotherhood	Sir Walter Scott, would-be aristocrat, eventual bankrupt
Amundsen, sensible Norwegian who took dogs and reached the South Pole first	Captain Scott, English gent who took ponies, came second, died
The Raleigh bicycle	The BSA bicycle
Anadin	Aspro
Cornets, leather boots	Saxophones, suede shoes
Great Uncle Jack	All wars, especially the First World War

Many of these were not popular options and for a time at school I basked in my father's perversity, wheeling around as the playground Messerschmitt to my classmates' Spitfires. But there were other and less satisfying reasons for a sense of difference. I had buck-teeth. Bigger children shouted after me: 'Hey, buck-teeth, buck-teeth, buck-teeth.' Even smaller children and girls did it, from a safe distance, so that I ran around the streets after them like an over-teased animal, flushed, hysterical and frustrated. I could find no redeeming example of what later became known as a role-model; buck-teeth people in comics and films were sometimes brainy ('Hi, Prof') but always risible. Even today I find it hard to forgive Walt Disney for his buck-toothed hound called Goofy.

One night, sobbing in bed, I heard my father muttering behind the door to my mother.

'We'll have to teach the laddie to box.'

My father had boxed in his youth, around 1916. He spread on the floor a sheet the size of a miniature boxing ring and for several nights we capered about in our socks and vests. 'Stick up your fists . . . now keep your left near your face and swing with your right.' It was no good. What I needed was an eight-year-old's equivalent of bayonet drill, fierce lessons in kicking and accurate stone-throwing, and what saved me in the end was dentistry rather than the Queensberry Rules. My mother took me to the dental hospital in Edinburgh where a man with a bow tie, the first I had ever seen outside the *Beano*, examined my teeth and seemed quite tickled with them. He called to other people in white coats, students I suppose, and they too appeared interested and pleased. I was a classic case. Plaster was poured into my mouth, I was told to bite, and a mould was made. Two weeks later I had a brace of pink plastic with a steel band. I wore it every night for years and got mornings off school to take the train to Edinburgh for monthly inspections. We travelled in steam-heated carriages with leather window straps and water-colour prints of British landscapes above the seats, pulled by locomotives with absurd names: *Wandering Willie, Jingling Geordie* again, *Luckie Mucklebackit, Roderick Dhu, The Laird O' Balmawhapple*. The train stole into Edinburgh through tunnels, then below a large monument to Scott, the bankrupt novelist, and finally into a station called Waverley after his novels. I lived among romantic fictions and demanded facts.

'Who was Jingling Geordie?'

'He wasn't real. Walter Scott made him up.'

'Why did he jingle?'

'You'll have to ask your father.'

But my father, like most people, had never read Scott and didn't know. Instead he would take out Burns from the bookcase and read aloud 'The Twa Dogs' or 'Holy Willie's Prayer'.

Often a chill mist hung over Edinburgh's streets and we would climb up frosted steps and through dark passages towards the disinfected warmth of the dental hospital. Always, the man in the bow tie was pleased: my teeth were making excellent progress, backwards. Eventually a new mould was made and held before me so that I could compare it with the original. At the age of eleven I was pronounced cured. Nobody at secondary school knew me as buck-teeth and the catcalls from my old enemies in the village died away. Some people may remember the early Fifties for the Korean war or the Coronation or the first erratic flights of the Comet, but I remember them for a triumph of dental science and receding teeth. Life could be altered; make an effort and one could almost be the same as everyone else.

Is living inevitable? Would everyone I knew always do it? I used to wonder about those questions and reached an early decision; the correct one, no. Two photographs in my parents' bedroom proved it. I learned not to mention them. One in a frame on the dresser showed a sepia baby in a white woollen hat; that was my brother George. The other, hung on the wall, showed a schoolboy tinted pink and blue; that was my brother Gordon. George had died before he was a year old, Gordon at the age of seven. I knew little about them. George had died too young to be the subject of interesting anecdotes and Gordon only occasionally sailed through adult conversation like a ghost overhead. The ghost had been bothered by asthma; he could do handstands; he took after my mother's side of the family. One evening, when we still lived in Lancashire, my father sat me on the back of the family tandem and we cycled across the town to a blackened gothic building which was the parish church. This for me was a new sight. Our usual itinerary included fish and chip shops, the houses of friends, parks, railway cuttings and canal banks, but rarely churches. Why were we here?

My father said: 'We've come to see where Gordon is.'

We went into the graveyard. I think I expected to see boy in the photograph leap from behind a tombstone l Magwitch. But there was nothing. My father pulled weeds from a patch of ground and looked preoccupied. Then an iron gate scraped shut and we pedalled home. My father told my mother about what we had seen. Sad voices in the kitchen:

'The weeds are thriving. Nobody seems to bother.'

'It's eight years ago now. Time flies.'

I never saw the grave again.

The morbidity came later. Individuals are like civilisations; they never entirely vanish unless they are very poor, or, like George, very young (and even he has his photograph). I knew our small house contained secrets. When my father was at work and my mother went out shopping I became a domestic archaeologist, digging through cupboards and drawers for evidence of an earlier way of life. I made several interesting discoveries: a large rubber contraceptive kept in a cardboard box and dusted with the kind of chalk found in puncture repair kits; a pile of magazines called *Health and Efficiency* which showed women completely nude; and then, underneath the sheets in the linen chest, a layer of toys and books which had belonged to Gordon. He had died in the middle of the war. Crude pencil drawings in scrapbooks showed warships firing at fighter aircraft. A comic featured a character called Musso the Wop. I pored over the *Radio Fun* annual and wished I had heard Tommy Handley, and the gang in *Happidrome*.

But this dying business scared me and I became obsessed by it. If it could take away a boy who liked *Radio Fun* and drew Spitfires so badly, was anybody safe? I saw myself as a likely target and began to work out when death would strike, measuring its progress through the family on different principles of incidence which gave me different results. These are the most vital arithmetical calculations I have ever made. If, for example, *age at death* was the principle then six years separated George and Gordon and, by an extension of the same interval, I could expect to reach thirteen. But if *date of* death was the principle then the outlook was considerably bleaker. My brothers had, I thought, died twelve years apart, the younger in 1943. That gave me until 1955. This year, next month, tomorrow even! I began to look for signs. The phrase 'Tropic of Cancer' stood out ominously in the school atlas. I perked up when adults mentioned atom bombs. One day, sitting on the station steps and looking out for old favourites – *Jingling Geordie, Luckie Mucklebackit* – I glanced south and imagined a mushroom cloud sprouting from behind the Pentland Hills.

In fact, my arithmetic was wrong. Ten years and not twelve separated my brothers' deaths, and I should have died in 1953, shortly before Everest was conquered. As 1955 progressed, death flew out of my mind, returned briefly with my worries about my father, and then vanished for a quarter of a century.

It turned out to be the year of the wonderful summer. For weeks the Firth of Forth stretched out blue and smooth below an unusual heat. I learned to swim in the sea and turned brown; the last traces of a Lancashire accent disappeared; my teeth were firmly on course to the vertical. I made friends and influenced people. In the long evenings we played street games and went whooping through the whin bushes on the hills, disturbing sailors and local girls who were exploring private parts in what they imagined were private places. An American battleship arrived and anchored in the Firth. Disposable versions of the condom I had seen in the drawer drifted on the shore, until the battleship steamed away and was replaced by a beautiful Cunard liner on a cruise round Europe with yet more Americans. The thin rubber flotsam gave way to the spongy husks of half-grapefruits, the flesh of which had been scooped out at shipboard breakfasts. Clearly, Americans lived and ate voraciously.

We were happy. But my father worried that the fabric of Scottish life had coarsened since his boyhood. He had pre-1914 memories of the village as a place of fishermen and ferrymen, and talked about riding to it from Dunfermline as an errand boy on a horse-drawn cart loaded with lemonade. Different kinds of people had come with the two world wars. Poles to the army barracks, Englishmen to the naval dockyard four miles away, Irishmen to carry hods and dig trenches in both. Sometimes the sweet smell of beer vomit filled the last bus home. The old scatological swearing – as thick as ess in the neck o' a bottle, ye couldnae chap shite aff an auld wife's erse – fought a losing battle with duller sexual imagery. Now when boys fought in the street they cried:

'Away, ya cunt.'

'Fuck off.'

'Ya wee hooer.'

And there was worse. One evening, as we walked along the shore to the old Lazaretto, we met Mr McDougall. I expected my father to stop and have one of his long conversations; McDougall was ideal material, a 'character' who'd knocked away some of the foundations of his council house and converted the space into a kind of bunker. A flagpole stood in his garden with a Union Jack fluttering at the top. The locals grinned when they passed this house and called it 'Fort McDougall'. But his children looked anxious and smelled.

'Fine night,' said McDougall on the shore.

My father ignored him and walked on. After a few minutes, he said: 'That man has just come out of Perth prison.'

What had he done?

'He'd been interfering with his daughter. Folk like that should be hung.'

The McDougall girl sat in the front row of my class but 'interfering with' had no more meaning for me than the local newspaper's frequent reports of men charged with 'lewd and libidinous behaviour'. Only much later did I discover that incest was a buried thread in village life, linked to some of the backward children we played with and tormented.

'Go on, Willie, say: *a cup of coffee and a chocolate biscuit.*'

'A cu o cohi anna chohi bihi.'

We chanted cu-o-cohi-chohi-bihi until some men coming

home from work told us to leave Willie alone. We were easily
scared by these people, who left early in the morning with
their old gas-mask satchels filled with sandwiches and
returned in the evening – the day's first sighting of fatherhood
– pushing their bicycles and exchanging pleasantries.

'A grand night for the garden.'

'That's a bitter wind.'

My father washed his hands and sat down to his tea. My
grandmother's plain Scottish cooking, boiled mutton and
potatoes, made him demand 'tasty' food and often his plate
was piled high with chips, baked beans, toast and fried eggs.
Then he might rise and put on his good clothes – suit, overcoat
and polished boots – and, smacking bay rum into his scalp,
run off down the stairs for the train that would take him to a
committee meeting of the Amalgamated Union of Engineers.
More frequently he fell asleep in his chair, to wake after an
hour and 'warm up' the wireless in preparation for a favourite
programme: *Take It From Here* or *Have A Go*, conducted in
the homely Yorkshire tones of Wilfred Pickles. We waited for
the weekly catchphrases:

''Ello, 'ello, 'ello!'

'What's on the table, Mabel?'

'Give 'er the money, Barney.'

He seemed to feel a kinship with Pickles, who was then one
of the BBC's greatest stars. 'He's quite a character,' he would
say. 'He lost a son you know.' My brother groaned theatrically
as the radio audience sang along with the signature tune
('Have a go, Joe, come and have a go') and went off to the
bedroom with Jelly Roll Morton.

I suppose that what all this amounts to is a working-class
childhood. I hesitate, not to fight shy of a cliché, but because I
still can't be sure; whenever I read phrases such as 'working-
class culture' or 'middle-class values' I feel dizzy from sociological abstraction and the need to be steadied by a fact or
two. Was it middle-class or working-class to read the *Eagle*
comic and the *Meccano Magazine*, or to listen to the genteel
Scottish tones of Auntie Kathleen on *Children's Hour*? All of

them evoked a different kind of boyhood lived in a gentler, richer climate where Dads went off to the office and attics housed the model railway. In none of them did downstairs neighbours like the Davidsons scream as unwatched chippans went on fire; none had characters like half-daft Noreen who would take her knickers down for a square of Highland Toffee.

And yet I never felt excluded. I don't think many of my generation did. The paradox can be explained rationally, and has been, and in all kinds of general ways. Britain may be one of the most class-obsessed countries in the world, but Scotland is less so than England; my family were members of the skilled working-class, keen to see their children educated; and we identified with fictional middle-class children because no other kind was on offer. All are generally true, but there was also something more particularly relevant. For all his socialist convictions I don't think my father ever saw social division in purely political or economic terms. He would make ritual attacks on the big local landlords, the Earl of Elgin and the Marquis of Linlithgow, and on people who showed how they 'fancied themselves' by sending their children to piano and elocution lessons ('Aye, but do they have books in the house?'), but it was an older moral force which generated the most genuine heat in him, and the class conflict as I most often heard it expressed was not so much between classes as internal to each of them; it was 'decent folk' versus the rest. This may be a simple social analysis; it was certainly a relevant one. A strict application of socialist theory would mean that our natural allies were the Davidsons (crash, thump; 'Where's ma fuckin' tea?') and that we would be bound to them for life. And bound not only to the Davidsons but also to another heart of darkness in our own family's past; the madhouse, illegitimacy, alcoholism, the chaos and poverty which my father had caught the last whiff of as his family completed their trek through the volcanic industrialism of Victorian Scotland.

The embers of Calvinism, at heart a seemingly narrower philosophy, freed him from class-bound loyalty and gave him

33

broader choice of the good and bad. This is hindsight and may be no more than an over-elaboration of one of my father's favourite concluding statements. *There's good and bad everywhere.* At the time his attitudes simply reflected the adventures of Lord Snooty in the pages of the *Beano*. Every week this classless little Etonian and His Pals would outwit the brutal ploys of the Gasworks Gang. My loyalty to Lord Snooty's side in this conflict was never in doubt; and neither, if he had read the *Beano*, would my father's have been. The Gasworks Gang, after all, lived directly underneath.

And so I never heard my father use 'working-class' or 'middle-class' as terms of approval or disapproval. The categories were far too broad and he liked clearer targets. Throughout the Fifties he took steady aim at the nearest approach to a class enemy: Edinburgh Scotsmen. It was a phrase of denunciation, like *kulak*, *aristo* and *Uncle Tom*. Leeches and perverters of history, off with their heads! Edinburgh Scotsmen didn't necessarily live in Edinburgh but the city symbolised their way of life. It had largely escaped the industrial revolution, its elegant terraces and squares were filled with lawyers, insurance men and generally people who, like Great Uncle Archie, 'did not get their hands dirty' and 'lived off the back of other folk'. They dressed their children in kilts but sent them to public schools based on the English model, where their accents were flattened out. My father said: 'They've sold their birthright for a mess of porridge.' Behind the joke lay a genuine grievance. Edinburgh Scotsmen did not *make anything*, other than wills, and yet it was their romantic and partial notions of Scottish history and Scottish dress which had captured the world's imagination; a Scot became a mean man in a kilt who drank whisky and supported a lost cause. They had 'made a fool out of Scotsmen'. The brightness of their kitsch obscured the dark complexities of a great industrial nation and the lives of people like himself. Or so my father thought, in the days before cranes and tall chimneys joined the clan system and Bonnie Prince Charlie in the pageantry of an old romance.

34

So far as I could see the village contained only one of these class enemies. Mr Huston lived in one of a string of Victorian villas near the station, which had been built speculatively in an attempt to woo commuters across the new bridge from Edinburgh. He wore a kilt and nailed brogues and had no obvious work outside some honorary position in the Church of Scotland. To the tumbrils with him! But once again my father's private hates failed in the face of individual humanity. During the time that I waited for my father to come home from work and was relieved to find him still alive, we would sometimes meet Mr Huston on the hill. He appeared majestically, kilt swaying, brogues sparking off the street like flintlocks, head up, chest out, bright eyes that took in the Firth and the hills beyond and seemed to say: This is God's own country.

My father would stop, pull up the lid of his cap and lean on the handlebars for a moment.

'Fine night, Mr Huston.'

'Grand night for a walk, Mr Jack.'

We pushed on up with the clicking bicycle.

He long outlived my fears for his death and when he did eventually die I didn't fear it so much as wish for it. It was, as many people said, 'a release'. He went on cycling back from his lathe until well into the Sixties. The new decade was good to us both. I left home at eighteen and gladly entered pubs, football grounds and dancehalls, surprising myself by defying ancestral gravity and not falling flat on my face. Films and television plays began to represent British life as we thought we knew it. When *Saturday Night and Sunday Morning*, the film of Alan Sillitoe's novel, came to the local Regal I was thrilled to see scenes of conscientious men working at milling machines and lathes. 'Poor bastards,' says Albert Finney in the role of the new British hero, the young worker who sticks up two fingers at respectability and grabs what he can get.

The film kindled a suspicion within me and for a time I imagined that this was the definitive verdict on my father, apparently a dupe who had worked for washers for nearly

35

fifty years. It was an ignorant, adolescent judgment; my father was not a 'poor bastard' and surprising things began to happen to him. I came home late one Saturday night and found him roaring with laughter at a satire show on television. 'My God, these boys are funny.' He joined the Campaign for Nuclear Disarmament and worked for it long after I, an earlier but more faint-hearted joiner, had left. He won a couple of thousand pounds on the football pools (a total ignorance of football led to the correct forecast; virtue, for once, had its reward) and took my mother on sea voyages to Egypt and the Soviet Union, two countries which had fascinated him since Howard Carter found Tutankhamen's tomb and the Bolsheviks stormed the Winter Palace.

He grew jollier and settled into a new role as a teller of quaint stories rather than bitter homilies against Freemasonic foremen and the unfairness of piece-work.

In 1967 he retired with a present of twenty pounds in an envelope and a determination to enjoy himself. He read books on Egyptology, went to evening classes in Russian, cultivated his garden and watched quiz shows and documentaries on television (satire had a setback when, in 1965, Kenneth Tynan, a perfect stranger, appeared in our living-room and said fuck; at that moment years of ess in a bottle, a lifetime's careful stewardship of domestic language, went for nothing). This is the passage of his life I know least about. We missed our connection somehow. I neglected him, no longer went out with him on the bike, barely listened to the stories I thought he would always be there to tell.

He took a casual job looking after the yachts which now moored at the pier where the ferry had once plied. The owners of this anchorage, 'the marina', behaved in a friendly way and invited him to their wine and cheese party. He talked about the invitation for a week and then declined with a question: 'What would I be doing at a wine and cheese party?'

The village filled up with new people as the old died; wives who wore jeans and loaded small cars at the nearest supermarket, husbands who drove what twenty years before would have seemed an impossible distance to work. Couples gutted old cottages and painted knock-through rooms in white, hung garlic from their kitchen shelves. In these houses the terms 'lunch' and 'supper' supplanted 'dinner' and 'tea', but their owners, searching for a past which could embellish their modern lives, went burrowing into history to uncover village traditions which had been invisible for forty years. The only village celebration of my childhood was the one which marked the Coronation, when New Testaments and children's belts in red, white and blue were distributed. Now an annual gala day was revived, with a bagpiper at the head of the procession, and a 'heritage trail' signposted in clean European sans-serif type as though it were an exit on an *autobahn*. Meanwhile most of the village shops closed and vans stopped calling with the groceries. Steam locomotives no longer thundered up the gradient and on to the bridge. The Davidsons went quiet and then dispersed. Old Huston died, and Edinburgh Scotsmen began to tiptoe out of my father's conversation like crestfallen actor-managers from the stage of an empty theatre.

He gave up reading newspaper stories which told of 'fights to save jobs'. Once he threw down the local weekly in disgust. 'There's nothing in here but sponsored walks and supermarket bargains.'

He cycled still, taking circuitous routes to avoid the new motorways and coming home to despair at the abundance of cars. Usually on these trips he would revisit his past. The Highlands, fifty miles away, were now beyond him, but even in his seventies he could still manage to reach the Fife hills and the desolate stretch of country which had once been the Fife coalfield. He brought back news to my mother. 'Do you mind the Lindsay Colliery? It's all away, there's nothing there but fields.' Factories had gone, churches were demolished, railway cuttings filled up with plastic bottles and rusty prams. My father worried about all this, and my mother worried about my father. There were disturbing signs that my grandfather's genes were bursting out from a lifetime's imprisonment.

'Where have you been, for Heaven's sake?'

'Oh I just got blethering to old Stewart on the hill there.'

He had always liked to argue. Now, more than ever, he liked to remember, partly because he was old and partly because a decent argument had become so hard to find. Dualism was dying out, a belief in anything other than the intimate present became rare. My father, who had spent years attacking capitalism or the Book of Genesis, the reputation of Captain Scott or the Aspro, could no longer find audiences to defend these items. 'Aye, you're right there,' people said, and went away. His old strictures, so radical in their time, such painfully constructed rebuttals of the orthodox, were neutralised by apathy. He made do with a Jehovah's Witness who kept an unsuccessful sweetshop near the shipbreaker's yard. They swopped contradictory texts from the Book of Revelations.

'He sells terrible sweets,' said my mother, wincing at the tartness of an ancient gooseberry crunch and remembering the chocolate gingers of their courtship.

'He's a harmless soul,' said my father.

Once around this time we visited an exhibition of old photographs in Dunfermline, his birthplace. One picture showed a street littered with horse dung and small boys standing in a cobbled gutter; the High Street, circa 1909. My father went up close. 'That's me on the left there. I remember the day the photographer came.' We looked at a boy with bare feet and a fringe cropped straight across the forehead. The photograph and the man beside it were difficult to reconcile. Quite suddenly I realised how old he was. He talked about writing his 'life story' and we encouraged him; for months of evenings and afternoons he sat in the easy chair with the chessboard and the foolscap on his knee, smiling and writing with his fountain pen.

He became, I suppose, like the people he had always cherished; a character. New people, friends of my brother's or of mine, often remarked on leaving him that he was 'such an interesting man'. Like the photograph, he was now of historic concern, and sometimes when I came up from London I expected to find him surrounded by tape recorders and students from the nearest university department of oral history. That did not happen. One day he collapsed into the potato patch he'd been digging. Cancer was diagnosed, eventually, but he never asked for the diagnosis and was never told. For many weeks my mother nursed him as he slipped in and out of pain and consciousness. The pills did not seem to work; he whimpered and cried aloud like an abandoned baby, an awful sound. The doctor decided to change the medication to an old-fashioned liquid cocktail of alcohol, morphine and cocaine. After the first dose he rose bright-eyed from the pillows and saw me, up from London.

'What's yon big lazy bugger doing here?'

Those were his last words to me, or rather about me, and my mother worried that I'd been hurt. 'He's never spoken about you like that before, I don't know what came over him.' We decided that it was bravado induced by alcohol, but I wondered. I remembered all the times I'd failed to help him in the garden; my uselessness with a chisel and saw; and my job, where I never got my hands dirty, or not literally at least. Or perhaps he was simply bored and had decided to liven people up. I wouldn't put this past him, given the circumstances of the first time I ever heard him swear. There's a poem by Sir Walter Scott, commonly invoked by patriots everywhere:

> *Breathes there a man with soul so dead*
> *Who never to himself hath said*
> *'This is my own, my native land!'*

My father, with an enduring distrust of patriotism born in the First World War, had his own version. I heard it as an eleven-year-old at my Uncle Jim's silver wedding anniversary. Our relatives gathered in a tearoom above the Regal cinema and had tea, sandwiches and bottled beer. Mr Shand, who drove locomotives (indeed I'd once seen him on the footplate of *Wandering Willie*), stood up and sang *Some Enchanted Evening*. Applause. Then Uncle Jim obliged with the *The Lullaby of Broadway*. Renewed applause. It was my father's turn. Words suddenly burst out of him:

> *Breathes there a man with soul so dead*
> *That never to himself hath said*

> *When his toe has kicked the bottom o' the bed*
> *'Oh ya bugger!'*

Laughter, looks of confusion from people who didn't know the original, shouts of 'just like Uncle Harry'. I blushed with shame. Later that night, walking up the hill from the last bus, my mother exclaimed: 'You and your poetry! Whatever made you say such a thing?' My father tutted with self-reproach. 'It must have been the beer talking. I was just getting bored with all that daft American nonsense.'

Death can always be depended upon for irony and the magnification of the insignificant. Driving to the crematorium to make the funeral arrangements I thought of the last word I heard him say; not his farewell message to me, but a later request for another drop of a favourite blackcurrant drink. *Ribena.* Accept no substitute; he had been a loyal consumer to the end.

The crematorium was a new building, concrete and glass, which had been built (as my father would have been the first to tell his mourners) near the site of one of the first railways in the world. The moorland to the east held mysterious water-filled hollows and old earthworks, traces of an eighteenth-century wagonway which had carried coal from Fife's first primitive collieries down to sailing barques moored at harbours in the Firth. Here my father had played in the summers before 1914, uncovering large square stones with boltholes which had once secured the wagonway's cast-iron rails. Here also we had gone for walks on Sundays in the Fifties, smashing down thistleheads and imagining the scene as it must have been when horses were pulling wooden tubs filled with coal. The world's first industrial revolution sprang from places such as this; it had converted our ancestors from ploughmen and their wives into iron moulders, pitmen, bleachers, factory girls, steam mechanics, colonial soldiers, and Christian missionaries. Now north Britain's bold interference with the shaping of the world was over. My father had penetrated the revolution's secrets when he went to night school and learned the principles of thermo-dynamics, but as its power failed so had he. His life was bound up with its decline, they almost shared last gasps.

My mother fretted. 'He wouldn't have wanted a minister at the service.' But there was no need to worry. The crematorium's manager was obliging and desperately cheerful. 'No minister, no bother. We can even take the cross down if you like.' The unforgiving essence of Scotland seemed to have been sucked out of the country with a syringe. 'Now what kind of music would you care for? A lot of old miners want *The Red Flag*, that's popular. But you can have anything you want. We had a widow up here a few months back who had *I'm Gonna Wash That Man Right Outa Ma Hair*.'

We settled for favourite tunes: the twenty-third Psalm, *All in an April Evening*. The ceremony lasted only a few minutes. We were out in the cold again before the undertaker's men, leaning on their big black cars, had time to finish their cigarettes. A lot of old men whom I did not know shook hands. 'He was a good man, your father.'

Most of the dead are retrospectively good, of course, but I don't doubt that my father lived up to the word in his lifetime. Still, it is difficult to define his goodness with any exactness and it would be wrong to imply that he possessed more than the usual measure. Christian morality and political utopianism had combined for a time to work potently on the imaginations of his generation, though the older idea tended to defuse the newer; a religion which in its modern interpretation stresses mercy, meekness and obedience may not be the best ally when there are barricades to be stormed. And my father, in his behaviour if not in his ideas, was a very obedient man.

I am thinking of the story of his missing left forefinger. He lost it as a young craftsman, after a fellow worker had taken a swing at a rivet and missed. As a child I would sometimes sit on his knee and feel the stump, intrigued by its unusual softness. I expected to find details of the accident in his manuscript; at least a paragraph, I thought. But there is barely a sentence: 'that same afternoon one of the older fitters knocked half of my forefinger off with a twenty-eight-pound hammer.' The accident has been subsumed into a much more important narrative, which began that morning and ended many years later, or perhaps never ended at all. That morning he had sworn at his gaffer, an elderly, upright man called Tam Davie, whose name my father always spoke with a respect bordering on love. Davie was an old Scottish ironist born in the middle years of Victoria's reign. He dubbed my father 'Snowflake' because his face was always blackened by oil and dust. 'It was Snowflake do this and Snowflake do that.' He endured this as an apprentice, but soon after his apprenticeship was out he gave Davie 'a volley, full blast, four-letter words and all.' Davie was grieved. He said: 'I've given ye three rises without your asking for them and yet ye would speak to me like that.' He threatened to report the bad language to my father's parents. My father was scared. A few hours later he lost his forefinger.

The next day Tam Davie walked across the street from the mill and knocked at the family's door. My father lay upstairs with his bandaged hand and waited for the storm to break. He lived in a stern house which struggled every week to obliterate the shame of my grandfather's Saturday evenings spent in the Cottage Inn. As a child, my father remembered, he had once clambered on to a forbidden wall and then fallen off. As he sprawled yelping on the ground his mother shouted from the back door: 'That's what God does tae bad bairns.' But now no sounds of scolding came up the stairs towards him; Davie, being an averagely decent man, had inquired only about the state of my father's hand. Such humanity! My father writes:

> I was so relieved and got such a good impression of Tam that there was nothing I would not have done for him to try to make amends. I never swore at him again. Four or five years later, when he was forcibly retired, I went round the factory with a notebook and collected over four pounds (a handsome sum in those days) and took him to the Co-operative Furnishing Dept, where he chose an 'uncut moquette' easy chair. He insisted on

having a 'spree' in the Tap Goth.* He said he wanted *all* the young lads to be there and I was to give their mothers his 'solemn promise that Ah'll undertake tae see that nane o' them touches strong drink.' And he did. We had a grand night on lemonade and pies. The older men had their whisky and they *all* gave us a song, every one of them.

I can see them all now. Auld Jimmy the blacksmith, with his long flowing beard, sang *Simon the Cellarer*; the second blacksmith, Jimmy Walls, gave us *Swimming Hard Against Life's Stream*; Johnny Marshall sang 'Oh my, look at the guy / Walking along the street / Oh, where did you get that funny face / Oh, where did you get those feet.' Well, Johnny was no Greta Garbo himself and while one of his feet was away for tobacco, the other was going for matches. But we all had a soft spot for Johnny and his song, and our laughter just about raised the roof. After a few more whiskies and many more songs, Harry Matson gave us *The Bay of Biscay*, and while we were singing *Auld Lang Syne*, Sandy Clarkston was struggling manfully (having had one too many) with the second verse of *Annie Laurie*.

He preserved the memory of this evening for the next half-century. This was perhaps how life should be lived, as a fellowship of the innocent and the well-intentioned who – somehow – had cleansed their souls of greed and aggression; who – somehow – not only produced but also owned the means of production; who – somehow – would free an empire from social and economic oppression but at the same time continue to make tablecloths for the Peninsular and Oriental Line. Gunfire would not be heard. The Winter Palaces of other régimes would fall silently, their occupants decanted into a new moral universe driven by hard work, fidelity, honesty and kindness. The last especially attracted him as an

* The Union Arms or Top Gothenburg, one of a chain of pubs in the Fife coalfield and its fringes run by the Gothenburg Public House Society, which borrowed an unusual idea from Sweden and tried to turn pub customers into teetotallers. The interiors of the society's saloons and bars were deliberately plain and uncomfortable; profits (which the pubs continued, oddly, to make) went towards the construction of wholesome amenities such as libraries and bowling-greens.

idea that might spread through the world like a chain letter. Kindness would repay kindness, *goodness and mercy all my life shall surely follow me.* Was it pure altruism? Would he, like Great Uncle Jack, have carelessly given away his own arse and shat instead through his mouth? No, I don't think so, goodness has its limits; but unintentionally he made a far greater sacrifice. His is the cruellest story.

Whilst serving on the *SS Nuddea*, a maladroit shipmate ('Chubby' was his *nom-de-plume*) was shunned and jeered at by all the other engineer officers. He was a bit of a bungler but I felt sorry for him and occasionally conceded him a little kindness. Now, as a token of his appreciation, he paid us a visit.

The year was 1933, the trough of the depression. My parents had moved out of their rooms above the off-licence by this time and were living in a small terraced house with a mud yard in a Lancashire street called Cemetery Road. My eldest brother George was nine months old. On Sundays they took him out in the pram and sauntered along canal banks, a substitute for Scottish countryside: 'the Bury canal, the Manchester canal, James Brindley the great engineer's canal at Worsley . . . we were so very happy.' One evening he took out his commonplace book and wrote:

> *A baby and mummy and dad*
> *Was ever a trio so glad,*
> *Since there's Georgie at home*
> *Dad cares not to roam,*
> *Where Mummy and Georgie may be*
> *There also is he*
> *For 'three's company'. See?*

Chubby must have written too. 'Dear Jock, pleased to hear you are fixed up with a shore job. I am not doing so well – at present stuck at home in L'pool between ships. It would be an easy trip over to see you and the wife, your old shipmate, Chubby!' I can imagine my father's response, all too well. 'He's a wee bit soft in the head,' he says to my mother, 'but there's no harm in him.' But there was harm in Chubby, a great deal of it. His brother lay sweating in bed with cerebrospinal meningitis, and when Chubby boarded the train he boarded in company, the *meningococci*.

Sometimes I wonder how he travelled; there was such a choice of railway lines in those days. Did Chubby and the *meningococci* take an express from Liverpool Lime Street along the world's first passenger railway, and then did he run down the long platform between Manchester Exchange and Manchester Victoria, once the longest station platform in the country? That way there might have been time for a cup of tea before he caught the local. Or did he and the *meningococci* come all the way in the same warm compartment, along the old Lancashire and Yorkshire Railway line through Wigan (Wallgate) and Bolton (Trinity Street)? Slower, but no fear of missed connections.

It doesn't matter, it's of stupidly arcane interest; this is what comes of a childhood watching railway trains. One way or another Chubby arrived in good order, throbbing with a secret life, at a wayside station called Farnworth and Halshaw Moor. No doubt my father met him next to the Virol advertisements ('Healthy babies need it'). No doubt he made much of little Georgie. No doubt my mother cooked a fine tea and they all enjoyed it. Quite possibly Chubby loosened his buttons and said:

'Ee that were grand. Care for a Woodbine, Jock?'

Eventually my father would walk him to the station and Chubby would slide down the window of his compartment and lean out through the steam.

'That's a great little kiddie you've got. Say ta very much to the wife.'

No harm came to this harmless man who unknowingly contained harm. A few days later, however, George became a hot little ball of fever. A few weeks later, he was dead. 'My Christian principles were severely retarded,' writes my father. 'For the first time I realised that a good seed sown can result in a crop of thistles.' He then tells a story from the funeral tea, a story I heard often as a child without connecting it to death.

They invited the neighbours, who had been kind, and ate in the parlour. There were not enough tinned pears to go round. 'No tinned pears for you then, Jock?' asks a weaver, seeing his empty plate. My father loved tinned pears as he loved any food from tins. 'No,' my mother lies, 'he cannae stomach tinned fruit.'

It was a trivial sacrifice remembered from a terrible time and told, I suppose, almost as a balm. But he neglects to record another incident from the day he took George to the graveyard in a horse-drawn cab, the baby's small coffin contained in a glass compartment beneath the driver's seat. I heard of it only once, thirty years later, one weekend when I came home from Glasgow. I had a bedsitter there, with a gas ring, a prized black corduroy jacket in the wardrobe, and a row of Penguin books on the sideboard. A quotation from Albert Camus was pinned above the fireplace, 'Man, on the whole, is more good than bad', but that weekend the optimism had been difficult to sustain. I'd been abandoned by a girl-friend and every popular song seemed to be freshly-minted, just for me ('How do you do what you do to me, I wish I knew . . .' Absurd new names had driven out the absurd old, Gerry and the Pacemakers, Freddie and the Dreamers had replaced the Laird O' Balmawhapple).

I came home in my black corduroy jacket. My father found me mooning gnomically around the house. He looked solemn. 'Worse things will happen in your life,' he said. 'Do you know what Granny Smith said to me the day we buried George?' Granny Smith had been a neighbour in Cemetery Road, cherished as my parents' first mentor of Lancashire life and always a focus of stories which exemplified Lancashire kindness and common-sense; I imagined her as a cheerful old woman who kept a row of ripening apples on the window-ledge. 'She said: "If you'd taken him to church and had him baptised, none of this would ever have happened."'

They rebuilt their family with two more sons; and there then began, so my father writes, 'what I have always considered the happiest period of my life.' They moved to a new council house with a garden and a bathroom in a street lined with young sycamores, Iris Avenue, and bought a tandem and a sidecar. The whole family, two adults and two children, would mount this contraption on a Sunday morning and cycle through the smell of cooking breakfasts until they reached the Pennine hills or the lanes of Cheshire, a release from the limits of pedestrian energy which had confined them to canal banks and the smudged grass of public parks. As his ultimate son, I was born too late to share this happiest of stretches, but I am not sorry; missing the heights I also missed the depths, and in any case it lasted only seven years. In 1943 two cousins in Scotland went down with diphtheria. One died. Their father was absent from home in the Royal Marines, so my parents asked my aunt and her surviving daughter to come down to Lancashire for a holiday. It was an ordinary kindness – my uncle and aunt would have done the same for us in different circumstances – though more careful people, of the kind who keenly follow weather forecasts and the stockmarket, might have kept their distance.

This time we know the route. The *corynebacteria diphtheria* took a familiar journey to our family, south across the Forth Bridge, changing trains and stations in Edinburgh, taking their passage through the hills and fells at Beattock and Shap. *Diphther* is the Classical Greek for leather, and leather is what happened to my brothers' throats. They became coarsened and then constricted; breathing was difficult; the heart muscles toiled.

My poor boys. Nobody ever prayed more sincerely or fervently than I did, but Gordon passed away.

Strangely enough, my father did not go mad, did not shoot vicars, aim kicks at the stubbornly healthy children of our neighbours, or take to arson. I don't think he even got drunk. Instead he became the complicated man I grew up with, swithering bafflingly between optimism and pessimism, preserving earlier memories and denying later ones, seizing the rare signs of justice on earth having failed to find it signalled from Heaven.

The struggle now began to start a new kind of life and, harder still, to form a new philosophy ... The final exposure had now been made of the lying Biblical tenet with which my mother had indoctrinated me: Galatians, Chapter Six, Verse Seven, *as ye sow, so shall ye reap.* Poor wee soul, he never did any harm to anyone, and as for the sins of the fathers being visited on the children and all that concomitant rubbish – it may be good enough for theologians and little children but surely must now be held by me in utter contempt. It was no easy task to throw overboard the forty years' indoctrination by my mother, the Baptist church and countless others. (But I mustn't blame my mother too much, she was a good woman .. she saw things in a different light, she had been brought up with an unshakeable faith in God, Queen Victoria and the British Empire under the strict discipline of the barrack square. She was very aware of the temptations to sin and the danger of falling into hellfire.)

According to the hieroglyphs on the tomb of Ti at Sakkara, Akhnaton, faced with a religious tradition dating back over two thousand years, took his courage in both hands and renounced it all.

Why not me?

I was now very sceptical and without faith, but I was in no doubt at all that I had been engaged in a struggle, not for self-preservation, but for the preservation of something outside self ... I eventually came to the conclusion that the hope of immortality was not born of any religion but was the result of human affection, the love of one human being for another, and the imperishable desire to be reunited with those we have lost.

I properly understood those words for the first time when I read them last summer as a man in early middle-age. I was seated at the upstairs window of a friend's house in Kent; a lovely old farmhouse with crooked roofs, creepers and beams, bought and maintained from the profits of film-work and advertising. Here Britain still flourishes. My view included a French car parked on a gravel drive and a wide lawn fringed with oaks. Beyond lay a shallow valley of cow pastures which ended with a wooded ridge, the last rise before England dips down to the Romney Marshes and slides into the English Channel.

I thought: my father tried so hard to make sense of his life. For years I had seen him as a florid Victorian building: over-decorated with anecdotes, steam-heated from the basement, festooned with enamel advertisements and pokerwork mottoes. *Drink Vimto . . . There's Good and Bad Everywhere.* But I had mistaken façade for structure. Underneath he was a piece of simple modernism. All he wanted was an answer to the question: why?

It was an August afternoon. A breeze ruffled the leaves and sent dandelion puffs floating over the grass. Suddenly I heard the piping note of a steam whistle, distant but unmistakeable. I put down my father's manuscript and looked out. There in the middle distance stood a small steam locomotive and four coaches among the hedges and the fields. It was a mile or so away, stationary on the track of one of those private railways – Britain has dozens of them – which have been preserved by the energies of people who in their spare time like to imagine themselves in a previous mechanical age. The locomotive whistled again, steam emerged and the soft thud of exhaust carried over the fields. Soon the train moved out of sight behind the grove of oaks; but its steam hung in the air for a moment, looking crisp and solid, before it drifted up towards the clouds, and frayed and disappeared.

London, Autumn, 1986

LAST RITES FOR THE WHITES

Rhodesia, Summer, 1977

The sun had gone down behind the mountains to the west when Wilson, the house-boy, served tea. 'No, not there Wilson. Here, on this table here,' said Peter Gresham. Wilson, an African of about thirty, smiled and moved the cups to a table on the terrace, parking them besides Gresham's walkie-talkie radio.

'Marvellous chap, Wilson,' said Gresham as Wilson padded back to the kitchen. 'Absolutely no chance of him joining the terrs.'

A 'terr' is Rhodesian slang for terrorist – white Rhodesians naturally do not call them freedom fighters or armies of liberation and get fairly testy with the word 'guerrilla' – and, though Gresham cannot see them, he knows they are 'out there' in the bush somewhere, or waiting to strike from camps just over the Mozambique border.

Gresham is fifty-five and manages a tea estate in the Honde valley, a cleft in Rhodesia's Eastern Highlands which runs north and east into Mozambique. The border is just four or five miles from his bungalow, to the east. To the west, the Inyanga Mountains, the highest in Rhodesia, climb suddenly and steeply to 8,000 feet and frequently disappear into white, fluffy cloud. It might almost be the English Lake District.

'Over there,' said Gresham, pointing to a small white blob on a green hillside which was steadily growing darker, 'that's our club. We had some tremendous get-togethers there in the good old days.' The 'good old days' is a reference to the period before 1976, the year the armies of the Patriotic Front stepped up the guerrilla war against Ian Smith's government. The club has a bar and a tennis court and a billiard table once exhibited for the excellence of its playing surface at a great Victorian exhibition. There the eight white families from Gresham's tea estate would meet other whites from the Abercorn estate, a few miles down the dirt track which ends abruptly at the Mozambique border.

Today it is unfrequented. Nobody leaves their bungalows after sunset. White women and children have been removed to Umtali, the nearest town. Gresham's wife went, along with much of Gresham's furniture. Some months ago terrorists lined up a score of Africans who worked in the tea plantations and shot them dead outside Gresham's tea factory. Land-mines, skilfully implanted in unmetalled roads, have killed others. Now the Gresham bungalow is surrounded by an electric fence and three sand-bagged bunkers. The windows are boxed over with wood and wire-netting to prevent hand grenades smashing through the glass.

The war has also changed Gresham's vocabulary. Army slang acquired during his years with the King's African Rifles has now been overlaid with the jargon of walkie-talkie radio transmissions and the new slang of the Rhodesian Army, who now guard his tea estate.

'These days life is just hassles, hassles, hassles,' said Gresham, using an odd word for a fifty-five-year-old former British army officer and ex-public schoolboy. The previous day a bus carrying African workers back from a football match had overturned and one or two people had died – an act of God rather than terrorism. Gresham spent much of his time shouting into his radio, trying to organise the recovery and burial of the bodies.

'Ghastly business, but it's Tango Sierra I'm afraid.' Tango Sierra? 'Bad luck or, um, tough shit.' He went on to explain other words. Stonk, that was a mortar attack. An egg was a landmine, gooks (borrowed from the Americans in Vietnam) were terrorists, freddies were members of Mozambique's

Frelimo army, revs were bursts of machine-gun fire, hassles were spots of bother, sudden raids from across the border.

Suddenly, in the darkness across the valley, a little circle of lights was switched on. 'Ah, there you are, the Blackpool illuminations. That's one of our protected villages.' Most of his 700 African workers now live in such villages, surrounded by barbed wire and defended by a couple of guards with FN rifles. The lights stay on all night. The workers earn a basic of six Rhodesian dollars for a six-day week (roughly six pounds) which, Gresham explained, included a special bonus for Saturday work. Absenteeism was high on Saturdays because on Fridays, pay night, a lot of people tended to get terribly drunk in the tea estate's beer hall (provided by the management) on native beer at eight cents a litre. The average wage for whites in Rhodesia is one hundred dollars a week, for blacks, ten dollars.

Gresham rose from his chair on the terrace. 'I think our presence is now required at The Hole in The Wall.' He led the way through the hall, hung with prints of earlier Elizabethan Greshams, and down a long corridor hung with stuffed animals' heads. 'Here we are, The Hole in The Wall.' A small room had been equipped as a bar. It was opening time and three army reservists were already drinking beer quietly with Gresham's assistant manager, Tony Huwgill. The reservists, intelligent men who in civilian life had jobs as accountants and game-park directors, carried FNs. Huwgill had an Uzi short-barrelled machine-gun, made in South Africa under licence from Israel.

On the bar were stacks of leaflets which Gresham and Huwgill distributed to their workers. They showed, in crude line drawings, smiling men with guns bending over dead and bleeding bodies. 'See the mad dog communist terrorists shooting old men and young girls with their communist AK guns,' said the copy. 'They do this because they want the people to be afraid of them. The communist terrorists say they are fighting for you. Do not let them deceive you . . . they have been turned into evil men by the communist camp instructors in Mozambique. The communist terrorists are now the murdering mad dogs of ZANU/ZANLA. Anyone who helps communist terrorists is helping to bring terror and death to the people.'

'A bit simple I suppose,' said Gresham, 'but it gets the message across.'

Dinner was announced. Wilson moved around the dining room with trays of roast potatoes and cauliflower. Huwgill, still in shorts, carved the roast beef. Gresham, now in cardigan and tie, uncorked a bottle of Rhodesian red underneath a portrait of Winston Churchill, then wrapped the bottle in a linen napkin. Certain standards were being kept up.

'Ah, so you spotted those spent cartridge cases outside your bedroom window did you indeed? Bit of a hassle there some weeks ago. Someone tried to shoot the cat.' Gresham winked at Huwgill and Huwgill smiled; both were being mindful of instructions from the Rhodesian Department of Information. Do not give too much away to foreign journalists, walls have ears, or, as a current Rhodesian poster has it, 'For his sake, keep quiet . . . think of National Security.' It shows a young blonde with her finger across her lips.

Gresham came to Africa because England was so cold. That, at least, was what he said over the brandy. 'Got a commission with the Honourable Artillery Company when I was seventeen. Trained on the Salisbury Plain in winter. It was bloody cold . . . I thought "Oh boy this is O for Out".' So then he joined the King's African Rifles and, after the war, settled in Rhodesia. First he was in jute, then he moved into tea and his present job eighteen years ago. Every three years he escapes the solitariness of the Honde valley on fourteen weeks' long-leave – 'to get A for Away, passages paid.'

But Gresham would not consider going A for Away for good, despite the presence of terrs and freddies, the occasional explosion of eggs, the danger of storks and the imminence of a black government. 'Dammit all, this country's been good to me. To take the gap [leave] at this point would be highly reprehensible.' Huwgill was more thoughtful. A black government had pushed him out of Kenya, he said, and the same thing looked likely to happen here. He was in his thirties, he had a young wife and two children. But his whole career had been spent in tea; tea was what he knew about. 'So where do I go? You tell me.'

A certain gloom came on after the brandy. Look at Black Africa, said Gresham, look at Uganda, look at that madman Bokassa in the Central African Empire, look at the tribal massacres in Burundi, the coups in Nigeria, the state Zambia was in. Was that what the West wanted to happen in Rhodesia? 'And please don't give us all that stuff about one man, one vote. I'm far too old and cynical for that . . . no, this is all about trade, you want to buy oil from Nigeria and flog them cars in exchange. We're just an embarrassment.'

As for Britain, don't talk to him about Britain. It was in a rotten state. Why, even the Royal Family wasn't what it was, even the Queen wasn't . . . but here Gresham suddenly smiled and, perhaps sensing that he was going too far, abruptly shut up. It was time to check the alarm on the electric fence and then turn in.

Early next morning he guided us down roads freshly swept for landmines to meet the Army convoy, the only safe way to get into the Honde valley and out again. His walkie-talkie was still beside him, Huwgill still carried his Uzi. But Gresham's resolute cheerfulness had returned. He apologised for the 'bad order' of his bungalow, that was what happened when your womenfolk went away. Now, because the terrs had been quiet recently, he was going to bring them all back, the poppets, to cheer things up.

The children would stay on at school in Umtali, however. As would the tea estate's accounts, which had also been removed for safety's sake. 'You see I want to die with my books clean,' said Gresham and chortled. Huwgill smiled. As usual, they were showing considerable pluck in the face of the enemy.

Every Sunday around three in the afternoon, Rhodesian radio broadcasts its version of *Family Favourites*. The woman announcer is reminiscent of Jean Metcalfe. In a voice of unflagging pertness she broadcasts messages of comfort and love to white Rhodesian men who have been called up and are now doing their bit, not in the comfort of barracks in BAOR 15, but 'out there' in the bush.

'Love from Mum and the two little ones . . . take great care and God bless, from Nigel, Biddy, Albert, Lynette . . . super to have you home, can't wait till next time, from Lynn and Sharon . . . praying for your safe return, love Donna . . . all for Junior Commandant Peter Donaldson. Head down and chin up Peter and keep out of range of those mortar attacks.'

Super . . . head down, chin up . . . these are the words which best convey the public spirit of the Rhodesian white. T-shirts and car-stickers proclaim that 'Rhodesia is super' and the word seems to have outgrown its roots, once set so firmly in an English world of tennis courts and small sports cars. Now sinewy men in camouflage army uniform will say 'super' when offered an English cigarette. Tough farmers refer to Rhodesia as a 'super country' with a 'super way of life'. And when, after a Sunday lunchtime drink, they are heaving their stout, sun-tanned thighs into their old Austin Cambridges and new Peugeots, they will call 'Head down, chin up' and 'Stay healthy' to their friends.

Perhaps the Austin Cambridges and Peugeots should be Hurricanes and Spitfires. This may be the dangerous Rho-desian farmland of 1977 but the mood is of Manston and Biggin Hill – or at least how we (and they) imagine that mood to have been. Peter Gresham has certainly caught it, but it is not just confined to farmers in lonely bungalows.

Gresham is not a typical Rhodesian – eighty per cent of the country's 265,000 whites live in towns, almost half of them in the suburbs of the capital, Salisbury – yet his attitudes are shared by most families, no matter how remote they are from the threat of landmines and mortars. The main reason is the call-up; every fit, white male between the ages of eighteen and fifty now spends part of his year in the army and the police reserve. All have learned how to handle a gun. Many have passed on their expertise to wives and children.

Fighting the war in this way has had a serious effect on the Rhodesian economy. Already hit by sanctions, its white, professional workforce now spends half the year absent from its desks guarding convoys and farmhouses. Somehow Rhodesia survives. 'Just think what Britain could be like if it had a spirit like ours,' said a young army lieutenant, a tobacco auctioneer in civilian life. Britain to him, as to most Rhodesians, was a country of drizzle, mean streets, strikes, race riots, unemployment.

The news of the Lewisham riots, given prominent coverage in that day's issue of the *Rhodesia Herald*, made him almost ecstatic. 'Now show me a race riot in Rhodesia. Go on. And just look at our regular army, nearly eighty per cent African and they're fighting the terrs alongside our chaps.' So far there have been no race riots in Rhodesia and the security forces are perhaps the country's one genuinely multi-racial institution, at least in their lower ranks. Africans join up largely because of the money and their loyalty is to the Army rather than to Ian Smith. There is, however, a five-year-old war going on which, by official Rhodesian estimates, has so far killed about 3,000 'terrorists' and 500 men on the other side.

The men who leave office jobs in Salisbury to guard remote farmhouses are called 'bright-lights', after the lights of the city they have left behind. A couple of them guard the home of Lady Wilson, a fifty-three-year-old widow who insists on living only 300 yards from the Mozambique border in the hills above Umtali. Here Lady Wilson (whose husband, Sir Ian Wilson, was the Speaker in the Assembly of the old Central African Federation) grows magnolias, azaleas and camellias in a garden shaded by New Zealand pines. Bullfrogs croak in the garden pond. Occasionally the house is raked by machine-gun fire. Lady Wilson, the founder of a well-intentioned but ill-supported movement called Women for Peace (she got the idea from the similarly-named group in Northern Ireland), is being incredibly hardy about the situation.

Every morning a 'bright-light' walks down the track which leads to her house to check it for landmines. We were now driving along the track in Lady Wilson's van at considerable speed. 'Here, you can ride shotgun,' said Lady Wilson, handing one over and producing a Webley pistol from her handbag. The pistol, she said, was a wedding present from her father in 1952. The Mau-Mau were active in Kenya in those days.

Lady Wilson drove us to see an agricultural school for young Africans which had recently been attacked by terrorists. Black attacking black is a frequent occurrence in Rhodesia – and a frequent theme of white Rhodesians: 'See, they kill their own.' The Smith Government flies Dakotas full of journalists to the scenes of such outrages, so that they may count the bodies and inspect the wounds of murdered tribesmen.

'All we want is that you people report the truth,' said a young army officer at the agricultural school, guarding the ruins of what had once been a worthy project designed to show blacks the techniques of the European farmer. But the truth in Rhodesia depends very much on whose side you are on: a recent public opinion poll in Salisbury showed that, while whites thought they were fighting a war against the spread of communism and anarchy in southern Africa, the blacks took a rather different view. They thought the cause of the war was racism.

The truth in this particular case was that a group of terrorists had vandalised several farm buildings and then shot three local village headmen in one of the dormitories. 'Shot in the guts I should say,' said the young officer, chirpily, 'you can see some second-hand grub on the floor.'

Not all white Rhodesians are plucky. More than 1,000 are leaving every month, taking the 'yellow route' and the 'chicken run' south to South Africa, east to Australia, even north to the much-despised United Kingdom (from whence some have returned, disgusted; their complaints of drizzle, socialism and strikes feature prominently in the local Press). No doubt far more would leave were it not for Rhodesia's stringent currency regulations. Each family is allowed out of the country with no more than 1,000 Rhodesian dollars. Some have been caught trying to smuggle out their wealth in the form of gold and jewellery (their cases, too, feature prominently in the local Press). The mayor of Bulawayo got so desperate that he hopped across to Botswana in a light plane.

This exodus makes Rhodesia a grand place for the optimistic house-hunter or property speculator. Jim Fox, a Salisbury estate agent, reckons that there are ten times as many houses on the market today as there were three years ago. Prices have dropped twenty per cent; excellent mortgage facilities are available at 7¼ per cent interest rates. Still, said Fox, your average Rhodesian was a remarkably pig-headed kind of person. Many people were actually still buying houses. 'In any other country they'd have packed their bags and buggered off long ago.'

The Salthouses are the kind of people Fox was talking about. Tony Salthouse is in his early thirties and runs a jewellery business in Salisbury. A Rhodesian, he came back from four years in the UK six years ago. His wife, Avril, was a secretary with a London cut-price store called Shoppertunities. Together they bought a house this summer for £28,000 in the Salisbury suburb of Emerald Hill, which is farther from the city than Avondale, Belgravia and Kensington but not as far out as Marlborough, Greendale or Glen Lorne. The name of every suburb shrieks with Britishness. Indeed in the late afternoon, when the sun is less fierce and the colours mellower, it could be the England of *Just William*: high green hedges, schoolboys drifting home in blazers and straw hats, icecream men who push boxes of wafers and cornets round on tricycles.

'Certainly you can come and see us,' said Avril Salthouse, 'but please don't write all the usual old clichés about swimming pools, servants and gin-and-tonics.'

Alas, the Salthouses do have a swimming pool and there was a liberal supply of gin-and-tonic. They also have two servants, a fairly modest number in Rhodesia, and two white, yelping dogs of the Maltese poodle breed. Tony Salthouse's parents had popped over for a drink before dinner. What kind of future did the assembled Salthouses see for themselves?

At first all four pledged their faith in Rhodesia, no matter how black the government. 'I'm committed to this country and as long as we're not victimised because we're white I'll happily stay,' said Tony Salthouse. He did not shrink at the prospect of black neighbours, or of sharing a hospital ward with black patients, or of sending any (potential) children to mixed-race schools. At present suburbs, hospitals and schools are all segregated; the Rhodesian telephone directory lists three numbers for the emergency ambulance service – for Europeans, Asians and Africans. But it was difficult to imagine the senior Salthouses tolerating black rule for long – or, perhaps of black rule tolerating them. Soon the conversation took the familiar Rhodesian turn.

Mr Salthouse Senior: 'The trouble is the children want to rule their teachers and they're not ready for it yet. Let's face it, the white man developed this country . . . before that they were swinging from the trees.'

Tony Salthouse: 'Come on now, Mum . . .'

Mr Salthouse Senior: 'All black politicians are looking for is a gold-plated bed and a Rolls-Royce. These blokes kill their own people. Look at Amin.'

Tony Salthouse: 'Come on now, Dad . . .'

Mrs Salthouse Senior: 'Anyway, they'll have to carry me out of this country in my coffin. The only place I'm going from here is Heaven. Next to Heaven, there's no place like Rhodesia.'

Rhodesia? Heaven? To an outsider it seems an unlikely comparison. The Smith Government is fighting a war which, by the admission of its own generals, it can never win; the landscape is often flat, brown scrubland; the capital has the architecture of modern Croydon and the social life of Croydon twenty years ago. Salisbury's streets have mock-boutiques with names such as Miss Truworth's, Zippers, What's Happening, full of freckled, leggy girls (the mini has not died here) who look like Englishwomen boosted into robust beauty by the Rhodesian diet of steak, eggs and orange juice. At night there is Jack Dent, playing his piano for dinner-dances in Meikle's Hotel. The waiters are black, the dancers and diners white. No one in improper dress will be admitted.

Dent is sixty-seven, a Londoner whose career took off after the Duke of Windsor stopped to chat to him one night in the early Thirties. That was in a nightclub called the Blue Train Grill. Now he has just finished playing a Scottish selection for Bill Irvine, the Rhodesian Minister of Housing, and is sitting at our table, describing his career and friendships: Dick Bentley ... Jack Warner ... Roma Beaumont, the soubrette ... the Café Anglais ... the Edward Hotel, Durban ... Ivor Novello. He returns to the piano and plays. Bill Irvine, the Housing Minister, leads his wife correctly, primly into the steps of the tango.

Or there is Eddie Calvert, the Man with the Golden Trumpet, starring at Salisbury's top nightspot, the La Bohème club. Calvert plays *O Mein Papa* and *Zambezi* and tells jokes. 'Why did I leave England? Two reasons. One, the wife. Two, Harold Wilson.' Cheers from the audience, which consists mainly of troops in camouflage and boots. Calvert says he hopes to open a nightclub – 'a five-star one' – in Salisbury. Like Dent, he has left Britain for good. 'England?' said Dent. 'Forget it, I'm finished with it, I'm Rhodesian now.'

It is difficult to know what inspires this kind of loyalty. The large majority of white Rhodesians are not the sons and daughters of colonial pioneers. Most came out from Britain after the war; 120,000 of them actually arrived after UDI in 1965; the accents of Liverpool, Glasgow and London are as common there as the tight vowel sounds of Ian Smith. They were attracted by the prospect of sunshine, servants, high wages, a fresh start. Now they seem to be rationalising their instincts for self-preservation into a kind of moral crusade.

In a dusty Bulawayo tobacconist's I picked up a free copy of a duplicated typewritten sheet headed 'An open letter to Rhodesians' and written (allegedly, anonymously) by an English family who had just arrived. 'Why did we come? Because we wanted our children to have as bright a future as possible ... because we were sick of the decadence creeping over Britain. What did we find? A people with a justifiable sense of achievement and the determination to fight for what had been achieved, despite the plottings and chicanery of a dishonest world.'

The letter also mentioned a 'materialistic World Conspiracy ... a Godless plan which only two nations [the other, one presumes, is South Africa] are showing the courage to fight.' Godlessness is certainly regarded as evil in Rhodesia. Christianity, if it can be judged by the number of its churches, has the country in its grip. Even the names of black nationalist leaders – Joshua Nkomo, Abel Muzorewa, Josiah Chinamano – speak of baptism and an education in the Christian mission schools. Robert Mugabe, perhaps the man the whites hate most, is, after all, a Catholic who likes Pat Boone records.

The Reverend Gary Strong, an Evangelical Methodist, would like to see Rhodesia preserved as a 'Christian society with a free-enterprise economy'. If the white man left, said Strong, then the economy would collapse and Rhodesia would be overtaken by extreme socialism. Recently he had been given the chance to quit the country himself and had spent two weeks in prayer, wrestling with the problem and eventually concluding that 'Gary, if people like you leave, there'll be a crisis here'. So Gary is staying, hating racialism on the one hand ('I tell you the worst racialists are new English immigrants') and terrorism on the other.

He agreed, however, that in moral terms the white Rhodesian is an odd human being. There is the obvious contradiction of a small, white, allegedly Christian community denying the vote to a black population, equally Christian but twenty-two times as large; and UDI was declared, among many other things, in the name of Christianity. And then there are other discrepancies within the white community itself. Rhodesian television shows pirated versions of BBC serials (*Dr Who*; *Softly*, *Softly*), but then takes great care to bleep out offensive words such as 'bastard' or 'a dose of the clap'. Rhodesia has high rates of alcoholism and divorce, but then it will not allow its alcoholics or divorcees to read *Playboy*. At least, though, the Rhodesian Board of Censors is kind enough to publish a list of the material it has banned. The one for 1976 includes *The Marx Brothers Scrapbook*,

Billy Connolly's biography and thirty-eight T-shirt transfers, described in careful detail ('Picture of two rabbits in attitude suggestive of coition,' and 'Picture of animated nut and bolt with legend consisting of five words commencing with the word "Smile"').

Every night at closedown, Rhodesian television plays the new Rhodesian national anthem. The tune is the choral movement from Beethoven's *Ninth Symphony*.

> *Rise, O voices of Rhodesia,*
> *God, may we Thy bounty share,*
> *Give us strength to face all danger and,*
> *where challenge is, to dare.*
> *Guide us, Lord, to wise decision*
> *ever of Thy grace aware,*
> *Oh, let our hearts beat bravely always,*
> *for this land within Thy care.*

Slides accompany the choir, changing with each line of the verse; the bush, Victoria Falls, the Kariba dam, Salisbury city centre. At the end the slide the camera lingers on is a shot of the statue of Cecil Rhodes – the country's founder and, next to Ian Smith, the whites' great hero.

Rhodes inspired the first white settlers to trek north from South Africa eighty-odd years ago. He thought vast quantities of gold were to be found there. As it turned out, there wasn't much gold, but Rhodes was not too disappointed. He had a greater ideal at heart. 'I contend,' he wrote in his *Confession of Faith*, 'that we (the English) are the finest race in the world and that the more of the world we inhabit the better it is for the human race.'

Rhodes' vision has now just about run its eighty-year course, stubbornly prolonged by 'the twelve good years Smithy has given us'. Most whites now accept the fact that Rhodesia will soon be Zimbabwe, that Salisbury will turn into Harare, that Cecil Square will be called something else (precisely what else is still terribly uncertain – Muzorewa Gardens? Sithole Circle? The Joshua Nkomo Piazza?), and that the statues of Cecil Rhodes will be torn down. But even in its twilight days white Rhodesia has much that Rhodes would take pride in.

He would no doubt be proud of Chief Justice Hector Macdonald, the judge who sentences terrorists to death. Macdonald, a born Rhodesian, lost a leg fighting for Britain in the last war and thinks there is much truth in Rhodes' *Confession of Faith.* 'The trouble with people of your generation is that you have nothing but a sense of shame for empire. I'm in no doubt that the British Empire was a force for good and not for evil.'

He would be proud, perhaps, of the white miners of Wankie (a town called after an African chief, Wange, and not, as Rhodesian wags would have you believe, because there is nothing else to do there anyway). They recently failed to muster enough votes to change the constitution of their miners' club and allow Africans as members. 'Munts? In here? It's a depressing thought,' said a white apprentice in the beer garden.

He would be proud of the many white Rhodesians who persist in taking their holidays at Victoria Falls, despite its occasional straffing by machine-gun and bombardment by rocket. *In the improbable event of an attack on this hotel,* reads a notice in the guests' bedrooms, *one, turn all lights out, two, lie down on the floor well away from the windows.*

And he would certainly be proud of Peter Gresham, still holding out in his front-line bungalow. 'What? A for Away, O for Off? No, to take the gap at this point would be highly reprehensible.' The writing may be on the wall, but many are refusing to read.

Don't Cry For Us, Argentina

The Falklands, Spring, 1978

Atlases of the world, published in countries other than Argentina, show the islands as a tight little group of pink dots clustered on the western edge of the blue South Atlantic. Cape Horn lies 400 miles to the west, Land's End more than 7,000 miles to the north and east. Their capital is given as Stanley and they bear the name Falklands, behind which comes the bracketed abbreviation (*Br*) signifying ownership by distant landlords – another group of islands, larger but similarly coloured pink, on the eastern edge of the North Atlantic. Argentine atlases are different. The islands are in the same place, certainly, but they are tagged with the words *Islas Malvinas*, their capital is *Puerto Stanley* and (*Ar*) is the abbreviation.

It is a piece of cartographical wish-fulfilment. Argentina claims the Falkland Islands, but does not, as yet, own them. The arguments between British and Argentine Foreign Offices have gone on at conferences in Lima and New York; the British Ambassador has been withdrawn from Buenos Aires. But despite the Argentine map the islands are administered still from Whitehall.

On the map the Argentine claim looks logical enough. Argentina represents the nearest land mass, the Patagonian coastline is only 500 miles away. On the ground, however, this logic confronts reality and quickly melts away.

A Sunday morning in Stanley in the month of March: the

smell of peat fires and the sound of Christ Church Cathedral's bells are being carried down the harbour on a south-west wind which has sprung from Cape Horn. On a good March day in the Falkland Islands the temperature can reach seventy degrees Fahrenheit and the wind speed may drop to nil. But inlet's head. Soon it will be moistening the lawns of such good days are rare and this is not one of them. It is cold, anorak weather; the wind is gusting at about seventeen knots – the mean speed for the movement of air in the Falklands – and with the wind comes rain. A curtain of it is moving steadily down the harbour inlet from east to west. Already it has smudged the view of the Royal Marines' encampment at the Government House and rattling down on the corrugated-iron roofs of Stanley itself. The people of Stanley will hear it, pause briefly to glance through their windows into John Street, Davis Street or Ross Road, and then continue with their preoccupations.

Monsignor Daniel Spraggon of St Mary's Church listens to its patter on his church's tarpaulined roof as he conducts mass. Mrs Des King of the Upland Goose Hotel anticipates its progress and brings in some sheets from her clothesline. Then she continues her preparations for the residents' lunch – packet onion soup, to be followed by one of Mrs King's many intriguing ways with mutton, to be finished off with portions of *crème caramel*, frozen in an English factory and then dispatched to the Falklands by ship.

Seconds later the rain reaches Mrs King's rival, a handsome, elderly lady called Emma who runs Emma's Restaurant inside the front room of her home at Jubilee Villas. The Villas (good sea views) comprise a short two-storey terrace in yellow brick, South London in appearance, with the date 1887 entwined on their front. Emma is also doing her best with a mutton dish, while a girl arranges the tables in her parlour. Emma's most frequent patrons are a small party of marine archaeologists, but after some weeks in the Falklands they have quarrelled and thus sit separately at lunch.

Emma and Mrs Des King are not the only rivals for the custom of Stanley's 1,000 people this Sunday morning. There is another, greater competition – for the ear of God – and here Monsignor Spraggon is clearly winning. Roman Catholics may number only eleven per cent of the Falklands' population, but they go to church. St Mary's is well filled. Anglicans, on the other hand, stay away in droves. Thus, as the rain reaches the red-painted corrugated-iron of Christ Church Cathedral roof, we find the Reverend Gerald Smith preaching to a congregation of a half-a-dozen small boys and girls in anoraks.

Mr Smith is dressed in robes of white and purple. His voice soars through hymns and dips into prayers, accompanied in the former by the fluting of his wife's recorder, but his efforts serve only to emphasise the great empty spaces of Christ Church. Once it was the seat of the Bishop of Eastern South America and the Falkland Islands. In 1889 Queen Victoria gave thirty pounds towards its building costs. But now the offices of the diocese have been removed to Buenos Aires and much of its congregation has drifted away – not to the pleasures of its parent country, Sunday newspapers or early morning television (for these are not available here), but to other, more private, pastimes.

Now comes Mr Smith's final prayer. For the people of the sheep-farm settlements of Bluff Cove and Fitzroy – they are in no particular peril; each island settlement has prayers said for it in weekly rotation – and for 'Elizabeth our Queen, for the governor of this island-colony and for all who live here.'

Behind the cathedral, rain is streaking down the glass-fronted box which houses the advertisement for this evening's attraction at Hardy's Cinema. *Guadalcanal Diary*, certificate A, starring Preston Foster, Lloyd Nolan, William Bendix. 'A great human picture of America's War in the Pacific,' it says, in prose which has not changed since it left the Hollywood publicist's desk some decades ago. 'A story written in the smoke of battle about US marines . . . ordinary men, wisecracking to the crack of sniper's bullets and joking about their lives amidst the terrors of savage jungle warfare. Here is all the unconquerable courage and heart-pounding action that gave the Sons of Heaven their first bitter taste of war.'

Alas, Hardy's Cinema suffers the same complaint as the cathedral; a lack of patronage. The projector has a long-standing fault on the soundtrack side and dialogue is frequently lost in a loud buzz.

Let us follow the rain east, and finally to the shop of Mr Des Peck, the Philomel Store, placed strategically adjacent to the pier where South American tourists descend from Argentine and Brazilian cruise ships in the summer months. The Philomel Store sells tinned beer, souvenirs, *Keep the Falkland Islands British* stickers and Smarties – *grazias de chocolate extra fino*, as Mr Peck's sign has them – to lure the tourist. Not that Des Peck has any great time for Argentines, 'Argies' or 'Latins' in the island parlance. Nor, indeed, for shop-keeping. As the bard, lyricist and tunesmith of the Falkland Islands Mr Peck is often busy composing. Today he is working on a poem which will be broadcast later in the week by the Falkland Islands Broadcasting Service, or Fibs as it is popularly known. His most famous work takes its inspiration from a great battle at sea – not that of *Guadalcanal Diary*, but one fought thirty years earlier between British and German fleets, just off the Falkland Islands in December, 1914.

> There will always be a Falklands
> With peace and Lib-er-ty
> That's why our Navy fought and died
> To keep our dear land free.

But soon Mr Peck lays down his pen and walks up Philomel Street towards the Globe Hotel. It is noon, opening time, and all over the length of Stanley, spread narrowly along its inlet, other men and women are following Mr Peck's example. They are donning anoraks, jumping into Land-Rovers and making for their favourite bar: The Rose, The Upland Goose, The Victory, The Globe. Stanley's bars are open for only an hour on Sundays – 'Glory Hour' – and everyone is determined to make the best of it.

The British traveller who eventually arrives in Stanley may think he has reached the end of the earth. He has, after all, flown far south to Buenos Aires and spent a day struggling with the Argentine bureaucracy for his 'White Card' – the *Certificado Provisorio* by which Argentina controls entry to and exit from the Falkland Islands. He has then flown farther south to Patagonia, itself almost a byword for mystical remoteness, to the small and scruffy oil town of Comodoro Rivadavia. And the next day, leaving the strong, sweet Latin smells of fresh coffee and tobacco behind, he has caught the Argentine Air Force's weekly flight across 600 miles of empty South Atlantic to Stanley, the last town going south before Antarctica. He has stepped from his Fokker Friendship into a settlement where the people walk at angles into the wind, their Anglo-Saxon faces red and broken-veined; whose banknotes are big, stiff and crisp like English ones used to be; where the fresh fruit and fish-fingers arrive four times a year by boat from Tilbury; devoid of trees, newsprint, market gardens; where the staple diet is often mutton, home-grown potatoes and canned beer.

He may think he has reached the end of the earth. But he has not. That feeling lies elsewhere in the Falklands – an hour by an old Beaver seaplane from Stanley perhaps, or a day (and more) by Land-Rover. For Stanley is regarded by islanders who live outside it as a kind of soft option, a place of bright lights, idleness and decadence. Those other Falklanders live on The Camp, from the Spanish *campo* for country (one of the very few Spanish words to make the trip east from Patagonia and insert itself into the slightly Australian English of the islands; the other is *che* for mate or comrade – hence *che-coat* for the national costume of the Falkland Islands, the anorak).

The Camp is spread across 4,700 square miles and two large and 200 small islands – East and West Falkland, Speedwell, Weddell, Saunders, Keppel – a land area more than half the size of Wales, but entirely without roads. It is inhospitable country, peat-bog and fell, dotted with place names which suggest its bleakness: Tumbledown Mountain, Mount Misery, Bluff Cove, No Man's Land. Crossing twenty miles of it by Land-Rover can take six hours on a good day.

The peat collapses, wheels go up to their axles in mud and bog-water, jacks and planks are produced, passengers are instructed to heave. It happens every mile or so and progress across country is slow and rough. About 800 people live in The Camp – the islands' total population is 1,800 – though this is not the most important demographic statistic, which comes with the mention of 658,000 sheep.

Sheep are the only reason that anyone at all lives on the Falklands. They are reared and sheared on The Camp and their wool provides the profit which makes the islands viable. That is why the men and women of the sheep stations view Stanley as Mancunians once did London: 'We make the money, they spend it.' It is a big sociological division, best illuminated by the small squabbles that go on over who gets the freshest shipment of fruit – and coming across an orange in The Camp must be like finding a grape in eighteenth-century Inverness – or the newest films from the film library. Stanley or The Camp? Each accuses the other. Then there is a time difference. The Camp sticks to its own time while Stanley swings an hour back and forth between summer and winter. Thus, flying by seaplane between Stanley and Goose Green, fifty miles away, we are crossing a time zone.

We are flying with the governor of the islands, Mr Jim Parker, who is accompanied by a shooting-stick and his wife, Deirdre. The Parkers were ferried to Stanley's seaplane base from Government House by their official car, a red-painted London taxi with the colony's version of the Union Jack flying from its bonnet. A taxi is cheaper than a Rolls-Royce, sturdy enough to cope with Stanley's few miles of ill-made road, and high enough to step into comfortably with a cocked hat on ceremonial occasions. Today, however, Mr Parker is dressed in tweeds and deer-stalker – clothes which befit his informal presence at the centenary meeting of the Darwin and Goose Green Sports Association.

Darwin's games are held every year at the end of the shearing season and go on for a week. They comprise dog trials and shearing contests, ladies' musical chairs and men's tug-of-war, catch-the-rooster competitions and numerous

69

horse races, rode over a steep racetrack on the moorland above the settlement. Until the Land-Rover arrived, the horse was the islands' chief tool of shepherding and transport. Many are ridden at Darwin by men whose families have looked after Falkland sheep for several generations, the descendants of Scots and English shepherds who arrived in the last half of the last century: McLeods, Binnies, Finlaysons, Mackenzies. In every race they rumble down the course from the horizon, standing in their stirrups to pass the ramshackle stand, the beer hut and the finishing line. The governor's wife presents a cup and the crowd breaks up, slamming the doors of its assembled Land-Rovers and bumping off down to the clump of red and white painted houses on the sea's edge: Goose Green, home of what were once the largest shearing sheds in the British Empire (or in the Southern Hemisphere – the people of Goose Green offer alternative boasts).

To the urban Briton with lingering notions of Imperial romance it is a pleasing picture. Here, in one of our last colonies, are weather-beaten sons and daughters of the Anglo-Saxon and Celtic races hard at play. Here are master and man on equable if not equal footing. The governor can be seen talking happily with sheep station managers and shepherds, his wife with the wives of each. Here are British exports of worth and quality. Land-Rovers, Smarties, Tennent's lager. Here is an absence of guilt. No natives have been expelled or subdued because the British came to the islands with an indigenous population of seals, geese and penguins and have only the blood of the native fox (long extinct) on their hands. But the picture is not without flaws.

I discover the first at that evening's dance in Goose Green recreation hall. Women aged from thirteen to sixty range themselves down one wall waiting to be taken up for the samba, the slow foxtrot and the Circassian Circle by men who are still drinking steadily. Whole tables lie covered with tins of the ubiquitous Tennent's lager (so ubiquitous that the cheesecake models on discarded tins smile up at you from the remotest bog and beach – *Linda Lying Low*, *Pat in Dreamland*, *Penny at Bedtime*). When the men have drunk enough to dance, however, it quickly becomes obvious that they outnumber the women two to one.

'That's the real trouble here,' says a young labourer, gripping my elbow and shoving a fist towards the ceiling. 'You either forget it or go blind.' He came recently to the Falklands from Britain – he'd read a headline in the *Daily Express* 'Young Britons Happy in Penguin Land' – and apart from the women problem was happy enough, saving 'ninety-nine per cent' of his £2,500 a year and living with his fellows in the farm bunk-house. Others take a more treasonable view. 'I'd let the Argies have this place tomorrow,' says a shepherd, 'if they would just send us over a couple of plane-loads of women.'

The problem is acute. Over the Falklands as a whole, men between thirty and sixty-four exceed women of the same age by three to two, and in The Camp it is especially bad. At the last census in 1972 the island of West Falkland had one unmarried woman over the age of nineteen and fifty-one unmarried men. The results are predictable. The Falklands have a declining population, increasing amounts of adultery and divorce, a little incest and illicit intercourse with girls below the legal age (though perhaps no more than in any isolated community) and much drinking. The presence of forty-two Royal Marines does not help. They cheer the population at large by showing the flag and wearing off-duty T-shirts inscribed, *Don't Cry for Me, Argentina*, but they also foster gloom among the islands' young bachelors. Each detachment serves a year at its base in Stanley, and each year half a dozen Stanley girls marry Royal Marines and leave the islands for married quarters in England.

So the birthrate declines and the population dwindles – over the past twenty-five years it has sunk from 2,300 to 1,800, with The Camp as the main source of emigration. But the reasons for this loss lie deeper than the availability of Royal Marines. They have to do with a feudal past and present, and an uncertain future.

John Davies, Elizabethan navigator and master of the ship *Desire*, is the man usually credited with the first sighting of the Falkland Islands. He saw them in 1592, being driven by a 'sore storme . . . among certaine isles never before discovered by any known relation'. The first recorded landing came one hundred years later when John Strong, another Englishman, put ashore to inspect the penguins. Strong sailed through the stretch of water which separated East and West Falkland (then known as Hawkins' Maiden Land or the Sebald Islands) and christened it Falkland Sound after the First Lord of the Admiralty of the day. But the French were not far behind. Their captains made a series of landings in the early eighteenth century and by 1722 a Paris printer produced a map bearing the legend *Iles Malouines*, naming them after St Malo, the port from which French ships sailed for the Horn and the South Seas. *Malouines* was later translated to the Spanish *Malvinas*, the word which now appears on Argentine atlases.

The French established the settlement on the islands in 1764 – at Port Louis, twenty miles north-west of Stanley – but sold it two years later to the Spanish crown for £25,000. Meanwhile in the intervening year, 1765, a small British fleet had sailed south to lay claim to the islands, begun a quarrel with the French and continued it with the Spanish. By 1770 Britain and Spain were poised on the edge of a full-scale war – a popular cause among the Opposition benches at Westminster, though not with the Government. It had enough trouble on its hands with the North American colonies and commissioned Dr Johnson to do a quick public-relations job on the case for appeasing Spain.

Johnson published his pamphlet, *Thoughts on the Late Transactions respecting Falklands' Islands*, in the following year. It is an admirable piece of Levin-like advocacy. Why, he asked, should Britain go to war for: 'The empty sound of an ancient title to a Magellanic rock, an island thrown aside from human use, stormy in winter, barren in summer, an island which not even the southern savages have dignified with habitation, where a garrison must be kept in a state that contemplates with envy the exiles of Siberia, of which the expense will be perpetual and the use only occasional, a nest

of smugglers in peace, in war a refuge of future buccaneers.'
That mood prevailed. The British garrison quit in 1774,
leaving behind a plaque full of bluster (*Be it known to all
nations that Falklands' Islands . . . are the sole property of His
Most Sacred Majesty, George the Third*) and the Spanish in
actual possession. They remained there for forty years, until
the wars of liberation broke Spain's stronghold over South
America and the newly-independent United Provinces of
Buenos Aires, later to become Argentina, claimed the island
for itself. Again, the claim was contested by Britain. In 1834
three boatloads of seamen and marines from the British sloop
Clio went ashore, struck the flag of the new republic and
hoisted the Union Jack – the colours that have flown there ever
since, despite the long and considerable protest of the Argentines.

British settlers began to arrive in the mid-nineteenth
century, along with imported Cheviot sheep and a London
company set up under Royal Charter, the Falkland Islands
Company. Throughout the past hundred years this company
has bought up sheep-grazing land. Today it owns about half
the total land area, more than 1.3 million acres. Even in
1896 the *Daily Telegraph* was moved to describe the Falklands as 'a strangled colony, fast in the grip of the land
monopolist' and some in the Falklands would say that the
position has scarcely changed today. 'This society,' says the
far-from-radical voice of the Reverend Gerald Smith, 'is
positively feudal.'

The men of The Camp live in tied company houses on
company land. They shop in the company store for goods
delivered by company ships, and have bills deducted from
company wages. Many of them use the company as a bank.
The wool they shear from the company sheep goes to Tilbury,
again by the company ships, where it is unloaded at the
company wharf, stored in the company warehouse and sold
on the company wool exchange in Bradford. Nor does this
monopoly apply only to land and sheep actually owned by
the Falkland Islands Company. By means of transport and
marketing, the Falkland Islands Company extends its in-

fluence over the islands' few other landlords. For better or worse, the Falklands are company islands.

This fact breeds apathy. There is little enterprise in the Falklands and their recent history is peppered with little projects, the bright ideas of outsiders, which have met early failure; canning factories, mink farms and the like. It also leads to a curious absence of any sense of history, Mr Des Peck and the *Battle of the Falklands* apart, or of a separate culture. When men retire in The Camp they lose their tied houses and go off to Stanley or back to Britain. Few old gaffers are left yarning round their peat fires; the collector of folksong, folklore and folkweave would be hard-pressed to gather material. The settlements aren't really settlements at all, says Gerald Smith, they're factory floors concerned with the production of fleece. 'And you must recognise that a lot of people here spend a lot of their time simply surviving. Cutting peat – a major preoccupation – or digging gardens for their only source of fresh vegetables.'

In 1975 the Foreign Office – disturbed, apparently, by 'the weakening of the colony's economy and the decline in its population' – commissioned Lord Shackleton to head an investigation into the plight of the Falkland Islands. Its report reached the important conclusion that the islands' economy had 'suffered historically from a lack of local investment and a continual flow of private funds out of the islands to the United Kingdom'. This stemmed from the fact that the island's landlords either chose to distribute their profits among their shareholders (most of them British) or to invest them in Britain rather than reinvest in the Falkland Islands.

Last year the Falkland Islands Company made £600,000 profit for its parent company Charrington Coalite Ltd, whose principal business is fuel distribution; registered office Buttermilk Lane, Bolsover, Derby. How the men of Buttermilk Lane came to own a sheep station in the South Atlantic is a complicated story of take-over deals which began when the Falkland Islands Company was taken over by Dundee, Perth and London Securities, a Slater-Walker outfit, in 1973.

Dundee, Perth and London was bought out by Charringtons Industrial Holdings Ltd, which in turn was subsumed last year by Coalite and Chemical Products Ltd. One of Coalite's other subsidiaries specialises in oil-rig platforms. The seabed between the Falklands and Argentina is thought to be rich in oil – the results of recent surveys are still awaited, but it may be that rigorous changes are in store for the economy of the Falkland Islands.

A notice outside the Royal Marines mess in Stanley warns its men against the dangers of the slackened tongue. *Need-to-know*, it says. *In a curious (gossipy) situation this principle is paramount.* A posting in the Falkland Islands is such a situation indeed. In a remote community of 1,800 people it is hard to keep anything quiet, though no doubt many adulterous husbands and wives have tried. Every morning a doctor comes into the radio-telephone hut in Stanley and listens as the sick describe their symptoms over the shortwave radio from outposts in The Camp – a valuable service both in terms of remedies offered to the patient and gossip provided for the Caps (other radio-telephone owners), who are naturally listening in.

'Doctor, I think I need more valium . . .'

'Doctor, I was sick again this morning . . .'

(Aha, so Mrs X is still depressed. And could Miss Y be pregnant *again*?)

But the future is what provokes the most serious curiosity among islanders. Britain has pledged that it will not change the constitutional position of the Falklands without first consulting the wishes of their inhabitants. And the wishes of the inhabitants are quite clear; they want desperately to stay as a British colony. The thought of being ruled from Buenos Aires appals them: 'I'd go . . . I'd quite definitely . . . what, stay here under some lousy Latin-American dictator? Not likely.'

Even the word 'Latin' as in Latin-American is used with a puckering mouth of distaste. Talking to the magistrate, Mr Harold Bennett, in his courtroom one day I mention my admira-

75

tion of a portrait of the monarch which hangs above the bench. 'Yes, so much better than the famous one by that Italian chap,' says Mr Bennett. Annigoni? 'That's the man. He made Her look so *Latin*.'

About exactly what, the people of the Falklands would like to know, is Britain talking to Argentina? The Argentines stress that the question of sovereignty comes before all else. Britain says they are discussing 'economic co-operation' as a priority – exploiting the South Atlantic's vast and as yet barely tapped resources of fish, for example, or the oil that may lie underneath them. Earlier this year a story leaked from a meeting of the two sides in Lima that an Argentine–British condominium was under discussion, with alternating governors from Buenos Aires and London. The Argentine Press referred to it, happily, as the *Falklinas* solution, but it horrified Stanley.

Nonetheless – and as a result of Anglo-Argentine agreement – the Falklands depend on Argentina now as they have never done before. Every piece of airmail, every civilian passenger who lands on the islands does so by permission of the Argentine Government. Before 1971 they came by ship from Montevideo in Uruguay. Now you have to be a detachment of the Royal Marines – who leave and depart by ship to Chile – to avoid passing through Argentina. Likewise the private citizen of Stanley now *has* to buy all petrol products – diesel, gasoline, lubricant, central-heating fuel – from YPF, Argentina's state-owned oil firm, which was granted a supplier's monopoly by Britain in 1974.

And, in fact, many Argentines now live happily off Falklands soil: the officers who look after the airline office in Stanley, two young women teachers dispatched by Argentina to teach the natives Spanish, the men who are building YPF's new oil jetty in Stanley harbour. Argentina has even established a base, scientific and/or military, on Thule in the south Sandwich Islands, a thousand miles from Stanley, but still a dependency of the Falklands. A ship from the British Antarctic Survey discovered it two years ago, but the British Government swore all who knew to secrecy in case the news upset people. This year the news leaked out and people, predictably, were upset.

A Monday afternoon in Stanley in the month of March: Sunday's rain has now blown east and sunshine is liding in patches across town and harbour. It turns roofs and pillarboxes a brighter red and burnishes the yellow anoraks worn by four marine archaeologists who are now crawling over a black hulk stranded at the inlet's edge. The hulk is the last remains of the *Charles Cooper*, an American packet of 850 tons which put into Stanley in September, 1866, en route from Liverpool to Melbourne with a cargo of North Country coal. The *Charles Cooper* leaked and needed repairs, but Stanley's Victorian shipwrights asked too high a price. So the ship was sold to an island company and served out the next hundred years as a warehouse for wool, condemned at Stanley to an immobile life at the end of the Falkland Island Company's pier.

The harbour is lined with similar hulks – victims of rough weather on their passage round the Horn and the avarice of local ship repairers and trading companies who would over-quote on the cost of patching hulls and decks, and then snap the ships up from their unhappy masters at bargain prices. They are also a reminder of the days when Stanley sat on one of the world's great trade routes, from Europe to the Antipodes, from New York to California, before the Panama Canal was cut and steam took the risk out of the passage round the Horn.

The sun shifts. First the granite of the war memorial glints, then the white paint glistens on the fence surrounding the home of Mr Terry Peck, chief constable.

The paint has been recently applied by the islands' only prisoner, a twenty-year-old youth doing time for unlawful sexual intercourse with a fifteen-year-old girl. His cell is next to Terry Peck's home and supper is supplied by Terry Peck's wife. Poetry comes to him over the prison radio courtesy of the chief constable's uncle, none other than Mr Des Peck of the Philomel Store, down by the pier.

That night Mr Peck's most recent poem is broadcast by Fibs.

We're only 2,000 people
Born and bred in Falkland Isles
You can always tell a Falklander
Because we're friendly and all smiles.

The record rack in the studio hut of Fibs contains two versions of the British national anthem. One is marked *Solemn*, the other *Triumphant*. Which version will they play, one wonders, when and if the problem of the Falkland Islands is finally solved?

STEEL STRIKE

Wales, Spring, 1980

There are two heroes in the life of Jack Reynolds. The first is Nye Bevan; predictable enough given that Mr Reynolds is old and Welsh and working-class and, like so many of his fellow-countrymen, admires a bit of passion in a man and his ability to turn a beautiful phrase. But the second comes as a surprise.

It is Ian Smith, late of the prime minister's residence, Salisbury, Rhodesia.

Old Mr Reynolds has a photograph of Mr Smith on the sideboard in the living-room of his old-age-pensioner's bungalow in Goya Place, Port Talbot. 'I admire a man who does well by his country,' says Mr Reynolds, though there may be a little more to it than that. In the photograph Mr Smith is shaking hands with Mr Reynolds' youngest son, John. He settled in Rhodesia for a time and led the country's judo team. Now he runs a nightclub in Swansea and prospers – unlike his elder brothers, Owen and Patrick, and unlike their sons.

The Reynolds family, John apart, have worked in the steel mills of South Wales for three generations. Jack, the grandfather, joined a tin-plate works in Port Talbot in 1920 at the age of fourteen. Owen, his eldest son, joined the same works at the same age in 1942. Alan, son of Owen, went to join his father in the rolling mills six years ago.

Today father and son enter their eleventh payless week in the steel strike. And, no matter the strike's outcome, they also face the sack. British Steel employs 11,500 workers in Port Talbot and says it must nearly halve that number. In South Wales as a whole about 12,000 jobs in steel are threatened. The multiplying effects of these cuts, the further sackings in the trades which depend on steel, could mean anything from 50,000 to 100,000 men and women joining the dole queue. Many in South Wales speak with unflamboyant certainty of 'de-industrialisation' and a return to the despair and privation of the Twenties and Thirties.

The chief feature of that great depression, in retrospect, was the passivity of its name – the Slump. Men remember years of idleness rather than riots. But the reaction this time to any great reduction in living standards is likely to be very different. Today's anger comes from a generation which has more to lose than its parents and grandparents, and it is being expressed in terms of violent resentment.

Jack Reynolds lived through the worst of the older awful time, yet he looks back on it without great sorrow. When I asked him if it had turned him into a socialist, he replied, quirkily as ever: 'No, I'm a royalist.' His sons say they are 'middle-of-the-road socialists'. They are intelligent and voluble men, wedded to notions of decency and fair-mindedness and quite liable to put in good words for the Royal Family ('That Charles now, I reckon we could have a good talk with him') and the occasional Tory (of Heath: 'a decent chap, old Ted').

But there is nothing quirky or ambiguous about their choice of villain. A mention of Mrs Thatcher or Sir Keith Joseph sparks total hatred, words of fear and loathing on the new road to Wigan Pier. Small wonder, they say, that Sir Keith was pelted with eggs on his recent Welsh visit; or, so Owen Reynolds likes to think, that the Welsh rugby team gave England such a tough time at Twickenham. 'I just wanted them to go up there and give it to the swine.'

Both Owen and Patrick say that the Thatcher–Joseph stance on steel is driving them out of their moderate corner – not into the arms of the Left, which is regarded merely as 'politics', but into something desperate and perhaps lawless. They fear that the old Welsh conspiracy theories might be right, that the country is run by public school men in the south-east of England. Look at Blunt, a traitor and one of their own. Didn't he go scot free? In Port Talbot you can pinch an empty milk bottle and be up before the beak.

'That Blunt thing was a disgrace, a terrible tragedy,' says Patrick. 'It left ordinary people like us disappointed and baffled.'

And later: 'We're not wild men. Our father brought us up to be courteous, always to treat other people with respect. But we're probably the last generation to have those qualities instilled in us, and I'm speaking for our generation when I say there'll be no violence – not yet at least. But I can't speak for the young. Look what they achieved in Iran. Today you have to realise that we see anarchy from all over the world on television. It's spoon-fed to us in our living-rooms.'

In South Wales now he senses a similar spirit. 'I can't describe it but I know it's there. It's like spotting a glum group in the corner of a Valley pub. You know there's been a death in the family. I just wish to God that Thatcher would get off her high horse before it's too late.'

The two brothers, their families and their father live on the same bleak post-war estate of council houses. Gardening does not seem a popular pastime in Port Talbot. Most gardens have been laid to concrete to accommodate the British-made saloon cars which the Port Talbot steel-worker is inclined to favour. One such car, attached to a caravan, is parked hard against Owen Reynolds' front door. These vehicles and the contents of the Reynolds' home would gladden the heart of any Home Counties dragoness, anxious to point out that the poor are no longer with us.

The house contains a telephone, a colour television, quantities of bright, curved and spongy furniture, a gilt mirror which celebrates Wales' grand-slam in the rugby internationals – and a bar stocked with bourbon, brandy, Cointreau. His brother Patrick's house also has a bar.

'You'll be thinking we all have bars in Port Talbot,' said Owen Reynolds, and I was.

He then pointed out that all this apparent prosperity was superficial and dwindling. The bar stock dates from a wedding anniversary last year, the television is rented, the car's on HP (Owen, aged fifty-one, is only now learning to drive). At the steel works he was earning £108 a week, pre-tax, in the loco-shunting yards. For the past ten weeks he had lived from his wife's wages; she works hard and repetitively making metal tops for whisky bottles.

'You may say I'm well off,' he said. 'But look at it this way. I have worked hard since I was fourteen. OK, I've raised children and there's nix in the bank, and I don't even own the roof over my head.'

Reynolds described his working life at the steel mill: a 'continental shift' system, working twenty-one days out of every twenty-eight at changing hours of the day and night. It sounded hard. But compared to his father wasn't he living like a prince? His answer amounted to a succinct summing-up of a theory recently expounded at great length in a book by Professor Peter Townsend. Poverty (or in Owen Reynolds' case, potential poverty) is relative rather than absolute.

'Nye Bevan said it: "The Arabs aren't going to live in tents all their lives." It's the aim of any generation of working people to have a higher standard of living than the one that went before them.'

He traced his family's social history. His grandfather, a collier, wanted his son to stay above the surface in the tin-plate works. That son, Jack Reynolds, worked in the rolling mills bending hot metal with shears so that sometimes the sweat would spill out of his wooden clogs. His son, Owen himself, went to work there but his father snapped his fingers and told him to get out to a pleasanter job in the same mill. Owen's son, Alan, works as a weighman – a nice job with chairs to sit on. His other son is a teacher in a comprehensive school.

Reynolds showed a photograph of himself posed beside a shunting locomotive. 'That's me in 1958, with prosperity just around the corner, or so I thought in those days.' There was indeed prosperity but it was brief. High wages in the Sixties meant that Owen could expect much more from life than his father. For one thing, the money financed his divorce (he has remarried since), an action rarely practised much beyond the rich in his father's time. It also meant more convivial social occasions, dances, camping holidays (though never outside Britain).

What the Reynolds brothers find unacceptable is that those days were the peak of prosperity for the British working-class; that in future people will have to make do with less. But didn't the unemployed in South Wales fifty years ago learn to cope? Owen thought the same would not happen again.

'You see in the old days you felt differently. There are no poor people if you're all poor people. It's only when you see the rich that you realise "God, I'm poor" and in those days in Port Talbot you never met them. Everybody was in the same boat.'

Today, together with Patrick's 'world-wide anarchy', the rich and the pleasures of being rich are continually flaunted in glowing colour on 21-inch screens in every Port Talbot house. Men on strike or unemployed occupy their days in front of the television. As we spoke last week a repair-man came to tinker with Owen's set – 'Get it right for God's sake,' said Owen in a voice that implied a blank screen would induce domestic revolution – while a breathless harangue from the local commercial radio station, Swansea Sound, encouraged its listeners to furnish their homes in 'elegant luxury' with the produce from a Swansea store.

Owen and Patrick listed their basic essentials for a decent life. 'A fair wage for a good day's work, a roof over your head and a larder full of food,' said Patrick, but then the list grew. A car? Yes. A telephone? Yes. A fridge? Certainly. As boys they were brought up by candle-light and oil-lamp in the Thirties, in a slum, now demolished, with an outside lavatory and a cold-water tap in the yard. In the Fifties a car and a fridge were luxuries. Now, both admitted, they could not envisage life without them.

Another essential has been added by the generation of Jack Reynolds' grandsons: the right and the need, much advocated by Mrs Thatcher, to own your own home. Owen and Patrick live in council houses and could endure the dole, should it come, on £8 a week rent. But many of the newly-married generation in Port Talbot have £150-a-month mortgages which dole money could not cover. Some of them, believing that Mrs Thatcher had the interests of the home-owning classes at heart, took her at her word and voted Tory. They are among the most bitter. The dignity of labour and the property-owning democracy sound hollow phrases when there is no work to dignify the home-owner and the mortgage is reclaimed.

But Owen's twenty-four-year-old son, Alan, still wants to buy a house. 'It's an investment, something you can pass on to your children. I'm not being snobbish about council houses, but I just want something better than the place I was brought up in. It's only natural, isn't it?'

Alan's grandfather seems baffled by these expectations. Gathered together with Alan, Owen and Patrick inside his bungalow, he thought the future could be much worse than the past.

'But those were bad days Dad, we were all so poor,' said Owen.

'We stuck together then though,' said his father. 'We helped each other, everyone was neighbours.' He looked out of the window across the windswept patches of grass to the sign that said Goya Place (Owen lives in Jasmin Close). 'You'd never believe it,' he said, 'but the man who designed this estate got the MBE.'

Alan had just returned from picket duty at a steel plant in Essex. The previous week he had stood at the gates of the Sheerness steel works. 'Did they draw their batons on you?' asked his grandfather, recalling, almost wistfully, one or two similar incidents from the General Strike. It was worse than that, Alan said. He had seen men being kicked on the ground. The scenes there, he said, had really frightened him.

Alan will almost certainly be sacked from the Port Talbot mills on the principle of last in, first out. He said he would use the redundancy money as the deposit on a house. And the repayments? 'I'm going to try for a job in the new Ford plant at Bridgend – they surely can't close that.'

He'd heard there were 2,500 vacancies – and 15,000 applications to fill them.

THE MAKING OF MECCANO MAN

Birmingham, Spring, 1980

Sir Harold Wilson first rose to public office as the ten-year-old secretary of the Huddersfield Meccano Club. Some years later, from a position even more exalted, he heralded the 'white-hot heat' of Britain's 'technological revolution'. As an old Meccano boy, the prospect must have excited Sir Harold, though as it turned out the revolution was never more than luke-warm and has now chilled considerably. British technology has collapsed like a badly-built Meccano crane. The factory that makes Meccano itself has closed; a paradigm of British inventiveness in the past and British decline in the present. Old Meccano boys throughout the world are perplexed and disappointed. Something, clearly, has gone wrong.

Such weighty thoughts fill the mind as we drive through the West Midlands to meet Mr Bert Love, honorary secretary of the Society of Advanced Meccano Constructors. Mr Love has a magnificent Meccano crane. It measures six-foot by four-foot high and took years to build. The components would cost several hundreds, perhaps even thousands of pounds, at today's prices. It is also one of the great joys of Mr Love's life; and on this point Mr Love is sensitive. By letter and telephone he has warned us that he expects his hobby to be taken seriously – as seriously as he himself takes it, which (having purchased a whole house in which to store nothing but Meccano parts) is very seriously indeed. Other journals have sought interviews, but they have been spurned. He got the impression they were after stories headlined *The Meccano Boy Who Never Grew Up* to provoke reactions of 'Fancy, a grown man . . .' from the sniggering readers. That is not our intention.

The drive to Mr Love's home in Hall Green, near Birmingham, takes us through the leafier Midlands suburbs. This looks like old Meccano country: houses, detached and semi-detached, with gravel drives and spare rooms big enough to cope with pre-war Hornby trains (o-gauge) and models made from the larger Meccano construction kits. Here those Meccano boys – pre-war children who survived in Meccano publicity until the Sixties – could lie on the carpet in front of a coal fire and build Tower Bridges. They had well-parted hair and cheeks with the sheen of apples. They wore long shorts and long socks, white shirts and school ties. Usually, too, they had a father. He smoked a pipe and helped with the difficult bits. Once a month he would return from the newsagent with the new *Meccano Magazine* as well as his ounce of St Bruno.

Perhaps you, like Sir Harold, were a Meccano boy. If so, you may know that there was more to your toy than met the eye. 'The boy who is Meccano-wise is the boy who is looked up to by his pals,' wrote the publicist for Meccano in North America sixty years ago. 'He is the boy who, as he walks along the railroad track, can explain to the other boys just why the bridge over the creek is built the way it is . . . the Meccano-wise boy is the boy who can answer the questions and, because he knows, he becomes the leader.'

This worked out for Sir Harold. But for others of us, the Meccano failures, those strips of green and red metal with the holes and the nuts and bolts were a baffling torture of construction which resulted in frustration and half-completed models. Saddened fathers stored away the red boxes at the top of the cupboard and next Christmas bought us something easier, like Lego.

We owe it all to a Liverpudlian butcher's clerk called Frank Hornby. He should be better known; his invention has influenced the imaginations of as many children as did the books of Enid Blyton or Captain W. E. 'Biggles' Johns. Hornby was a Victorian, born in 1863 and a devout believer in the works of Samuel Smiles. He read *Self-Help* and *The Lives of the Great Engineers* and took to making models for his children. The big breakthrough – combining self-help, engineering, models and children – came in 1900.

'One snowy Christmas Eve I was taking a long railway journey,' wrote Hornby fifteen years later, 'and as I sat in my corner seat my mind was, as usual, turning over new schemes for my boys' enjoyment.' His immediate problem was a scarcity of parts for a 'fine model crane' then under construction. And then, Eureka! (or Cripes! in Meccano-boy language) Hornby had it! He would make the same kind of part, perforated with bolt holes, so that they could be bolted in different positions and at different angles. 'I tell you, boys, that I was pleased when I hit upon this solution to our trouble, but I had no idea then that the few hours' close thought which I had given to my hobby were destined to change the entire future course of my life and work.'

Hornby called his invention Mechanics-Made-Easy and patented it in 1901. It was a simple idea – half-inch wide metal strips with bolt-holes a half-inch apart – but immediately successful. In 1907 he coined the name Meccano. By the First World War Jaeger were manufacturing Meccano sweaters and Hornby had made a million and was earnestly outlining his philosophy in a small book entitled *Frank Hornby: the Boy who made a Million with a Toy*. Samuel Smiles had not been forgotten: 'The Boy Scouts' idea is to do a helpful deed every day. Meccano is built on the principle of helpfulness. It gives every boy the opportunity to learn (while he is playing) how to do things that will help him to be successful when he becomes a man.'

A greater boom followed. During the Twenties and Thirties Hornby's products invaded nearly every middle-class home in the Empire. Meccano begat Dinky toys. *Meccano Magazine*, founded in 1916, grew to 130,000 copies a month. There were editions in German and French; *The Meccano Instruction Manual* even ran to Russian and Cantonese. And in the middle of this period Bert Love, then aged six, bought his first set for sixpence at a Bournemouth jumble sale. It was only a ooo set in a range that ran from ooo to oo to o and then from numbers one to seven. But it emerges as a major turning-point in Mr Love's life.

Mr Love's home is easy to identify because he has decorated the porch with Meccano parts. Inside are Mr and Mrs Love, moving carefully among heaps of old but rare Meccano to offer us sherry. Their life can be charted in two ways. Either as an average couple's triumph over the common obstacles of life; they have stuck together, raised three children and provided them with good educations. Or as Mr Love's steady progress from the ooo set to the pinnacle of Meccano achievement – the building of the giant block-lifting crane.

The young Love resolved to build this soon after his purchase at the jumble sale. It was featured, together with the neat schoolboys and the pipe-smoking father, on the cover of the lowliest Meccano packet. What Meccano failed to tell its young clientele, however, was that this crane was impossible to build without having to go to the expense of buying the largest set in the range. And even then you needed extra parts.

Mr Love has computed that before the war the biggest set, the 'millionaire's set', cost the equivalent of eighteen weeks' wages for somebody like a skilled bricklayer. Its price then was £42 (today, still packed in wooden boxes, it costs £500 and Meccano sell only about fifty a year). But the boy Love persevered, converting each set to the larger size (a 2a set, for example, turns a number 2 set into a number 3) to clamber slowly up Meccano's steep south face. The moment of truth came soon after the war. Mr Love had to abandon Meccano during his time in the Navy, but quickly returned to it on the floor of the home of his newly-acquired mother-in-law in Rothesay. There he discovered the awful fact: even with the largest set, the crane could not be built.

Lesser men might then have stamped on every tiny girder, bracket and bolt. But Mr Love pledged instead that, one day, he would build a bigger and better crane than anything Meccano had advertised. He would do a Frank Hornby. He would make new parts himself.

Today the result sits in the upstairs bedroom of his other house, Meccano House, which he bought a few years ago to cope with the over-flow of Meccano which was threatening to submerge the home the couple actually live in. It stands only two back-gardens away, filled with thousands of pounds worth of old boxed sets, model pumping engines and fairground machinery. All of it looks like precisely what it is – old Meccano – for the Meccano modeller has always been concerned with the abstract principles of construction rather than verisimilitude.

It was not always so: Frank Hornby originally intended his little girders to be covered with painted cardboard so that a model, say, of a grandfather clock (and Mr Love had a full-size Meccano grandfather clock in his hall) would look like a grandfather clock. But the parts themselves were so aesthetically pleasing that few modellers bothered. First they appeared in plain chrome, then in blue and gilt, then in the much loved red and green. Today they are in blue, white and yellow.

Mr Love has examples from every period, as befits the honorary secretary and co-founder of the Society of Advanced Meccano Constructors, a breakaway from the Midlands Meccano Guild. 'They allowed children as members,' says Mr Love, with total disapproval. His society's twenty members include a surgeon, a quantity surveyor and a deputy bank manager. Every day letters reach his home requesting advice or rare parts, from Britain and overseas; from men building small Eiffel Towers in France, trans-Danube bridges in Hungarian living-rooms, railway engines in Argentina. Meccano stretched beyond the Empire.

Last year Mr Love, now fifty-five, retired early from teaching mathematics so that he could devote more time to his hobby, though 'hobby' sounds a feeble term to describe so grand a passion. He is a precise, some might say a severe, man. No-smoking signs decorate his home and there was a nasty moment when I reached out to take a piece of Twenties ephemera – *The Meccano Book of Engineering*, price 3d – from one of his many piles. It was like a man with a blowlamp approaching *The Book of Kells*.

'No, you can't touch it!' he shouted. 'I'll sit beside you and turn the pages if you want to look.'

He himself has appeared on the cover of a more recent instruction manual. The photograph shows him as a lovable Meccano dad with sweater and screwdriver, posed behind a crane with his real-life son in the foreground. It seems, however, that Love Junior never really took to the 'joy of inventing'; perhaps it is hardly a surprise.

And so we say farefull to Mr Love, to let him re-read notes by 'Spanner' in old copies of *Meccano Magazine*, to peruse requests for thinner washers and threaded strip couplings. It is a happy picture, spoiled only by the rapid sinking of the sun in the golden west. For it seems unlikely that the famous label – 'Meccano, Binns Road, Liverpool' – will continue to appear on these famous products. Frank Hornby died in 1936. His sons, like Mr Love's, were interested in other things. Sir Alec Issigonis used Meccano to design the transmission of the Mini – one of its many industrial applications; it was indeed more than a toy – but by then the rot and the losses had set in at Liverpool.

Lines Brothers, a firm which made plastic toys, took over the Hornby firm in the early Sixties. As an old Hornby Dublo (double o gauge) boy I remember this with a shudder. They too went bust a decade later. Airfix (more plastic) took over the Meccano side, Hornby trains went to a firm in Kent. Both are now in serious financial trouble. Airfix doubt the Liverpool factory will ever produce Meccano again, despite the sit-in of a thousand workers when closure was announced late last year. It was losing £50,000 a week towards the end. The management said the workers were lazy, dishonest and drunk. The workers said the management were incompetent. No surprises here.

Earlier this year the Maharishi Mahesh Yogi, the great meditator, showed interest in buying the plant if the work force could agree to two hours' meditation every day. He wanted to produce micro-chips. But the factory's unions had reservations over the meditation. Perhaps the best solution is to demolish the factory and sell the bricks to Meccano enthusiasts. This is a serious proposal. A former editor of *Meccano Magazine*, Mr Chris Jelly, says he has had requests for Binns Road bricks from across the world. Such is the loyalty implanted in the breast of the old Meccano boy.

Airfix, meanwhile, say they will continue to market Meccano as 'aggressively as ever'. They have introduced new parts and new packaging. But where will the parts come from? Ah. Many years ago Hornby opened a wholly-owned subsidiary in France – Meccano (France) Ltd. It is now independent and prospering.

The parts will be imported.

THE RETURN OF THE
BRIGHT YOUNG THINGS

Oxford, Spring, 1981

'Introversion,' said Paul Golding, 'is a terribly overrated virtue.' Golding spoke as we took tea and cake in his rooms in the village of Eynsham, a few miles from the spires of Oxford. He is a third-year student of languages who wants to be an interior designer. He is not himself of an introverted nature; indeed of all the young men I met in Oxford last month he was the most literally gilded, his face having received a skilful application of cosmetics.

Golding passed more cake and spoke sharply to his poodle, Oscar. Discotheque music came from his gramophone: 'Trash,' said Golding, 'but trash done well ... you know I can like anything provided they do it well.' This is a common sentiment in Oxford (and elsewhere) these days.

He said his father was a businessman in the Canary Islands who'd sent him to boarding school, Stonyhurst, in Lancashire, where he had not been happy. 'I was undoubtedly the most unpopular boy in the school – and the brightest. I was much more sophisticated than the average English child. I was loathed because I was arrogant, and because everyone fancied me.'

More tea, another mouthful of cherry cake. He reflected on gilded youth. 'What these people are saying, basically, is let's have a fun time ... I suppose if I looked on it from the outside I'd loathe it, but the fact is that most of these people are very talented, very nice and very beautiful.' Who were they? 'Well, most of the really wonderful people went down last year.'

Some, however, remain: Pandora Mond, daughter of Lady Melchett; Domenica Fraser, daughter of Antonia; Nigella Lawson, daughter of Nigel; Nicky Shulman, daughter of the *London Standard* drama and film critic; Rupert Soames, grandson of Sir Winston Churchill. They are a tiny minority of Oxford's 7,000 students, but they do constitute an exclusive group. They meet three or four times a term for dinners and parties. They form clubs and elect themselves to office. They are photographed for *Tatler* magazine. Friendships formed at Eton or Winchester (Harrow at a pinch) are their basis; female qualification for membership is usually wealth, wit and beauty. The women enjoy dressing-up. The men enjoy getting drunk; 'hog-whimpering drunk' in the words of Rupert Soames.

Paul Golding himself stands a little apart from this small throng. He runs his own club, the Kay-Whyte Club, named after the KY brand of lubricant jelly. 'Also,' said Golding, 'because Kay is such a nice androgynous name and Whyte is a pun of Anthony Blanche in *Brideshead Revisited*' (the novel by Evelyn Waugh). Golding passed an album containing photographs of Kay-Whyte dinners. Men and women in a variety of historical costume seemed to be having a remarkable time.

'That's me as Nijinsky in the ballet *Scheherazade*,' said Golding, pointing to a picture of a youth clad in gold reclining on a couch. 'And this is me looking like my mother.'

I wondered what Golding believed in. 'Beauty, love, success, respect,' he said. And what did he not believe in? 'Money and reputation.' But then, as Golding said, I had to remember that he was a rarity at Oxford even among the gilded. 'I'm very, very, very rare indeed.' Others hired their clothes from theatrical shops, were into para-punk or Gucci-Fiorucci. They liked Scott Fitzgerald and the dreadful David Hockney. He made his own clothes and loved the Renaissance.

At length he and Oscar walked me to the bus stop. I thanked him for his time. It had been an informative afternoon.

*

On the bus I read a few more pages of the Penguin *Brideshead Revisited*, recommended by some as a key to the present goings-on. The characters rather than the theme or plot of this fine novel are what concern us here. Its early chapters are set in the Oxford of the Twenties and dwell on the drunken, innocent and affected climate of that time. Here, for example, is Anthony Blanche:

'My dear ... I think it's perfectly brilliant of Sebastian to have discovered you. Where do you lurk? I shall come down to your burrow and ch-chivvy you out like an old st-t-toat.'

It is commonly said (though Waugh denied it) that Blanche was based on the aesthete and Italophile, Harold Acton. Golding met Acton in Italy before coming up to Oxford ('he promised me I'd find the Oscar Wildes of the future here, which unfortunately has not been true').

Echoes, then, of the aesthete Blanche/Acton in the activities of the Kay-Whyte Club. Other Oxford clubs, on the other hand, did not sound at all aesthetic: the Assassins', the Bullingdon, the Dangerous Sports Club, the Piers Gaveston – named after Edward II's catamite, who died shortly after Edward met his end by buggery with a hot poker. No, these did not sound like supper tables where one chewed the fat about Botticelli. The Waugh character that influenced behaviour here had to be *Brideshead Revisited*'s Sebastian Flyte.

'There's no doubt that Sebastian Flyte has been an enduring and terrible influence on the behaviour of some Oxford men,' said the editor of *Tatler*, Tina Brown. 'But what has changed in Oxford is that it's fashionable again to be rich and smart ... in the Sixties and the Seventies the rich and smart went on existing but were rather more on the defensive.'

Flyte is certainly rich and smart – and often drunk. He enters the novel by vomiting through an open window – into, rather than out of, some college rooms on the ground floor. Later he asks his close friend:

'Ought we to be drunk every night?'
'Yes, I think so.'
'I think so too.'

This sounded more like a conversation one might hear at, say, the Assassins' Club. The menu for that club's most recent dinner comprised: consommé, sole, quail, sorbet, château-briand, crème brulée, cheese, fruit, coffee. Accompanied by: Muscadet, Côtes du Rhône, Burgundy, Sauternes, port and 'limitless' champagne. That kind of thing can set a young man on his hands and knees, hog-whimpering the while.

But the girls I met that evening did not agree that the bright young things of 1981 were simply throw-backs to the Twenties. Melanie Walters and Caroline Kellett groaned at the mention of *Brideshead Revisited*, despite the fact that they were drinking gin slings in a cocktail bar with palm trees and cane chairs – a setting almost created for a film of the book. Melanie and Kellett (she is known, for some reason, by her second name) said that of course everybody read Waugh before they came up, but that life in Oxford these days was rather more ordinary and intelligent.

Still, their club, the George Club, did not include girls from comprehensives among its seventeen members. Kellett assured me that this was by accident rather than design. 'It doesn't need money particularly, it's much more a hierarchy based on style.' What style? 'It's panache, elan, flamboyance and a certain amount of intelligence. For God's sake, it's a cultural and aesthetic standard as well as a question of self-projection. You can come from any class and have it.'

As for dressing-up and/or falling down: 'All through history important people have shown themselves perfectly capable of going over the top. This is the time when we can do that sort of thing, for the rest of our lives our position in society will be much more low profile.'

By this time we had moved to supper in an Italian res-taurant, where Kellett eschewed wine (she does not like the taste of alcohol) and instead snorted down four or five vodkas and orange. Both girls are pretty and have already made appearances in the pages of *Tatler*, a magazine that Kellett would rather enjoy working for, she thought. Melanie Walters is studying Arabic and would rather like to deal in Islamic Art with Sotheby's. Neither had much interest in politics – feminism was thought a waste of time.

'Most students at Oxford are basically apathetic about politics,' said Kellett. 'We've all learned that extreme views favour a minority rather than a majority. Our generation believes that the future lies in self-belief. Everyone here, even the Northern Chemists (drudges in the sciences, up from comprehensives), are out for themselves. If you're at all bright you know you screw other people before they screw you.'

Rupert Soames was next on the list. We met the next day at lunchtime in the cocktail bar of the Randolph Hotel. Soames had just returned from his second interview with Morgan Guaranty, a smart merchant bank, and was in fine form. 'Booked a table for lunch at the Trout in Wolvercote,' he said, 'but booked it in the name of Johnson, so we don't have to turn up if you'd prefer not.'

We strode out of the hotel. Soames had a cheery word for the head porter, who also had a cheery word for him. These fellows, I thought, must plop from the womb with a vote of thanks – plus some instructions – for the midwife.

We drove fast in his new car towards lunch. 'Annoyed about that picture the *Sunday Times Magazine* took on Sunday,' said Soames. Annoyed because it was a corny Fleet Street idea of gilded youth? 'No, no. Annoyed because I wasn't asked to be in it,' said Soames, and laughed. At Eton he was Master of the Beagles; last term he presided over the Oxford Union; he reads politics and philosophy at Worcester College and runs a mobile discotheque called A Touch of Class.

We strode into the Trout. Soames had a cheery word for the chef ('Hallo there, chef'), and the chef had a cheery word for him ('Nice to see you again, sir'). Outside the sun sparkled on the weir.

'Look, I suppose if you must call us the *jeunesse dorée* you must, but it's a pity there isn't another word for it. What is it? Well, basically it's this. We're a group of people who've come up to Oxford with a base of friends from school, and on the whole we're richer than the average student and we tend to have famous parents.

'The fancy-dress part is simply to turn the party into an event; you either make people drive a long way to your place in Northumberland or you make them dress up. So we give parties a theme, and in Oxford these themes can be disgusting at times.'

Such as? 'Clitoris allsorts,' said Soames. We smiled into our beer.

'Of course people get drunk, absolutely hog-whimpering drunk, and there's lots of straight sex about, though I'd also say there's much less homosexuality and bisexuality than you might expect.'

Unusually for this group, Soames is interested in politics ('family's steeped in it, you see') and will talk at length about the state of the nation. I mentioned the Oxford Monday Club's recent display of sieg-heil salutes and its allegedly fine rendering of the Horst Wessel song. 'Don't take them seriously, it's a fairly silly institution. And they were drunk,' said Soames. 'Absolutely hog-whimpering.'

He continued. 'You see, students went through the Sixties thinking the world was organised in a bad way and that they could do something about it. Absolutely wrongly as it turned out. Now people take themselves less seriously, which is very, very attractive. Oxford's a charmed existence before you go out into the world and take a job of high responsibility. Also it's a wonderful place to meet a wife, there are so many lovely and clever girls about.'

Soames stopped. 'You haven't asked me about my ambitions,' he said. I apologised for this neglect and asked. 'To be rich and to love and marry a beautiful woman.'

How rich? 'Very, very rich. As rich as one possibly can be.'

On the drive back, Soames said that the people he liked

best in life were the people who made him laugh; that he would never leave Britain for reasons of tax; and that if he died now he would die happy because he'd done so much with his life. But he also said he'd taken out an insurance policy to pay the school fees of the family he hoped to have one day. He is now twenty-one and unmarried.

Finally, to tea with three leading members of the most socially important dining clubs. It was a charming occasion in a scruffy terraced house in south Oxford. I provided scones and apple tart. They furnished tea, jam and laughter. Robin Howard, a Wykehamist, reads theology at Exeter. He is the Doge of the Vile Bodies Club – named after the Waugh novel; members must attend dinners dressed as Waugh characters – and a member of the Piers Gaveston. The Gaveston has thirteen members, including one Catamite and one Master of Debauchery. Howard said he would like to join the priesthood, if he reaches the conclusion that God exists.

William Sieghart, an Etonian, reads PPE at St Anne's. He is a member of the Keats Society, which has little to do wtih truth or beauty. The title comes in extraordinarily handy, said Sieghart, when he approaches hotel-keepers for the hire of rooms. Little do they suspect that the draughts of warm south will be ordered quite copiously, or that the evening may end in smashed chairs, vomit and (sometimes) copulation under the table. At a recent dinner Sieghart overheard a waiter say: 'Mark my words, Reg, there's been an orgy here tonight.' Sieghart had also been interviewed by the Morgan Guaranty bank that day. He said he wanted to be 'a millionaire within ten years – I'm blindly ambitious on that score.'

Robert Stirling, another Etonian, reads French and philosophy at Lincoln. He is the Bludgeon of the Assassins' Club and wants to be an art dealer.

Together we went to the lavatory to inspect the club photographs hung on the wall. The same faces appear in each: Robin, William, Robert, Nicky, Kellett, Melanie. The face that appears with perhaps the greatest regularity is that of the late Nicholas Kermack, a big, smiling boy often placed centre in the front row. Two months ago he died in this house, of asthma.

On the train back to Paddington I finished *Brideshead Revisited*. It ends in the Second World War amid melancholy yearning for times past. And I could not help remembering a sentence offered, unprompted, by Rupert Soames.

'The *jeunesse dorée*, as you call them, may not care much about politics, but I'm certain that if the Russians came in they'd be the first into the trenches and the first out over the top.'

Perhaps.

SCENES FROM THE LIFE OF A BELEAGUERED GENERATION
Summer, 1981

I spent most of last summer talking to young people. Occasionally colleagues, friends and relatives would ask what I was doing and I would tell them. They would then express varying degrees of alarm, boredom and sympathy – and sometimes a surprising curiosity, as though one had returned from a long stay with the Marsh Arabs. 'What are they actually *like*?' they would ask. 'How did you find them?'

It was not an easy question to answer and my replies tended to be based on who I had last seen. They ranged from 'fatalistic and angry' after a morning spent with unemployed West Indian boys in North London, to 'cheerful and pleasant' after a day at a Boys' Brigade camp on the Isle of Wight. I had not, in fact, expected to like the Boys' Brigade – I share a common prejudice about an organisation which combines military drill with evangelic Christianity. The truth is that I was touched by a simple notice which had been pinned to the mess-tent wall. *Remember our motto*, it said, *think of the other fellow first.*

The Scouts had a similar effect on Donald McCullin (hardly a man, one would have thought, to take to camp-fire sing-songs with enthusiasm). He returned from photographing a Scout camp in the Welsh mountains aglow with praise. 'If anyone says a word against the Scouts to me in future,' he said, 'I'll punch them in the throat.'

These reactions were probably the result of too long among

disaffected youth and attitudes of sometimes chilling nihilism, where every institution or idea is called a 'con' or 'laugh'. Job schemes, Mrs Thatcher, Tony Benn, God, these are all 'cons'. Schools, newspapers, fulfilling work, these are all 'a laugh'.

Such total disenchantment with the social fabric can be frightening – or heartening if you favour revolutionary change – but neither the disenchantment nor the fear it causes are new phenomena. Anxiety about the fate of the young, particularly the urban delinquent boy, has existed in Britain for at least the past hundred years. Neither the Scouts nor the Boys' Brigade would have been born without it. 'Fear and self-interest,' writes the historian John Springhall, 'had as much to do with the setting up of the early youth movements as altruism.' Thus William Smith founded the Boys' Brigade in the 1880s as a means of controlling the rowdy working-class children who were sent to his Glasgow Sunday School; and Baden-Powell gave us the Boy Scouts because he feared that the 'deterioration of our race' – apparent to him in the 1900s – would soon lead to the degeneration of Empire.

Both organisations still flourish despite nearly a century of popular mockery. They and the Girl Guides have more members now than ten years ago. Their creeds still emphasise God, Queen and duty to one's fellow men and women. But they did not, in the end, do much to stem Glasgow's crime rate or the Empire's collapse. They no longer contain – if they ever did – the kind of young person who inspires puzzlement, concern and fear in the adult breast. They represent the difference, to quote my colleague Philip Norman, between 'young people' (anoraks, orienteering, A-levels) and 'youths' (glue-sniffing, rowdy, criminal).

It is impossible to estimate how many young people/youths fit these popular stereotypes and this report cannot pretend to be sociology. There are in the United Kingdom today about 8.2 million people aged between thirteen and twenty-one. They represent nearly fifteen per cent of the population; two-thirds of them are defined as working-class; males outnumber females by 200,000. Nearly a quarter of the girls marry before they are twenty. A quarter of the boys will be convicted of crime worse than a motoring offence by the time they are twenty-five. Nearly 1.2 million under the age of twenty-four are on the dole, 638,000 of them aged sixteen to nineteen. They drink more but smoke less than they did ten years ago. Solvent abuse (glue-sniffing) is widespread. It is cheap – a tin for £1.70 will last two days. Evo-stick and Thix-O-Fix are favourite brands. About sixteen per cent of the school population will get one A-level or more; about twelve per cent will leave school with no qualifications whatsoever.

With these statistics in mind I set out to discover what a broad sample of British youth believed and how they behaved. I spoke to about a hundred in all – at some length – in schools, hospitals, summer camps, detention centres, in the army and the police, employed and unemployed. They were white, black and brown; some wore hair *à la* Mohican, others dressed like characters from the early novels of Evelyn Waugh or tarts from the more sado-masochistic salons (Britain must surely have produced the most bizarrely-attired young in the world). I moved around: Hampshire, Yorkshire, London, Birmingham, Liverpool, Newcastle, the Hebrides. We talked about work, race, right and wrong, patriotism, crime, religion, schools, parents and what was to become of us all. It can be said that I rarely returned to my hotel of an evening either (a) unsurprised, or (b) abrim with confidence in the future.

Two stories spread around Britain in the wake of the summer's riots. Neither of them appeared in the Press nor on television and neither is true, so far as one can tell. But both were believed or half-believed by a wide variety of the people I talked to, and as an indication of the kind of country many young people believe they are living in, both are worth re-telling here.

I heard the first from Asians in Southall, from senior pupils at a Hebridean comprehensive, from some Newcastle punks and from young Yorkshire miners. All believed that the riots in London, Liverpool and Manchester had so scared the Government that it had imposed censorship on newspapers and the broadcasting media. Equally serious disturbances had occurred in other towns, so the story went, but they had gone unreported. Glasgow – notably riot-free – was a favourite location in this story and D-notices to Fleet Street editors appeared in the more sophisticated versions. In others, it was simply a case of 'them – you know, the media, Mrs Thatcher and that' conspiring to keep the country from imminent anarchy.

The second story had a more limited circulation – I heard it in Yorkshire and London. The most complete version came from an eighteen-year-old boy serving three months in a detention centre near Wakefield – a customer for Mr Whitelaw's 'Short, Sharp Shock'. I had asked about his future. 'Pretty bad,' he said, 'unemployment's never going to get any better. I'm not supposed to tell anyone this but the other day my Uncle Cyril and my Auntie Dot got sent ration books through the post. They'd got *Not to be used until February 1982* marked on the front. Then a couple of days later they got a letter saying there'd been a mistake and could they please send the ration books back and not tell anybody about them. That's true, that. Y'see they'd sent them out too *early*.'

These stories have a ring of the Phoney War about them, and indeed during July, the month of the riots, whole conversations among adults in London pubs might have been reproduced from a Lyons Corner House of forty years ago – jotted down by a snooper on Blitz morale from the Ministry of Information. Chats over a pint went along these lines:

'They say it's Highbury's turn tonight.'
'I heard it was really bad in Hackney.'
'They say there's not a window left in the Seven Sisters Road.'
'They sent all the kids home from school early down our way.'
'They're boarding up all the shops in Kensington High Street.'
'Ken High Street! Never.'

Adults took it badly. Soon their conversation switched from

where it had happened to why. Unemployment; police relations with the black community; the influence of television; the destruction of working-class communities in once great Victorian cities; the breakdown of family life; the abrogation of parental discipline; the failure of the Church to give guidance. Each of these theories about the behaviour of the young had its advocates and opponents.

'If it's all about being on the dole and living in a high-rise flat next to a motorway then why hasn't it happened in Glasgow?'

'If it's about police methods then why did it happen in Handsworth where all the bobbies go around on bikes telling you the time?'

'You can't blame it on unemployment. Half the kids I saw on telly last night were still at school.'

Young people, I discovered, had a more direct line in reasoning. Many of them described the riots as 'daft' or 'a laugh' (two boys in for a Short, Sharp Shock said rather sniffly that 'most of 'em weren't proper riots at all') and the rioters as 'thick' or 'mongols'. Few, on the other hand, doubted that rioting had been good fun or that it had worked. Young people had shifted themselves sharply to the centre of adult consciousness. A mining apprentice in Yorkshire put it like this:

'Rioting's just like gang-fighting really. You've got one set of lads chucking bricks at another set of lads who're wearing a daft uniform and they're chucking bricks back at you. But with all this unemployment it had to come, hadn't it? It gave them a reason so they went and kicked hell out of the coppers. It's proved a point and it's made the Government act. That unemployment march [organised by the TUC] hardly showed – the Press made 'em look bad and all. But the riots worked. If it's a start and they keep on then that's good. Otherwise the Government will just hand out a few jobs and that'll be that.'

According to Lieutenant-Colonel Prideaux, 'Wherever you go, an idle person is a dangerous one.' Prideaux commands the Royal Green Jackets at their base – the Rifle Depot,

Winchester. His particular speciality is junior recruits, the fortunate sixteen- to eighteen-year-olds who have escaped the dole queue by securing a place in the British Army; last year 33,000 boys applied for 10,000 places.

Prideaux poured coffee ('black, white, pink?') and moved the biscuit plate around. Barks of command penetrated his office window from the depot's drill square. 'Inout Inout Inout, Outin Outin Outin, Updown Updown Updown, Downup Downup Downup.' Recruits were being rehearsed in gymnastics for their passing-out parade. I asked about the problems of bringing discipline to bear on boys these days.

'Yes,' he said, 'I think that before we probably accepted discipline a lot more readily. Today it's difficult to see where they'd get any idea of discipline *from*. Still I'd say that on average about seventy-five per cent accept it and about twenty-five per cent ask why they have to do something and we explain why. But if they really question authority with a capital A then it's unlikely they're going to be the sort of chaps who will want to stay in the Army.

'When they arrive we make them sit round a bonfire and get each one to stand up in turn and tell his life. Most are incredibly shy, but there are the occasional chaps who go on about how they played merry hell with their schoolteachers, or how they skedaddled from school, or how many girls they've had, or how they can drink fifteen pints of beer at a sitting. He's usually the chap who folds later on.'

Prideaux seemed to view this state of affairs with a fair measure of satisfaction.

Why did they join the Army? 'One, unemployment. Two, an active life. Three, learning a trade. Four, every young man sees himself as roughie-toughie – it's Audie Murphy and war-film stuff, I'm afraid. And these days an enormous number come from broken homes – indeed, that's often the reason given for joining.'

And what interested them once they were in? The answer was another brisk enumeration: 'One, when are they going to eat. Two, when are they going to get paid. Three, when are they going on leave.'

The recruits themselves bore out much of what their colonel

had said. Their chief enthusiasm was for the near future. The past was considered a hopeless place, the present exhausting ('they're not idle here for a split second,' said the colonel) and the horizons of County Armagh or West Germany too far off to contemplate. The past meant school and civvy street. The prevailing attitude among the boys towards school was contempt.

'The only thing that school taught me was how to doss . . . we used to walk around during the lessons and the teachers couldn't do nothing about it . . . skivers make it hard for you in school if you want to learn . . . some of us only turned up for our school dinners . . . if they hit you in school you'd have your dad up, wouldn't you? Your parents can't complain here, because you're on your own.'

Social class (which still sharply divides the British Army between officers and men) did not worry them. Of officers: 'Sometimes we can't understand their orders because their accents are a bit funny.' Politics did not interest them. Of unemployment: 'Some of the kids on the dole at home are having an ace time.'

Of Northern Ireland: 'It's your parents who worry; they see all that stuff on the telly. Soldiers say they enjoy it.' Their idea of a good time was 'a night on the piss', though the expense was regretted. 'You go into the pub,' said a seventeen-year-old from East London, 'and it's one fiver after another. You get a bird who drinks Pernod and it's all gone in a couple of hours.'

Their ideas of right and wrong contained few absolutes. Breaking windows in empty houses (most had done it) was thought to be a perfectly respectable pastime; breaking shop windows was wrong 'unless you didn't like the geezer who owned the shop'; shooting people was (obviously) not wrong, *unless your target couldn't see you*; on the other hand any kind of violence towards women, especially old women, was wrong; cat-strangling was also wrong, though it was not unknown.

The dozen boys I spoke to were all white, from working-class homes in London, the Midlands and the West Country. The Green Jackets, however, do recruit a fair number of black youths.

Slowly the conversation drifted through patriotism ('We're English, aren't we? I mean, we're God's gift') and the riots of this summer ('daft – just to get yourself noticed') towards the thorny and ever-present subject of race.

'Yeah we got coloured geezers, sambos and that,' said one of the louder boys, 'but we all take the piss. I mean last month we pretended to be the Ku Klux Klan. We put pillow-cases over our heads and went around the barracks at night moaning and wailing and telling them all that Maggie Thatcher was going to kick 'em all out. But everybody gets the piss taken out of them, they know it's only a joke like. There's this Paki, we call him Abdul. We say, "Give us a fag, Abdul, you nig-nog" and he says, "Aw piss off or I'll get my tribe down to have a go at you." I mean it's a joke for him as well. We all do it. The corporals take the piss just as bad.'

They do. The next day Donald McCullin was photographing a black recruit behind the parade ground. A corporal passed them. 'Oi,' he shouted, 'remember to show 'im your lips.'

I asked a young officer if this kind of behaviour presented problems. He said: 'Well occasionally we do get blacks ganging up together in a black power kind of thing – we call them the coon clans – but fortunately we've got some excellent black NCOs and they sort things out pretty quickly.' In fact the Green Jackets tend to be regarded as a sloppy, pinko outfit by other units in the British Army; by, for example, the Household Regiments who appear to such stunning effect in royal pageants. The Household Regiments do not accept black recruits. 'It's not official policy, you understand,' said a cavalry officer, 'it's just that we won't have them.'

'Boys can be incredibly beastly to one another,' said Colonel Prideaux. 'The townies are beastly to the ooh-arrs [country lads], the white boys can be bloody to the black boys. I always treat them all exactly the same. Sometimes I'll get a black boy who says I'm picking on him because he's black. I always tell them: "Look I don't give a monkey's if you're black, white, pink . . ."'

Imagine a camp version of Quentin Crisp and you have Andy.

I met Andy on a Saturday afternoon in the King's Road, Chelsea. His hair is dyed blond and coiffed; tight trousers; vivid lipstick; cheeks dulled with face-powder. All his energy has been poured into his appearance; he is devoted to the way he looks, though he thinks he may change himself soon; you can't stay looking the same way for too long. He hopes to be noticed and now he has been. He is delighted. This is how famous people become famous, entire careers can be based on looks. It is a more attractive route than working and in any case work is in short supply. And yet Andy is as working-class as any of the crop-haired recruits in Winchester barracks. He lives, unemployed, in Croydon. His father is a postman: 'a yobbo, a scruff,' says Andy. What does his father make of all this? 'He keeps saying that what he really wanted was a son.'

In North London, three black teenagers talk about their future:

'I can't see over the age of twenty-five.'

'Me, I feel I'll be dead soon.'

'Anything could happen. You got so many problems – the Government, the police, unemployment. You could be spending your entire life in jail or something.'

These three were taking part in a twenty-week course in a fashionably revamped warehouse – a course designed to teach the benefits and skills of self-employment to the unemployed. It is the only one of its kind in Britain for the 'under-educated, under-twenties'. Most of its participants are black; many have criminal records; few come from stable families. Their tutors display enthusiasm but say they are battling with a well-founded pessimism among their charges. I asked the boys I met if they blamed anyone or anything for their unemployment. 'It's not our country so how can you blame anybody?' said one, and the others agreed.

None said they felt themselves to be British: 'I'd like to go back to the West Indies. OK, maybe it's harder to make a living there but it's your own place and you're not under any pressure, know what I mean? It's a bad thing to deprive anybody of, seeing their own country.'

Politics: 'The more I think about politics the more it pisses me off. The white man rules the world. You've always been so *busy*. You're like leeches, man, you suck out our countries. I mean the blacks don't even rule their bits of the world. The Jamaicans don't run Jamaica – it's the CIA who runs Seaga (the right-wing Jamaican prime minister), isn't it?'

One boy wore a Rastafarian badge; red, green and yellow. I asked about a return to Africa. 'Yeah, let's have all the whites from South Africa over here and all us blacks in South Africa ... Idi Amin, now, I really rated him.' (laughter)

And then came a recurrent theme: the uselessness of school. Here Albert, who wanted to be a sound recordist, was the most articulate. 'My school didn't care who made it and who didn't. The teachers don't make a good appearance to the people. I mean who's going to listen to a scruffy teacher. If a teacher came to school dressed properly it would look as though he bothered, wouldn't it? But they come all scruffy, faded cords and all, and if a man comes in looking like a tramp, who's going to bother with what he's telling you? The only guy who bothered at our school was the head and he was the only guy who scared us. He wore a tie and a suit and he looked good.

'Teachers know nothing about people. They don't know how to treat them or nothing. Here they *ask* you to do things – "Would you please open that window? Can you tell the class what happened in 1939?" Stuff like that. If they ask you, you've got a right to say yes or no. So you say no 'cause it's easier. So they let you relax on the radiator for the next half-hour. In Jamaica they don't muck about asking you, they *tell* you.'

This may be the received wisdom of West Indian parents, but none of these boys seemed to get on with their parents (or at least mothers; fathers were rarely mentioned). 'Everything I did in their eyes was wrong. You see I mixed with white kids and I learnt their dirty habits and that was all wrong.'

Another voice: 'White people! All they know about you is surveys, surveys.'

Albert: 'I'd like more black speakers to come to the course (as would their tutors, but small businessmen who are also black are difficult to find). I'd like to see black MPs. I'd like a poor person to run England. When they've got money in their pocket, their heads're full of fashion.'

A fine morning on the Isle of Wight. I walk through green fields under blue skies towards the tents of the Lambeth and Southwark battalion of the Boys' Brigade. Boys, black and white, are playing football; tonight they will have a wide game in which their officers will dress up as members of the KGB and hide in the woods and the boys will have to find them. I have come among Christians. Outside each tent, awaiting my inspection, are neat little piles; each contains a Bible, a cap, a belt and folded blankets. A boy recites the Objects of the Brigade:

> The advancement of Christ's Kingdom among boys and the pro-
> motion of habits of obedience, reverence, discipline, self-respect
> and all that tends towards a true Christian manliness.

We settle down to watch the football game. I remark on the absence of swearing among the exclamations rising from the players. 'We come down heavy on that,' says an officer, a draughtsman in his mid-thirties from South London. 'It still amazes me how we can do it and get away with it, and it says a lot for the boys that they can see the difference and respect it. You see that Jamaican boy leaning against the goalpost? He still calls you Sir. Most boys straight from Jamaica do, but within a few months it all begins to go.' The officer looked wistful, as though he were watching the last great Atlantic liner being slowly towed towards the breaker's yard.

Over lunch in the mess-tent (grace, cheese sandwiches, orange squash) I ask an officer's wife if it is not dispiriting, this effort to promote true Christian manliness in the summer of 1981 among youths of sixteen. 'Oh no,' she says, 'even if we keep only one boy, his spirit is precious to Our Lord.' Later I ask a sixteen-year-old if the prospect of unemployment does not worry him. No, he says, he's more scared of nuclear war. 'But I've got faith – it's that that keeps me going, really.'

*

Nuclear war worries young people more than any other issue. Time and again when I asked about the future, their replies suggested there would not be much future to care about. 'I'm against these nuclear weapons,' said a boy burglar receiving the Short, Sharp Shock. 'It's these third world countries that are going to start it all off. Just imagine Cambodia with a nuclear bomb! They could hold us to ransom for food and stuff. I reckon they should install fall-out shelters in every back-garden.'

A group of punk girls I spoke to in Newcastle were even gloomier. 'We'll be punks till we're grannies,' said one, 'but we'll likely be in little pieces long before then. We support CND but it's a hopeless cause like. It's depressing.'

'Everybody's got it in them to kill,' said another. 'We think we're higher than the animals but we're not.'

Not everyone, however, has decided to lie down in fancy clothes and wait for the bomb to drop. The young membership of anti-nuclear campaigns is growing rapidly. In Stornaway, on the Hebridean island of Lewis, I met members of a group called *Sith*, the Gaelic word for peace.

NATO wants to build a base on the island; earlier this year *Sith* organised the first protest march Lewis has seen for many years. The nucleus of its membership is drawn from the local comprehensive, a school with a fine academic record. They described themselves variously as socialists, anarchists, vegetarians and radical humanists – and also Christians, for Lewis is nothing if not a Christian (or at least Calvinist) island.

Its downfall from this state of grace has been predicted often enough. Louis MacNeice went there before the war and wrote:

> *It's no go the Herring Board*
> *It's no go the Bible*
> *All we want is a packet of fags*
> *When our hands are idle.*

But the Bible and Sabbatarianism are still holding up remarkably well, all things considered. The comprehensive school headmaster told me that he now considered it safe to be seen on Sundays strolling round his garden or driving his car, but still unsafe to be seen digging the one or washing the other. Oddly (or not oddly) I found more optimism, wit and articulate debate here among young people than in any major British city.

'You've got to hope,' said one girl in *Sith*. 'If something doesn't change soon we've had it. But I think things are starting to change. When we grow up, things will change.'

Many of their parents opposed what they were doing, but they did not dislike their parents because of this. Sometimes they complained of adult complacency. 'Our parents are horrified by what's going on in England,' said one boy, 'but also I think they rather enjoy watching it on television. It's almost as though they're saying: "Oh, look at that. Isn't it terrible? But at least we're fine and cosy up here."' Teachers, however, were not at all unpopular: 'All of us here were brought up to respect teachers. You should respect them. Teachers are there to teach you things.'

Would they stay on Lewis? Most of the boys thought not. 'You have to leave. Against us are the people who believe in the ultimate righteousness of their own community. Most opposition to NATO here isn't because people are anti-nuclear; it's based on the fact that NATO might fly their planes on a Sunday or the runway will destroy the local peat bog. They're out of touch with society and society's problems.'

Two members of the peace group in Stornoway are trying to correct that. They have become skinheads – thought to be the only skinheads in the Hebrides. They have the uniform but they lack convincing aggression. One boy blushed and refused to speak when I addressed him. The other, a crofter's son, said he wore Doc Marten boots and cropped hair so that he would be 'unacceptable'. But wasn't he acceptable? 'Och yes,' he said, with a shrug, 'unfortunately.'

To a ceremony in Southall at the home of Mr S. P. Gupta (MA, according to the bell-push). The ceremony is Indian and traditional: *Rakhi*. Mr Gupta's two clever and polite sons

– students at Cambridge and East Anglia – are to become 'brothers' to the pretty daughters of another Mr Gupta who runs an Indian snacks shop in Southall High Street. The families assemble. A cloth is spread on the floor. The girls tie gay pieces of cord round each boy's wrist ('with this bond of love I call you my brother') and pop Indian sweets into the boys' mouths. The boys reward them with a pound note each. Now the Gupta brothers are pledged to protect the Gupta sisters. Why is such a ceremony considered necessary?

'The time may come when the brother has to help the sister,' says Mr S. P. Gupta. 'If the sister is having a hard time then it is the brother's duty to intervene – even if the person giving her a hard time is her husband. We do not call it intervention, we call it help. Other than sex, you see, marriage is not considered a private relationship. It's a family relationship. We'd consider it insulting to approach an outsider – the social services, for example – for help in a domestic dispute. The family is considered a better institution because the family knows us and loves us. If they don't do this, their duty, we're surprised. "What has happened?" we'll ask them. "Has your blood gone *white*?"'

And then the Guptas and their sons get into their car and drive to Newcastle, to inspect the potential bride that Mr Gupta has selected for his younger son.

It was an attack on Indian womanhood, so the people of Southall say, that sparked off the Southall riot in July. Skinheads arrived in buses from East London one afternoon and began behaving yobbishly and violently in Asian shops. The Indian, predominately Punjabi, youth of the town then marched on the pub where the skinheads had gathered and burned it down; an act that earned the approbation of many non-Asian young people. Skinheads, the Hebridean variety apart, evoke widespread fear and dislike. They are thought to be 'thick' and 'vicious'. It would be a mistake, however, to imagine that they hold a monopoly of anti-black or, more precisely, anti-Asian attitudes among the young. 'It's them Pakis I can't stand,' said a young Yorkshire miner. Why?

'They smell.' No, they don't. 'Well their breath smells then.' Not particularly. 'Well there's summat about them that smells is all I can say.'

Or a young Manchester shop-breaker: 'Sometimes we do Paki shops. OK, it's still not right but I just don't like Pakis. I hate 'em. They just shouldn't be in this country. I think they're worse than West Indians. It's the food they eat, that curry. They stink of it all the time.'

Part of the reason why white youths pick on Asians is, quite simply, that they feel they can get away with it; West Indians are a much tougher proposition ('You don't want to go tangling with that lot'). This, however, is beginning to change. The Southall Youth Movement, according to one of its leaders, Balraj Singh, grew out of young Asians who were 'fed up with being bashed about in the school playground'. Many adult Asians view the movement with suspicion. They say it models itself on the aggressive behaviour of white youth and they fear it will damage the interests of their own community; and certainly the Southall Youth Movement's chauvinism can seem like a mirror image of the terraces at, say, West Ham. Its members are anti-politics, anti-liberal and anti-middle-class.

'We don't have a political ideology,' said Singh. 'We're dealing with kids who are half-illiterate and kids like that can't grasp ideas like capitalism and the working class. We believe in our own culture.' Neither does he believe in the 'race relations business' (though the movement receives a grant). 'The communities here are already segregated. The Asians go to Asian shops, the English go to English shops, there's no mixing after school. Multi-racialism and multi-culturalism are figments of the imagination. The only place there's mixing is the Community Relations Council, where the Indian middle-classes eat sweet curries [ie modified to Western taste] and drink wine.' Singh called this group 'Coconuts – they look brown but they're white inside.'

He said the future looked grim. Britain hadn't much to offer: no jobs, racial tension, hopeless schools. On the other hand, young Asians were 'here to stay and fight' and looked

increasingly to militancy rather than moderation as a gua-
rantee of their future.

Some Asian parents have reached other solutions. Many of
the more prosperous families, I was told, were now sending
their children back to the subcontinent for their education.
There, staying either with their grandparents or at boarding
schools in hill-stations, they would learn good manners, respect for their seniors and (with luck) gain enough knowledge
to pass the Oxford and Cambridge entrance exams. Others,
particularly the Sikh community, would like to establish their
own school in Southall, just as West Indian families have
done in Tottenham, North London. Many of them imagined
that British schools would be based on Dr Arnold's Rugby.
The appearance and behaviour of white children frightened
them.

Some might be rather worried, for example, by the appearance of Bobby, a girl punk in Newcastle upon Tyne, who
colourfully sported spiky hair, tribal make-up, bondage
trousers in tartan, spiked jacket and big boots. What did she
think of school? Put it this way: 'If I had kids I'd save up and
send them to grammar school.' Her friend Meg said she would
teach them at home.

Bobby and Meg and their friends Mel and Trigger meet
regularly in an old warehouse (where else?) which serves
Newcastle youth as a 'community arts centre'. They are all
punks, all girls and all unemployed. They are now learning
photography by taking pictures of one another – Bobby was
the current 'character study' – and journalism by publishing a
magazine. They interviewed me when I was there. 'Go on,'
said the community worker, a former hippy, 'ask him why
he's wearing *a suit.*'

They also belong to an anarchist group. 'They haven't got
many members and they don't really know what they're
about,' said Trigger. 'They just go paint-spraying *Anarchy*
and *Peace* and that.'

They were reasonably happy not to be working ('it can be
very boring, work') and remarkably tolerant of everything,
apart from 'society' and people who were intolerant of them,

though at the same time they did like people to note their appearance. What did being a punk mean? 'It's giving people something to laugh at . . . you get thrown out of pubs, you get picked on by the police . . . you make more friends this way, people come up and speak to you like.'

They did not like skirts (some had never worn them), high heels, marriage ('men are only good for one thing'), skinheads, political parties, newspapers ('biased and cheap'), or violence – despite their studded jackets and hefty boots ('if we scare people then that's because people are narrow-minded'). They did not believe in God ('conditioning'). They liked the local bands (PM Tension, Total Chaos), pizzas, biscuits, the *Hammer House of Horror* series on television but not the *News at Ten* ('we're not interested in what other people do'). Homosexuality was OK. 'Gay folk are canny, they're better-natured than other lads and they're different, like us,' said Trigger.

Trigger had a long history of petty crime and local authority care. She had sniffed glue: 'You just stagger about – people shouldn't have to get that bored but they do.' All four liked getting drunk. Scotch Ale was good, but cider was cheap. Mel: 'I can drink seven pints afore I'm sick.' Meg: 'I really like Pernod – the times I've been sick is when I've had too much Pernod.'

They said, yes, they were anti-social. Any question of individual wrong (outside hitting old ladies over the head) was countered by mentioning greater wrong-doing elsewhere. For example:

Question: 'Isn't vandalism wrong?'
Answer: 'So is dropping bombs on people.'
Question: 'Isn't dropping litter wrong?'
Answer: 'Look at all that rubbish they dump in the sea.'

This was the most common form of moral argument I met. 'Why pick on us?' was a recurring theme. 'If it's wrong for us to sniff glue, how come you can kill yourself with cigarettes . . . if it's wrong to carry offensive weapons, why is it right to sell them?' No doubt one can think of many kind and lucid answers to these questions. If one is pressed for time, however, the temptation is to switch the argument from morality to consequences. To say: 'If you behave in what the rest of us consider to be an unacceptable way, then the results for yourself will be extremely unpleasant.' In brief, the Short Sharp Shock.

Mr William Whitelaw, the Home Secretary, introduced the Short, Sharp Shock after Conservative pressure for 'a deterrent regime' inside establishments for young offenders. Four detention centres now practise it – including New Hall, near Wakefield, which takes seventeen- to twenty-year-old boys from Yorkshire and Greater Manchester. Its old army huts house about one hundred boys, each serving three months (two, with good behaviour) for offences which include stealing cars, vandalism, arson and threatening behaviour. About fifty per cent of them are there because they stole. They have on average two or three previous convictions. About sixty per cent of them will appear in court again within two years. About ninety per cent are registered as unemployed when they get here and the same percentage will leave without a job in prospect.

When the boys arrive they get a haircut (except skinheads, who must grow their hair to regulation length). Ear-rings are removed, uniforms issued. Then they begin what is, in theory at least, a punishing schedule of work and drill. It goes: 6.15, rise and clean dormitory. 6.45, wash. 7.30, breakfast. 8.00, divide into working parties. 8.00–12.00, dig fields, look after pigs, tend gardens, weave in weaving shop, etc. Then lunch, followed by an afternoon of drill, physical education, more work, and tea. 6.00, classes in woodwork, metalwork, how to read telephone directories, etc. 8.00, polishing shoes and buttons. 9.30, lights out.

They get a day off every second weekend and attend church service (the Chapel of St Wilfrid) every Sunday, where the vicar tends to stick to old favourites (*Onward Christian Soldiers*) because many of the boys cannot read fast enough to sing unfamiliar words in the hymn book. It sounds punishing; it looks punishing, the sight of boys being bullied round a drill square; but does it deter boys from crime any more than the rather more relaxed regime – no drill and more education – that it replaced?

The staff of New Hall are sceptical, for various reasons. The officers said it was still too little, too late: boys were not going to be shocked out of criminality at eighteen and the officers still lacked the power 'to run them ragged'. The warden thought that the environment was 'a sedative in a sense – regular meals, regular work, regular bedtime – it provides a form of organisation for people who are often mentally disorganised'.

The probation officer took a different view: she thought that it 'stimulated them mentally and physically – remember these are the kind of lads who stayed in bed till three in the afternoon at home'. The tragedy was, she said, that they would return to jobless towns and broken homes where New Hall's disciplinary code would be absolutely meaningless.

But the most damning evidence came from the boys themselves. A thief from Manchester: 'I can't say whether I'll go out and pinch again or not, but I can tell you that drilling hasn't made any difference. It makes it better, I think. I enjoy it, it passes the time more quickly and it makes us fit. Next time we'll just run faster from the coppers, won't we?'

Another thief, from Rotherham: 'I've been in and out of children's homes all my life – me mam's fault, she was always boozing and going out with men. She's been married five times. This place wasn't as hard as I thought it would be. PE's a bit hard, but it's only making us fitter. Drill was what people weren't supposed to like, but they do. There's *not enough* of it to my liking – they could have a drill session before dinner as well as after it. When I leave here and my probation officer says: "Now, John, what had the biggest effect on you at New Hall?" I'll say "All that drill – it was really horrible, it really hurts." Then they'll give us more of it, which is good because it's a lot easier than working in that weaving shop.'

He said he could think of many ways to make New Hall harder. They could be forced to rise earlier, or made to live in cells rather than dormitories. 'Then there'd be nobody to talk to and life would be more boring and much harder because of that. I had a cell in the remand centre and it was much harder than here.'

He was leaving the next day for home and a stepfather he hated. 'I say I won't get into trouble again, but there's always temptation. I might see fifty quid on the sideboard and just fuck off with it.'

Adulthood used to capture youth with the serious, stabilising stuff of work and marriages and family life. Teddy Boys became foremen, bought Ford Consuls and semis in Essex, became Teddy Boys in their spare-time. But for many young people in Britain now that road is closed; they face a future without work and without money. The youth culture of the Sixties promised freedom from the 'enslavement' of work and the 'oppression' of adult values. That promise has largely been fulfilled, though rather more harshly than its prophets predicted. The young now live in a kind of ghetto, marooned there because they lack the money or the will – for the adult world no longer seems such an attractive place – to scale the walls.

Will they be vandalising phone booths and spraying *Peace* and *Anarchy* on walls when they are thirty-five? Will they still be listening to Blondie? Will rioting become as regular as the Boat Race? Baden-Powell, should he be living at this hour, would be seriously perplexed.

THE RISE OF THE
FOUR-LETTER WORD

Autumn, 1982

Workers on the assembly line at British Leyland's car plant at Oxford returned to work last week after a strike promoted – at least in part – by what they claimed was the management's use of bad language. Managers, they said, had sworn abrasively at members of the workforce.

The dispute, the so-called 'swearing strike,' caused some cynical eyebrows and questions to be raised; it was difficult to believe that the strikers themselves spoke with the chastity of Sunday School teachers. Surely this was a mote-and-beam situation? Where had they been living all these years? Had they never watched a television play, or been to a football match, or (even) passed a school playground? Was this simply not a good excuse to down tools and (as it were) bugger off to the pub?

I telephoned David Buckle, the Transport and General Workers Union official in Oxford, to discover the precise words to which his members had taken such exception. Buckle was reticent. 'I have a lady secretary sitting beside me,' he said, 'but if I say the words were effing bastards and effing pigs, you'll no doubt get my meaning.'

Indeed we do. Mr Buckle could have employed the adjectives frigging or naffing, or even played totally safe by going for blanking baskets, and we would all know the real words which lurked beneath the euphemisms. He was simply observing the old courtly virtues – virtues which this article also intends

121

to observe – by trying to avoid potential offence or embarrassment to either the woman beside him or the stranger on the telephone. 'Gordon Bennett!' or 'Sugar!' it was tempting to exclaim in reply, 'that's pretty strong stuff, Mr Buckle.'

But the temptation was resisted, for even a brief investigation of the current state of British swearing reveals a complex of attitudes which must be taken seriously – and a central paradox. People of all classes and stations in Britain probably swear more today than at any time in recent history – and here we are talking of the hard Anglo-Saxon stuff, not the quaint 'bloodies' of yesteryear – but the sheer commonness of four-letter words has not greatly reduced their capacity to shock or offend.

It depends upon who is swearing, to whom, and where. For example, a man might tolerate a friendly 'f . . . off' from a male colleague, but not the same words from a female colleague or his boss or (Heaven forbid!) his wife. Equally, a reader of fiction might take no exception to the forty-nine f . . .s on one page of Martin Amis's novel *Success* (page fifty-two, actually), but the same person, watching television, might be shocked by a similar dose of the word in a documentary or film.

Channel Four, which started broadcasting the day after the Oxford car men downed tools, discovered this rather quickly. Like the rest of the broadcast media, the new channel has a duty under the Broadcasting Act to ensure that its output offends neither 'good taste' nor 'decency'. More specifically, under guidelines produced by the Independent Broadcasting Authority, it is asked 'to avoid the gratuitous use of language likely to offend', although its use can be defended (after nine o'clock and the children are thought to be in bed) on the grounds of 'context' and 'authenticity'.

Several films shown on Channel Four have needed this defence. *Network*, *Semi-Tough* and *Remembrance* were all peppered with four-letter words which the station, which likes to consider itself an 'adult' channel, chose not to cut. 'Our position,' says a Channel Four spokesman, 'is that we wouldn't want to censor the language of the film-making talents we are able to display.'

The BBC behaves differently. According to Alan Hart, Controller of BBC1, it frequently chops bad language out of late-night films – but then the BBC has been living with political opposition and Mrs Mary Whitehouse for rather longer than Channel Four.

Mrs Whitehouse is already heading in that station's direction. Last week she wrote to the attorney general asking him, in her own words, 'to fire a warning shot across Channel Four's bows.' She and her fellow members of the National Viewers and Listeners Association have been counting words.

In one episode of the soap-opera, *Brookside*, Mrs Whitehouse bagged one *bastard*, one *sod-off*, one *If-I-was-on-fire-you-wouldn't-piss-on-me* and one *Have-we-buggery*. She is reasonably happy to repeat these words down the telephone, but draws the line at her real concern, 'the Anglo-Saxon word'. Even in her letter to the attorney general, she says, she refers to it as 'eff, dot, dot, dot'.

In the Sixties Mrs Whitehouse battled unsuccessfully against 'bloody' – she counted forty-four examples in one episode of the BBC series, *Till Death Do Us Part* – and today senses that she is about to depart on a similar crusade against the Anglo-Saxon word. 'It's my impression,' she says, 'that there have been more four-letter words on Channel Four in a fortnight than on any other channel in a whole year.'

Mrs Whitehouse may be trying to stop the flood after the dam has broken, but she is determined to win this time: 'I'll put my reputation on the line. Unless something is done, and done quickly, we'll have four-letter words littering our programmes in future, just as "bloody" does now.

'What we're talking about is the crudeness and coarseness and innate vulgarity of these words. They tend to destroy the nuance of feeling which language exists to express. They reduce sexual experience to a harsh and crude act. They're destructive to our culture and destructive to relationships. People, ordinary people, are concerned and frustrated beyond measure.'

Mrs Whitehouse's view that language is changed from the top of the social heap rather than the bottom, by a conspiritorial liberal élite rather than by the crowd, may puzzle anyone who has ever listened to the dreary adjectival swearing of (say) a skinhead. But it does get some support from Professor Randolph Quirk, the vice-chancellor of London University and a distinguished writer and lecturer on language.

Professor Quirk uses four-letter words as a doctor might handle the human body; quite dispassionately. The telephone line rang to the sound of Anglo-Saxon, probably in contravention of the obscenity law contained in the Telecommunications Act, 1981. It was true, he thought, that there was 'a greater spread' of swearing in Britain today. But, he added, 'we in the so-called arty circles often don't realise how much further we've gone in this direction than the rest of society.'

He recalled the outrage caused when Kenneth Tynan said f . . . on television, the first person ever to do so, in 1965. 'I couldn't understand the fuss. It was a word we'd used in the senior common room for years. And then I found myself with a group of engineering and medical students one day and discovered that they had been absolutely appalled by Tynan. You see, swearing not only affects different classes in different ways, there can even be differences between professions.'

He thought that today society had 'a more honest recognition' of a language that has always been with us, though suppressed. The *Concise Oxford Dictionary*, for example, included the Anglo-Saxon words for the first time only in the Seventies. He did admit, however, that this recognition clashed with what he termed the puritanism of much of the population, and particularly the working-class. (I am not sure if the professor used the word 'puritanism' pejoratively, but he certainly seemed to take a dim view of New Zealand, which he described as 'very prissy, linguistically.')

Which raises another great paradox in British swearing; the working-class, after all, are the people who are supposed to have been swearing, unrecognised, for years. But they have bound the habit with rules and regulations, appropriate and inappropriate times and places. Many abhor the fact that the old Anglo-Saxon has crept out of its prison in the mine, the mill and the public bar and is now threatening an assault on the living-room.

Alan Bleasdale, the writer whose BBC series, *The Boys From the Black Stuff*, so vividly revealed the lives of the Liverpool unemployed, charts this progress quite specifically: 'I first heard a woman swear in 1967. She was a teacher in the same school as me, and I was appalled.' Bleasdale went abroad in 1971, returning in 1974. 'When I left I'd never heard a girl pupil swear. When I came back, I found beautiful little eleven-year-olds shouting "you f ... ing twat" down the school corridor. I was appalled again.' Nonetheless, the word frigging featured often in Bleasdale's recent series. Authenticity, presumably, was the criterion here.

Working-class communities may prove the last bastions of the courtly virtues. As Bleasdale says: 'The people I grew up with still can't bear to hear a woman swear, and very few working men will swear in front of their wives unless they [the men] are drunk.'

Whether women need or appreciate this protection is another matter. Sometimes, one feels, it is sensitive men who should be supplied with ear-muffs. Earlier this month I talked to an old miner in Wigan who had been unlucky enough to watch and hear Pamela Stephenson's performance at the lunch for 'The Woman of The Year'.

'That Stephenson woman. . . .', he said, puzzled. 'It beats me why academic types like that have to swear. I mean it's degrading, isn't it? We swore down the pit because we were driven to swear. You need to swear if you're up to your arse in water and it's as black as night. But there's nothing clever about swearing, is there?'

Professor Quirk would disagree. In his book * he welcomes

---

* *Style and Communication in the English Language*, Edward Arnold, 1982.

the continuing trend 'away from old constraints and rigid-
ities'.

But his chapter on swearing, entitled 'Sound Barriers and
Gangbangsprache', closes with a bleak rider.

> I find it no easier than anyone else to view sympathetically the
> abuses and perversions of what I have been trying to see as broadly
> beneficent trends. Obscene and brutal language is certainly more
> audible, not merely among the idealistic and "progressive" but
> also among muggers, the "Paki-bashers", the black hoodlums
> and white back-lashers and it is not surprising if the relaxed con-
> straints are linked in the minds of many not with an enhanced
> democracy but with more sinister fascistic trends, street violence
> and mob rule. There is nothing liberal or "liberated" in getting a
> thrill out of linguistic flashing at old ladies . . .
>
> The porn merchants, like the poor, have always been with us,
> as have the cruel and the brutal and the mentally retarded. We
> must take the roughnecks with the smoothies and accept that any
> major social movement will spawn its deviants.

Such fair-minded sentiments are perhaps easier to take on
board if one reads them in some civilised spot far removed
from a railway carriage full of Millwall supporters, boy soldiers, or (who knows?) professors of linguistics. Place most
people in the midst of Professor's Quirk's gangbangsprache
and they will still show a strong desire to leave at the next
station.

Four Journeys

1. WIGAN, AUTUMN, 1982

George Orwell spent less than a month in Wigan in 1936 and from that experience produced a book with a title – if not a message – that has never been forgotten.

The Road to Wigan Pier has sold more than half a million copies in its Penguin edition alone, and has rarely been out of print since Victor Gollancz and the Left Book Club accepted it for publication in 1937. Its 200 pages of description and polemic cover a good deal of ground. At first hand, Orwell investigated the working conditions of the miner and the domestic situation of the unemployed; he stooped and coughed his way down pit-tunnels and through the front doors of slums, for he was a tall man and often troubled with his chest; he talked to idle men on street corners; he made many notes. And then, the external journey over, he turned in on himself to examine his own reactions – the reactions of an old Etonian and former imperial policeman in Burma – towards the social class whose cause he espoused. Did the workers smell? Could they ever learn to love Socialism when Socialists were often, in Orwell's view, fey people who wore sandals and drank carrot juice? Finally, he issued a clarion call to the English middle-class to join the struggle for Socialism – defined by the author as 'justice and liberty' – in a book that ends '... for, after all, we have nothing to lose but our aitches.'

But that is not what many people, and particularly people

in Wigan, remember about *The Road to Wigan Pier*. The passage that sticks in the Wigan memory – and sometimes the Wigan throat – concerns Orwell's days and nights in a Wigan lodging house, described so horribly and vividly in the book's first eighteen pages. For who can forget the chamberpot kept under the kitchen table, or the great white folds of tripe, or the thumbprints left on the bread by the landlord's black hands?

In this way Orwell made Wigan famous and, in the long run, there is no such thing as bad publicity. Today, with the tripe shop and the chamberpot junked down the same well of British history as Wigan's coal mines and cotton mills, most people in Wigan look back with a strange detachment and wonder that it was ever like that. There is even talk in Wigan of a memorial to Orwell: a bust in the carpark opposite his lodgings above the tripe shop, perhaps, or a plaque on the canal-bank near the site of the long-demolished Wigan Pier itself.

People who remember those days are less amused. 'He gave a very poor picture of Wigan, did Orwell,' one old man told me as he changed gear in his Japanese car. 'The majority of Wigan folk weren't like the people in his book. He lived with the dregs.'

Any writer, any voyeur, who goes to Wigan in the steps of Orwell may soon reach the same view. Orwell sought out the worst lodgings he could find, spurning cleaner accommodation and the advice of the working men he had befriended. Orwell knew good copy when he saw it; perhaps only one home in 15,000 Wigan homes kept the chamberpot under the table but Orwell found it.

I pondered the point glumly in the lavatory of my own Wigan lodgings this winter. They were the cheapest I could find – six pounds a night with breakfast, compared to Orwell's one pound a week, full board – but of the squalor that shocks I could find no trace. The toilet roll was encased in knitted wool with a plastic fairy on top, a verse by Mabel Lucie Attwell was nailed to the wall:

> *Please remember – don't forget*
> *Never leave the bathroom wet*

> *Nor leave the soap still in the water*
> *That's a thing we never ought'er.*

Middle-class gentility, the quality so derided by Orwell, seemed to have stretched its gloved fingers down into this particular section of the working-class. Some, further up the scale, may have lost their aitches; but many, lower down, have discovered the knitted toilet roll cover. And why not?

It was a Sunday evening. Church bells rang over Wigan, which is a religious town as English towns go. A third of the population is Roman Catholic, the descendants of Irishmen sucked into Lancashire in the last century to fill a vacuum of jobs in coal and cotton. My landlord came from this stock, his terraced house built on ground riddled with the empty coal seams which had been burrowed by his forefathers. At that moment he sat downstairs, listening to *Songs of Praise* in the kitchen. Cheerful hymns rang up the stairs and against the flush and Yale-locked doors of the empty bedrooms.

Most lodgers went home for the weekend, leaving me and a middle-aged man called Bill to share the house's second television in the parlour. Bill, who had no home to go to, said only three things but said them often:

'Aye Aye'

''Ey up'

'That's the stuff'

Occasionally he would smoke part of a cigarette, nipping it carefully with his fingernails and replacing it in the box if it looked as though it might contain a few more puffs. 'He's a funny chap is Bill,' said the landlord over breakfast one morning. 'Never says owt. We inherited him when we bought the place eight years ago. I said to him one day, Bill, I said, what happens if anything happens to you like, I mean who do we get in touch with?'

And Bill said nobody, not a soul, he had no mother or father or brothers or sisters, nobody in the whole world. 'Well,' said the landlord, 'that's maybe as all right for you to say, but where does that leave *us*?'

Nonetheless, the landlord was a kindly man with a strong philosophic streak. He had worked on the railways and in the police before entering the boarding house business, since when he and his bedrooms had seen all sorts: men who had run away with fancy women from Warrington; men who had been evicted by their wives and then died alone, of cancer ('towards the end, the only thing he really cared for were his cigarettes'). In the morning, retrieving the bacon, egg and fried bread from the serving hatch, he would be cheerful. 'Champion!' he would say to those who asked after his health.

He and his wife had just celebrated their Ruby Wedding anniversary. The room where the meals were served lay littered with presents, still in their boxes. Brand-names held the eye: a Calypso Seven-Piece Water Set, a Goblin Teasmade. They added to the tide of ornamentation in plastic, glass and brass which threatened to overwhelm the room. An electric organ stood in one corner, a trolley of sauce and vinegar bottles in another. The walls had pictures of eighteenth-century squires having a good time – smoking long pipes, drinking wine, eating grapes. The landlord moved deftly among this clutter in his slippers, dispensing fried food and lightly singing lines from popular songs. 'Do you really want to hurt me?' he would ask of himself as he placed the teapot on the table.

He was proud of his wife, a confectioner to trade, who baked pies and cakes. But other objects of affection lay well in the past; in the time, forty years ago, when he worked as a fireman on the old LMS. He still bought magazines filled with pictures of steam engines. One evening he cornered me in the hall and reminisced about engines of the *Black Five* and *Baby Scot* classes, and the different steaming qualities of good Yorkshire and bad Lancashire coal. ('Terrible stuff. You could shovel in a couple o' ton, look like a proper Al Jolson, and still get more heat out of a fridge.') And then, in mid-reverie about the difficulties of the steep ascent to Shap, he suddenly said 'Ey up, 'ere's the boss' and his wife came through the front door.

'I was just telling 'im about my days on the railway,' said the landlord.

The wife said a sharp 'Oh aye' and gave me a look which might have been pitying; and which, as it happened, was misplaced, for many British males under the age of twelve and over thirty-five can be drawn into a story which involves the *Royal Scot*, falling steam pressure and the signals against you just out of Carnforth. But our talk, broken off, was never resumed. The next day – there being a shortage of bedrooms – I moved to a room above a noisy pub filled with afternoon drinkers. Flannelette sheets were exchanged for nylon.

I was sorry to move. Orwell's landlord, the dreadful Mrs Brooker, would constantly whine: 'It does seem 'ard, don't it now?' Mine had a less certain verdict on the human predicament. 'Eh,' he would say, 'you just can't weigh up human nature, can you?' But wealth moderates despair. The landlord's Volvo Estate lay beached outside the house with the inappropriateness of a dead whale on a British shore, in a narrow street that had long since ceased to ring to the sound of clogs.

Weighing up human nature is indeed a difficult business. Today Wigan suffers the same chronic unemployment that it did in Orwell's day. Nearly twenty per cent of the working population is on the dole. All the town's cotton mills have closed. The Wigan coalfield has been worked out. Here, you might suppose, is a part of England close to breakdown, a forcing house for revolution or at least the petty anarchy of riots. Yet – and this sets one of the great puzzles of contemporary Britain, especially for the Left – a cry of 'Justice and Liberty!' does not seem likely to bring Wigonians pouring on to the streets.

Perhaps it never would; perhaps it never will; perhaps enough justice and liberty have been dispensed, to make the call redundant. Certainly Wigan, perched on its little hill above the Lancashire plain, seems about as close to revolt as Weybridge. The first thing that strikes me, coming up from London, is that it's a very *clean* town: no graffiti, not much litter, little smoke. The old market is thronged, baker's windows display great piles of carbohydrate: ring scones, sultana scones, plain scones, brown scones, barm cakes, finger doughnuts, parkin, meat and potato-pies. Many of the shop fronts are in the mock-Tudor style, the result of a planning decision made in the Twenties by the local corporation; so that, the writer H. V. Morton noted in 1927, 'in twenty years there will not be a better-looking or more original manufacturing town in the North of England.'

Wigan's present appearance may not justify that boast, because today quite a lot of it is waste land punctuated by ring roads. But another of Morton's observations still rings true. He had expected to find a place 'of dreary roads and stagnant canals and white-faced Wigonians dragging their weary steps along dull streets, haunted by the horror of the place in which they are condemned to live.' Instead he found 'a spa' in comparison to the towns of the English Midlands.

Morton wrote only ten years before Orwell, but the Slump had yet to bite and Orwell may, in some senses, have seen a different town. Writers, however, tend to find the things they seek, be they horrible lodgings or mock-Tudor streets. In my case, I wanted to discover people who could tell me why Wigan, or indeed Britain, was not more distressed by its own condition.

There were many answers. Some people pointed to the town's Roman Catholicism as a breeder of stoicism and good behaviour. Others said its working-class were innately conservative (they are if exemplified by the two great trade union leaders born in Wigan, Joe Gormley and the late Les Cannon). Many felt their town was peculiarly blessed. Go east and you came to Bolton and Blackburn, towns which had 'more darkies than Calcutta'. Go west and you were in Liverpool or, even worse, the Liverpudlian overspill town of Skelmersdale. Nearly everybody spoke of Liverpool and its inhabitants with dread. 'They should build a wall round the place,' said one man, 'just like the one they have in Berlin.'

'Bewildering, isn't it?' said Sydney Smith, owner of the largest and most famous newsagent's and bookshop in Wigan. 'All these folk on the dole and yet trade still prospers.' I had been pointed in Mr Smith's direction because he was one of the few people left who remembered Orwell in Wigan; he had, in fact, lived in the same street as Orwell's first digs – the house the author quit for the tripe shop because the former was too boringly clean. Smith remembered him as 'a tall fellow who wore a hat and a raincoat and spoke in a language different to Lancashire . . . I remember some folk thought he was a nark of some kind, what these days you'd call a snooper from the Social Security.'

Mr Smith, like almost everybody I met in Wigan, was a very decent person. 'Decency' was a quality Orwell cherished in the English working-class; Wigan is still alive with it. Mr Smith took me to watch Wigan Athletic being beaten one–nil by Newport County in the rain. He took me home to meet the wife. He took me to the site of Orwell's lodgings – a grassy mound, the statutory saplings and the statutory rain. Meanwhile he recalled interesting things. There were a 1,000 old mine shafts within five miles of the town centre. The Wigan Coal and Iron Company had once been a larger consortium than Krupps. Occasionally, with a distant smile, he would recall poverty. 'The unemployed used to say "Let's go to Woolworths and have a warm" . . . I can remember the days when the top of an egg were a luxury.' (Sadly, the pith and truth of these remarks is diluted because we have all watched too many Hovis commercials.)

But Mr Smith's most interesting revelation concerned the present; the sales of magazines stocked by his shop. Here they are, and remember this is in a solid Labour-voting town with hardly a middle-class to speak of.

Tribune	7	copies
Labour Weekly	12	,,
New Statesman	13	,,
Economist	22	,,
Investor's Chronicle	22	,,
The *Lady*	36	,,
Private Eye	200	,,
Computer magazines (25 different titles)	2,500	,, per month

In other words, the *Lady* magazine sold more than the three Socialist weeklies put together; *Private Eye*'s jokes, London gossip and maverick conservatism sold fifteen times more than the *New Statesman*; computer magazines made all of these seem small beer. Sydney Smith said that it astonished him too, this great Wigan interest in computers; and then, as a man who remembered the top of an egg as a luxury, he laughed with bafflement and delight.

Others are equally baffled but less delighted. Neil Turner, the secretary of the local Labour Party, and his wife remarked wanly that 'real solidarity' in Wigan was pretty rare. They had spotted the phenomenon known to sociologists as 'privatisation', whereby people stayed inside their own homes and busied themselves with computers, video machines and roof repairs. The working-class, in particular, had become much less communal. Not that this, said Mr Turner, was a threat to Labour in Wigan where the two hardest things to find were 'a job and someone who voted Tory'. But he was disappointed that so many felt that 'they can't do anything to change anything'.

He drove me on a Sunday evening to one of Wigan's many Labour Clubs on a housing estate, Marsh Green, on the outskirts of the town. Labour Clubs have many detractors among the politically-minded in Wigan. 'Bingo and beer! It's bloody sickening,' said one trade unionist. 'Ask that lot who Keir Hardie was and nobody would know. Ask them the shop that sold the cheapest Guinness in Wigan, and *everybody* would know.' Still, the clubs draw people out of their homes when other entertainments – cinemas, theatres, proper nightclubs – have failed. Their bingo, beer and snooker are remarkably cheap, and on my night at Marsh Green they had a singer who did a passable imitation of Stevie Wonder.

At the bar, I met a young, plump man who had not worked for two years. Did he think he would ever work again? 'Eh,' he said in the face of probability, 'I certainly 'ope so.' The next day, at home before his coal fire in his council house, he confessed that he had never considered the possibility of never working until I had asked him. 'It's a thought, intit?'

He'd worked as an upholsterer for fifteen years after leaving school and the house was well and softly furnished. He and his wife and two small children lived off a total of £73.60 a week – £63.10 from Social Security, £10.50 family allowance – a sum which aroused some resentment from one or two working colleagues in the Labour Club who, after they had paid tax, did not take home a great deal more. In 1937, Orwell found a similar family – father unemployed, two small children – who were living on £1.60 a week from the dole. Orwell itemised the family's budget, and the comparison with today is interesting. First Orwell's list, converted from shillings and pence:

Rent	45p
Clothing Club	15p
Coal	10p
Gas	7p
Milk	4p
Union fees	1p
Insurance	1p
Meat	12½p
Flour (2 stone)	17p
Yeast	1½p
Potatoes	5p
Dripping	4p
Margarine	3p
Bacon	6p
Sugar	9p
Tea	5p
Jam	3½p
Peas and cabbage	2½p
Carrots, onions	2p
Quaker Oats	2p
Soap, etc	4p
TOTAL	**£1.60**

Now the weekly budget of today's unemployed family of four,

the Armitages in Marsh Green, spent from a total income of
£73.60

Rent	£20
Coal	£10
Electricity	£4
TV (a slot meter – 50p for six hours)	£4
TV licence stamp	£1
Telephone	£2
Interest on £400 loan for washing machine	£7.50
HP on husband's suit and shoes	£2
Food	£18
TOTAL	**£68.50**

To itemise the food consumed by the Armitages would
require too long a list, but it can safely be said that the family
are not living high on the hog. Their diet consists mainly of
carbohydrates – more than a quarter of the food bill goes on
bread, pies and cakes – and tinned food, which Mrs Armitage
buys on her fortnightly trip to the local Asda Superstore. She
can rattle down her shopping list as though it were carved on
her heart ('Let's think now . . . two jars salmon paste, one big
tin meat balls, one bottle orange squash . . .'). Often the
quantities seem tiny: two cartons of yoghurt, ten fish fingers
per fortnight for a family which includes two growing children.

Of course, the lists then and now show startling differences.
Which unemployed Wigan miner in 1937 could have imagined
that his unemployed grandson in 1982 would be able to afford
a telephone, a washing machine and forty-eight hours of television a week? But the similarities are also striking. Both
families are in hock to 'Clothing Clubs'. Neither buys fresh
fruit. Both eat a lot of bread (though the woman in 1937
baked hers, a habit Orwell considered 'wasteful'). Mrs
Armitage laughed at the idea of a visit to the butcher's: 'It's
mainly corned beef we have for Sunday dinner. My sister
jokes about it, but it's surprising how good it tastes.'

Another striking similarity is how little either budget allows for expenditure outside the bare essentials of being fed and warmly housed. True, the Armitages have a surplus of £5.10 a week where the pre-war family had none; but a fiver a week will not go far on clothes, bus fares, the occasional packet of cigarettes or pint of beer, the everyday wear and tear of household goods.

'We've had no new shirts or dresses since Christmas ten months ago,' said Mr Armitage, 'though we did buy a pair of shoes for the little lad in September. You see you can't get credit when you're on the dole. The only time we go to Wigan (ten minutes away by bus) is to sign on or go to the wife's mother's. Sometimes we walk. It takes about an hour. It's surprising how many people you see walking these days.'

The Armitages have never been abroad, though Mr Armitage spent his two redundancy payments on holidays for the family in Blackpool and at Butlin's in Skegness ('When we had money we squandered it,' said Mrs Armitage). Last year, during Wigan Wakes week, they stayed at home and 'took butties' on day trips to Blackpool, Southport and Chester Zoo. 'It were heartbreaking for the wife to see other folk going away with their suitcases,' said Mr Armitage. 'She cried for two days.'

So were they angry? Mr Armitage: 'Not really angry, more frustrated. You just can't make ends meet so it annoys you.'

Were they more political? Mr Armitage: 'I suppose unemployment has got me more involved with the Labour Party which I weren't before. I go to ward meetings, but it's really only to pass the time. But they can't do any worse than this present lot, can they?'

Did they envy the better off? Mrs Armitage: 'If they've worked for their money they deserve it.'

Did television advertising upset them with glimpses of goods they could never afford? Mr Armitage: 'No, not really. Oh, there is one that frustrates me, for a steam-iron. Ours is dry and it's buggered.'

Mrs Armitage said she herself didn't watch much television. She was a great reader, anything to do with the eighteenth and nineteenth centuries. Her sister brought her paperbacks from a stall on Wigan market: you paid a deposit on a book and then got some money back when you returned the book, which you then put down on another book. And so on, the deposits getting cheaper as the books got more worn. In this way she had read most of Catherine Cookson.

'I love her books,' said Mrs Armitage, aged twenty-eight, mid-way through summarising aloud a particularly vivid Cookson chapter on a mining disaster. 'They make your problems look like nothing.'

I left the Armitages to their tea of tomato soup and bread and walked back to Wigan through the dark: across a field and over a stream where an abandoned fridge glistened like an iceberg; past the Asda Superstore and various ruined buildings labelled Video Centre, Brake Centre, Exhaust Centre; past Wigan Pier itself. Wigan Pier (it should be explained) was an old coal wharf on the Leeds and Liverpool Canal which eighty years ago became a music hall joke, Wigan being a grimy town far from the sea. It was actually demolished seven years before Orwell reached Wigan, but the joke survived. Today the local council wants to posh up the canalside and the surviving warehouses so that they might serve 'important leisure, recreation and education uses'. The cost, from public funds and private enterprise, will be two million pounds. They call it the Wigan Pier Project.

Difficult, I thought, to know what Orwell would have made of this idea. With the Armitages he would have been on surer ground. 'It may be,' he wrote, 'that the psychological adjustments which the working-class are visibly making is the best they could make in the circumstances. They have neither turned revolutionary nor lost their self-respect; merely they have kept their tempers and settled down to make the best of things on a fish-and-chip standard . . . Of course the post-war development of cheap luxuries has been a very fortunate thing for our rulers. It is quite likely that fish and chips, art silk stockings, tinned salmon, cut-price chocolate, the movies, the radio, strong tea and the football pools have between them averted revolution.'

I took another Orwell quote with me when I went to the factory of Wigan's largest private employer, Heinz of the 'Fifty-Seven Varieties'.

We may find in the long run that tinned food is a deadlier weapon than the machine gun.

This did not go down well inside the biggest tinned food factory in the Commonwealth. Every year the 3,000 employees of Heinz in Wigan produce 960 million tins of processed food in conditions of the strictest hygiene. They are proud of the nourishment provided. To say the least, they think it unlikely that the world incidence of botulism – and Heaven forbid it should ever strike Heinz – could possibly be damaging more bodies than the machine gun; or that their excellent baked beans could be damaging any bodies at all.

About 200 different varieties of can and recipe pour out of the factory – everything from steamed puddings to those unappealing combinations that babies are thought to like – but the king among these is the baked bean. Per head of population, Britain eats more baked beans than any other country in the world; and – an interesting fact – while the total market in tinned food has shrunk over the past decade, thanks to the domestic freezer, the sale of baked beans has actually increased during the recent recession. Heinz has forty per cent of the baked bean market. Every single Heinz baked bean consumed in Britain comes from Wigan. Wigan is the baked bean capital of the world.

Therefore, with hygienic white coat and cap and something called a snood to prevent particles of beard falling into the tomato pulp, I went to the Bean Department, which works a continuous three-shift system much as coal mines do. The process looks remarkably simple. You take dried white beans in sacks from the bean markets of North America. A machine sorts them for size and the removal of the un-bean such as grit. Another machine cleans them. A further machine blanches them. They are then poured at high speed into tins and topped up with tomato sauce and, sometimes, sausages. The tins are sealed and then cooked inside large, sterile ovens. A further machine applies the labels.

The noise is appalling. Every minute, twenty-four hours a day, five days a week, 2,000 tins of baked beans clatter down the production lines.

'There's no doubt about it, baked beans are an excellent food,' said the factory manager, Mr Ken Evans. 'Children love them. They're high in protein, low in fat. If you want an unbiased recommendation, let me point you to the F-plan diet in the current *Vogue*.'

This, however, is not the reason for their popularity among the unemployed on the Marsh Green housing estate, which lies just across the road from the factory. The people of Marsh Green buy the tins – at a large discount – which Heinz cannot sell on the open market because they are badly dented or the food inside them is the wrong colour. Mrs Armitage, for example, frequently buys twenty-four large damaged tins of sausage and beans for £3.60; a snip. And when the Armitage family tire of sausage and beans – which they do, Mr Armitage in particular being 'sick at the sight of them' – then Mrs Armitage has a novel recipe for stew. *Vogue* please note. Take one damaged tin of oxtail soup. Take another of vegetable soup. Mix in pan. Heat. Serve.

In Orwell's day the unemployed hunted after waste fuel rather than waste food, scrambling for odd bits of coal on the spoil heaps of the Wigan coalfield. 'An extraordinary custom . . . well worth seeing,' Orwell wrote. 'Indeed I rather wonder that it has never been filmed.' Elsewhere in fact it was filmed, with the result that the sight of ill-dressed men scavenging for coal as the waste comes rushing down the slag-heap is one of our most enduring, indignant images of the Thirties. A damaged can of baked beans represents an altogether more boring proposition for a film-maker. I do not wonder that it has never been filmed.

But you can still find coal and indignation in Wigan if you

look hard enough. Mr Bill Bridge, an unemployed electrician who helps run the town's Unemployed Workers Centre, was very indignant indeed.

'I don't talk to the capitalist Press. Nothing against you, you may be all right, but I know your editors won't allow you to tell the truth, they'll change the things you write.'

Mr Bridge had experience of reporters and had taken at face value their shabby excuses ('It wasn't me that wrote that, honestly Mr Bridge, it was *the sub-editors*'). I told him I worked for a fair and open-minded newspaper. Mr Bridge laughed. 'Bet it didn't support Arthur Scargill, did it?' Well, no, that was probably true, but on the other hand . . .

Mr Bridge, another decent Wigan man, saw my troubled search for the other hand, and relented. The trouble with good-minded Liberals, he said, was that at bottom they didn't understand the working-class and their problems. 'They didn't in Orwell's time and they don't now. Orwell knew he could get out of Wigan any time he wanted. The only people who can help the working-class are the working-class themselves.'

The trouble was, he said, that Britain had 'the most cunning capitalist society in the world' which had always managed to restrain and contain any outbreak of real Socialism. Also, the working-class had never bothered to educate themselves. The Labour Party and the Labour Clubs were bloody tragic; the fact that the parents of Wigan were willing to sit back and accept the fact that seventy per cent of their children would leave school without the prospect of a job, that was also bloody tragic. His hope lay among the young unemployed. 'You can't live with any dignity on the dole. That was true in 1937 and it's true now. But once you've taken someone's dignity away, they've nothing else to lose. That's when they'll fight the system we live under.'

He drew comfort from an old Socialist saying, remembered from his childhood in the Thirties:

> *We can manage without them*
> *They can't manage without us.*

But can't they? On my last day in Wigan I drove with Donald Anderson – a local historian and, that rare thing, a private colliery owner – to find the site of the pit Orwell had gone down. We passed through many old mining villages, their streets still busy with people buying barm cakes and (presumably) computer magazines. Mr Anderson explained that all these terraces, all these people, were there because, between the years 1820 and 1840, the old Lancashire landlords suddenly realised they were sitting on a vast untapped source of wealth: coal. 'It was like the North Sea oil boom,' said Mr Anderson, 'Wigan became one big mining camp.' Rural labourers from the south of England and Scotland, as well as Ireland, moved here for the money. Mr Anderson's own grandfather, a tunnelling contractor, came south from Aberdeen.

But what *purpose* did the population serve now, outside the few who produced baked beans or (another Wigan factory) Tupperware? Mr Anderson said he had no answer to that one.

Now in his seventies, he has worked fifty-five years in the coal industry. Few people in Britain can be so knowledgeable about the history of coal: seams, shafts, black damp, water, the habits of miners. Recently the workers in his drift mine had broken through to the galleries of a pit abandoned more than a hundred years ago. His men had found the imprints of clog heels in the coal dust. They were the size of half-crowns. They came from children's clogs.

We moved to the churchyard next to the black waste which marks the site of the Pemberton Colliery, whose 3,000 miners and fat seams once made it the sixteenth most productive pit in Britain. Mr Anderson identified the graves of pump men, deputies, under-managers. He pointed to the adjacent graves of Thomas Cook and Thomas Holcraft. 'Funny,' he said, 'but Cook sacked Holcraft. There was a terrible row. Now they're playing footsie-footsie six foot under the ground.'

Eventually, down a rough track across fields, we reached Orwell's pit. 'There used to be some terrific pits hereabouts,' said Mr Anderson, 'three-thousand-ton-a-day collieries.

The spoil heaps, great conical mountains they were, we called them The Three Sisters.'

We stood among the saplings in what is now known as The Three Sisters Recreation Area. There was bird-song, the distant rattle of a tractor, but no sign that here generations of men had toiled underground for miserable wages so that, in Orwell's words, 'you and I and the editor of the *Times Lit Supp*, and the Nancy poets and the Archbishop of Canterbury and Comrade X, author of *Marxism for Infants*' might live decently. No winding gear, no spoil heaps, no shaft, nothing but green.

'Never mind,' said Mr Anderson, 'you can say you stood on the *site* of Orwell's pit.' Adding: 'You know this land used to be Lord Gerard's pheasantry. It's nice to know it's going back to what it was.'

We leaned on the farm gate and looked over at Wigan on its hill. The only chimneys visible belonged to the power station, and that itself will close within the next few years.

I had intended to end my Wigan journey there, leaving me and Mr Anderson leaning on the gate and ruminating about the transience of work and capitalism's changing nature. But that is not my most vivid memory of my trip to Lancashire. That comes from Blackpool. Many people in Wigan recommended me to Blackpool for the last week of the illuminations. There, they said, I would see vast crowds and wonder 'Recession . . . what Recession?'

So I went. The crowds were indeed huge, drifting up and down the prom in the cold drizzle of late October, watching the brown sea come tumbling in from Ireland. I took note of the scene and then went into Yates's famous Wine Lodge for, as Sydney Smith would say, 'a warm'. The place was filled with jolly men and women drinking champagne (£1.25 a glass) and fortified wines. Here, I thought, is the North Country as ever was.

Then, at the table in front of me, a young man produced a carefully-folded piece of paper from his wallet, examined the white dust within, and sniffed it powerfully well into his nose. His two friends took the paper by turn and did the same.

For a moment I imagined, naively, that this was a novel, Lancastrian way with Beecham's Powder.

2. THE COTSWOLDS, WINTER, 1982

The almshouses in Chipping Campden look very picturesque and very old. A London merchant called Sir Baptist Hicks built them in late medieval times from the profits of his prospering Cotswold wool business. Today they are much photographed by tourists and sometimes used by television companies for historical serials which need a backdrop untainted by the late twentieth century. But they also still house the kind of people for whom they were built; the poor and elderly of the parish, old Cotswold folk who are not (yet) played by actors which is a surprise given that the town ('the most beautiful High Street in Britain') looks as though it has been assembled by carpenters from Paramount Studios.

At ten o'clock on a winter's morning I walked past the church which contains the remains of Sir Baptist Hicks – the church bells calling the few faithful to prayer – and knocked at random on an almshouse door. A voice told me to come in. There I found Mr Eric Teague, sitting next to his portable television and not watching a programme from the Open University. I took a seat by a table covered in sticky jars of sauce and jam and, ready to listen to tales of haymaking and the good timekeeping of the Great Western Railway and composing my features into what I hoped would be the appropriately wistful response, asked Mr Teague if life in the Cotswolds had changed much since his boyhood.

'Course they 'ave,' said Mr Teague. 'They're much more sexier. I mean there's a good deal more sex about than there used to be, ain't there?' Mr Teague approved. He asked what it cost in London these days. I replied that as far as I could gather the going rate in my own neighbourhood – Finsbury Park's famed red-light district – was somewhere between £10 and £30. And how much, Mr Teague asked, did a London hotel cost these days? About £30 to £50 a night. 'Well,' said Mr Teague, 'you'd be better off spending the night in a knocking shop, wouldn't you?'

Mr Teague laughed and laughed and then began to cough, until tears and spittle ran down his chin. 'But don't you be writing that stuff down,' he said. I continued to write. Mr Teague picked up his stick and began to hit my ankles – swish, swish, cackle, cackle – later switching his attack to my notebook itself. 'Eh,' he said, 'but you're a rum bugger.'

Eventually we managed to restore some sort of decorum to the conversation, though not for long. Despite his age and his plastic hip, Eric Teague was easily the liveliest person I met in the Cotswolds, where the usual idea of an animated evening seems to consist of a supper shared in a hotel dining-room by two couples who talk interminably about an absent third couple called John and Sarah who have just bought an old farmhouse near Stow but may split up and move separately back to London, Sarah keeping the BMW. But then, as J. B. Priestley wrote, 'you cannot estimate the life of a people by the wealth of dramatic material it offers you.'

Soon Mr Teague was remembering the songs his father had sung: *The Preacher in the Village Church*, *The Grandfather Clock*, *The Old Rustic Bridge*, *The Old Armchair*. Soon Mr Teague was singing himself, his voice crackling in competition with the Open University. 'Here's a good one, a dirty one mind you . . .'

> *When I was in service down Rosemary Lane*
> *I had a kind master and mistress the same*
> *Till one afternoon, when the sailor came to tea*
> *That was the beginning of my miseree*

> *Oh the oak and the ash and the bonny willow tree*
> *Will all be growing green in North Americkee*

It was time to call in the photographer, David Montgomery, who is not one of your quick in-and-out men with a battery-driven Nikon. He takes with him an assistant and lights and a tripod. Bearing this in mind, I asked Mr Teague if he would mind being photographed. The response was electric; like the moment in *Sunset Boulevard* when Gloria Swanson hears the word *camera* after twenty years of neglect from the studios. 'Course not,' he said, 'bring them in.' They came and found their subject enthusiastic. How would they like him? Standing up? Sitting down? Outside? Inside? Smiling? Solemn? He'd been photographed many times before, sometimes by people from American magazines who promised to send his picture but never did.

Here, in fact, was a pleasing example of the continuity of Olde England. Fifty years ago, J. B. Priestley visited these same almshouses to find that a film crew had been there before him. The film crew had filmed the oldest resident, Old Polly, and given her a ten-shilling note for her trouble.

The Cotswolds and the dwindling number of their original inhabitants seem to have represented a dream of the essential England for most of this century. 'The most English and the least unspoiled of all our countrysides,' wrote Priestley in 1933. 'We ought to take the whole of that exquisite countryside and lay it on our consciences. It could be turned into a sort of national park ... a district acquired by the nation itself, which would not, however, turn away the people who work the land. The beauty of the Cotswolds belongs to England, and England should see that she keeps it.'

The book that contains these words is Priestley's *English Journey*, which relates a tour around the country made by the author in the middle of the Slump. Many of the places he visited have changed utterly. Southampton, Liverpool, Bradford, the Potteries, Newcastle – their inheritance of Victorian industry and trade may have been tottering in the Thirties but it was not entirely defunct. Priestley hated many of these towns: 'a wilderness of dirty bricks ... what you see looks like a debauchery of cynical greed.' He was distressed and depressed by their unemployment: 'the dole is part of no plan; it is a mere declaration of intellectual bankruptcy. Nothing is encouraged by it except a shambling, dull-eyed poor imitation of life. The Labour Exchanges stink of defeated humanity.'

The Cotswolds, on the other hand, offered Priestley a glimpse of what English life could, and maybe should, be like. 'There is not, I imagine, much distress anywhere in this region . . . people look comfortable here . . . the towns are without those very squalid patches you often find in country towns . . . the average standard of life in these parts must be fairly high.'

Much the same might be said of them today, partly because much of what Priestley wished for has happened. Leave aside the facts that the land has not been nationalised and that many of the people who once worked it have been driven away by the tractor. The Cotswolds have been cherished. The forty-mile-long ridge of limestone hills that climb up the eastern side of the Severn valley, almost from Bristol to the Black Country, are legally protected from change. They have been designated an 'Area of Outstanding Natural Beauty', the largest in the country. They include more than fifty separate conservation areas. Their towns and villages contain more than 4,000 listed buildings. Fewer than one in ten of their workforce is out of work. Their houses of mellow stone, which catches the sun so beautifully, have become the retreats of the rich and famous.

So would J. B. Priestley raise three cheers for what has happened in the Cotswolds, the ostensible preservation of quintessential Englishness? Or would his praise be stinted by a view of the wider England, where more people than ever before – more even than in 1933 – are leading 'a shambling, dull-eyed poor imitation of life?'

Today Priestley lives on the northern edge of the Cotswolds, just outside Stratford-on-Avon. I made his house the point of departure for the journey south, up the valleys and across the wolds and through the antique shops of essential England.

The interview was not a great success. The author is eighty-eight and lives in a fine house, built over several centuries, with a door opened by his secretary. But neither old age nor an autocratic lack of hospitality can be blamed, for Mr Priestley was sharp and welcoming. The problem, probably, is that the author is tired of remembering things for the benefit of other people. 'Interviews,' he said at one point, 'are a dead loss. They take time. You don't get paid for them. All you get is misrepresented.'

I shall try not to misrepresent Mr Priestley. The truth about our conversation is that the author was far more interested in a book I had brought along with me than in any banal questions about the past, present and future of England. The book was a Penguin edition of his own *English Journey*.

'You know,' he said more than once, 'I've never seen this before.'

'But Jack,' said his wife, the archaeologist Jacquetta Hawkes, 'you *wrote* it.'

He said he realised that, but the particular edition was new to him. We talked briefly in his study (or perhaps library), Mr Priestley sucking a pipe. He said he loved England and he loved the English; they were a kind people and had not, he thought, changed in any fundamental way. Yes, he was a patriot, though he had got 'fed up' with all the fuss made about the Falklands. No, the sight of modern Bradford, his birthplace, did not make him melancholy. As to questions of class, social justice and the future, Mr Priestley sighed at those and said: 'Difficult' or 'Dunno'.

I rose to leave and Mr Priestley pointed to the copy of *English Journey* which still lay on the sofa. 'Yours or ours?' he asked. Mine, I said, but would he like it? 'Yes,' said its author, 'I should like that very much.'

An evening bus runs from Stratford to Chipping Campden. It takes a strangely complicated route and carries few passengers. Only one other person, a young girl, climbed off when we eventually reached the most beautiful High Street in Britain. At night in winter it has the beauty of a mausoleum. The hotel was cold. I went out to a restaurant and ate pheasant which tasted like cold porcelain. Walking back down the

High Street I decided that middle-class middle England was a thoroughly miserable environment for the outsider; it offers few prospects of communal entertainment or chance meetings, it is so intensely *private*. The outsider walks past the lighted windows of Chipping Campden like a poor boy in Dickens. Through the mullioned panes he may glimpse careful interiors; revealed stonework, a log fire, chintz cushions, prints, a standard lamp. Once these houses contained the working population of Chipping Campden. Today even the humblest of them will cost at least £50,000 and they mainly contain migrants from the West Midlands. Most of these migrants are retired people. The native and unmortgageable young – those who have not quit for the cities – live outside the town in council estates. This is a common pattern in the Cotswolds, and indeed of most 'desirable' villages in England.

Therefore many Cotswold villages lack life. They are lovely shells, periwinkles inhabited by hermit crabs.

In India old people who face the prospect of death will often spend their money – if they have it – on a one-way ticket to Benares, the most sacred Hindu city. To die in Benares means a certain passage to a better life. But the English are not really a spiritual people; stand outside a Cotswold church and count the dozen who enter. They retire and spend their money – if they have it – on pieces of an earthly Heaven. They move away from the plains of the Thames and the Severn and the Trent. The blacks, the crime, the unemployed, the growing shabbiness of everyday England are left behind. They turn their cars off the M1, the M4 or the M5 and climb into the triangular stretch of country that lies between. Like Mr Priestley, these people love England. In fact they might be said to worship it. The Cotswolds are sacred in their own way.

Once inside the sanctuary, Cotswold-worshippers devote their energies to the appearance of things. That a place such as Chipping Campden looks as it does owes as much to individual enterprise and historical accident as it does to the Town and Country Planning Act. Money from the old English wool trade gave Campden its fine stock of medieval buildings. The centuries of decline that followed ensured they were not replaced. The Cotswolds were, in hindsight, lucky enough to miss the Industrial Revolution. Only a couple of railway lines penetrated the hills. No coal or iron was found beneath the limestone. Crude twentieth-century developments – the demolition of market halls, the erection of brick bungalows – might have begun with the motor car, but by that time the Cotswolds were in the grip of an early conservation movement.

It is odd to think of it now (and whisper it before the log fires of Bourton-on-the-Water), but the inspiration behind this movement was Socialist. William Morris found that the domestic architecture of the Cotswolds illustrated his belief that 'art must be for the people, not for the connoisseur; it must be by the people not by unassisted individual genius'. Medieval architecture was superior to Victorian because it was the product of the people's 'associated thought and labour'.

A small tide of Morris's disciples – craftsmen, medievalists, Socialists – thereupon flooded the Cotswolds. One of them, C. R. Ashbee, brought 150 men, women and children from London to Chipping Campden, where he founded the Guild of Handicrafts in 1902. The guild repaired, restored and, where necessary, rebuilt. This idealism, aided by the innate conservatism of the great landlords, paved the way for the popular worship of Olde Englishness.

Today it sometimes reaches a puritanical extreme. Telephone boxes in the Cotswolds, for example, are painted battleship grey instead of red so that you don't notice them. Or consider the great Bourton-on-the-Water litter bin controversy, front-page news in the *Evesham Journal*, which has cooled relations between Bourton-on-the-Water parish council and the village's conservation society. The subject, said the *Journal*, arose at a recent council meeting when . . .

> . . . Mr R. Grave referred to a letter in which a member of the society described the new bins as 'starkly litter bins'. 'What else can they be?' he said.
>
> Mrs K. V. King said she felt the new bin immediately on the edge of the village green could be put adjacent to a tree so that it did not look so conspicuous.

Mr. R. H. Dix said the whole object of a litter bin was to be conspicuous. 'To hide them is to defeat the object,' he said.

Sinners can be punished. The owner of a cake shop in Chipping Campden painted his door bright pink. The wrath of the Campdenites became great. They wrote to the planning authority, which said there was little it could do. Woe, woe, and a great wailing arose even unto the adjacent parishes of Blockley and Bourton-on-the Hill etc. Then the ladies of Campden hit upon a plan. They boycotted the cakes. Today the cake-shop door is painted a demure off-white.

Does anything else happen in the Cotswolds? I asked the question of the *Evesham Journal*'s man in Chipping Norton, Mr Peter Robinson. No scandals, nobody drowned – in fact nothing to laugh at at all?

Mr Robinson said no, conservation was the big running story in these parts, though Chipping Norton had in fact recently experienced its first murder – a domestic affair – for the past twenty-five years. Mr Robinson was born and bred in Chipping Norton and has spent all his working life there – thirty years of reporting the town's affairs. He is not ashamed of this fact and he is proud of his town, resenting, like many other people, the local government reorganisation of 1974 which robbed the ancient borough (1606) of its aldermen, mayor's regalia, and real power. If the *Down Your Way* team has not already visited Chipping Norton, then it should do so immediately and make Mr Robinson its first port of call. My guess is that his musical choice will be either something by the Huddersfield Choral Society or Bing Crosby.

He has never been tempted by Fleet Street or even Banbury. He retains a moral scruple which makes one proud to belong to the same profession.

'You know,' he said as we drove across the wolds towards a meeting of Blockley Parish Council, 'you have to laugh at some of those national newspapers. They ask you to do the most ridiculous things.' Recently Mr Robinson had received a telephone call in the early evening, interrupting his composition of a piece on the Chipping Norton Rotary Club.

' 'Ello Pete mate,' said an unknown voice, familiarly, having just familiarised itself with Mr Robinson's name in the directory of local newspaper correspondents. ' 'Ow would you like to earn some real money for a change?'

Mr Robinson said y-e-s, what money had they in mind and what was to be done? The voice identified itself as the newsdesk of a well known Sunday newspaper and said 250 green ones.

'We've a little cracker of a story here,' it continued. A Lincolnshire vicar had run away with his housekeeper in a blue Cortina. The voice had good reason to believe that the couple had driven to Chipping Norton, more specifically to the White Hart Hotel. Would Mr Robinson nip along there smartish, grab the manager, ascertain the number of bedrooms occupied and for how long, phone London with the details, and then engage the vicar and paramour in innocent chatter until a photographer arrived?

'No,' said Mr Robinson.

'Look, are you a reporter or what?' said London.

'I am indeed,' said Mr Robinson, fingering his notes on the Rotarians, 'but I would like to spend the rest of what I hope will be a pleasant working life on good terms with the manager of the White Hart.'

'Jesus Aitch Christ,' said London.

And so the conversation continued, Mr Robinson arguing that if the vicar hadn't killed anyone or embezzled church funds then as far as he was concerned he (the vicar) was in the clear; London wheedling with Mr Robinson because it knew no other newspaperman in Chipping Norton. At last a compromise was reached. Mr Robinson would walk to the hotel carpark and then telephone London if he spotted a blue Cortina.

'And I *did* see a blue Cortina,' said Mr Robinson at the conclusion of his story. 'But I didn't phone back. Blow them, I thought, the old vicar might have found some love in his life at last.'

We arrived at Blockley and the meeting of its parish council. English parish councils these days have very little power. They can 'observe and comment on' planning decisions made higher up the local authority scale. They can spend their allotted portion of the rates on items such as maintaining the village hall and cutting the grass on the village green. They are not, however, a waste of time.

About a dozen members attended at Blockley, including the distinguished figure of Sir Robert Lusty, the London publisher. A ripple went round the room when the chairman announced that, as well as the usual gents of the Press from Cheltenham and Evesham, there was 'a man here from the London *Sunday Times*'. No doubt Blockley now expects one of those stories which begins: *Blockley (pop. 1,800) is the kind of English village which sends American tourists scurrying for their Instamatics. Beneath its rustic surface, however . . .*

Therefore I shall reach for the house-style book and try not to disappoint. *At approximately 7.48 pm Mr John Malin, a silver-haired local businessman, knocked on the table and called the meeting to order. Much of what happened in the next two hours will not be readily understood by the layman. Four facts, however, can be stated with some certainty:*

o Local street lights sometimes go out unexpectedly and are a hazard to the old and infirm.

o The council agreed to raise its contribution to Evesham's Citizens' Advice Bureau from £5 to £10.

o Dog turds continue to plague Blockley. The chairman read a letter from a Mr Pike which said that many dog-owners 'stood and watched' while their pets 'performed' on the parish footways. A short exchange of views followed. A councillor: 'Yes, and they usually appear to do it on very short grass.' Another councillor: 'Untidy owners have untidy dogs.' Sir Robert Lusty: 'Perhaps Blockley dogs need a lecture from Barbara Woodhouse.' The council agreed to commiserate with Mr Pike but drew back from a suggestion that it mounted an advertising campaign along the lines of 'Blockley is beautiful – let's keep it that way'. A woman councillor said she had never considered Blockley beautiful in any case, which prompted an angry retort from Mr R. Barrymore Lingard, who said that in his opinion Blockley was a very nice village indeed. Woman councillor: 'Nice certainly, but not beautiful.'

o The council agreed to look for a site for a wooden bench which had been kindly donated to the parish by the landlord of The Crown, in memory of his mother. One councillor wondered if the bench was vandal-resistant.

'Ah,' said Mr Robinson as we drove away, 'the essence of English democracy.' It was. The council had been well-mannered, well-minuted and well-attended. It cared passionately about Blockley. But it had also demonstrated its Englishness in a rather less benign way (*Beneath the innocent surface* etc). It had tried to keep the most important item on its agenda a secret from the ratepayers of Blockley.

The story is terribly complicated. It concerns a tree root from a tree which may or may not stand on the council's common land. The root had damaged a drain and water from the drain had damaged private property and the owner had complained. To put matters right would cost about £2,000. Either the council or the council's insurers would have to fork out, depending on the precise location of the tree. To raise £2,000 would mean that the council would have to double the rates. It decided to do this as a safeguard. It could not keep that decision secret, but for some reason – which I never understood – the chairman thought that the *purpose* of the rates rise should not be revealed to the public. So when the root and drain issue came up for discussion, reporters were asked to lay down their pens; the council 'was now going into committee'. It went in and out of committee twice, before the public's right to know was secured by the men from the Evesham and Cheltenham papers.

Pragmatism rather than morality won the day. The reporters pointed out that the headline *Mystery over Blockley* rates rise was more damaging than *Drain may cost Blockley £2,000*, and in the end the council agreed.

'That was a daft business about the drain,' said Mr Robinson later, adding that daftness often made his job worthwhile. It was one of the essential differences between Chipping Norton and Russia.

There is a lot of money in the Cotswolds. Money from cigarettes; Lord Dulverton, a member of the Wills family, owns the Batsford estate. Money from merchant banks; Baron von Thyssen at Daylesford, Cyril Kleinwort's daughter at Sezincote. Money from show-business, money from antiques, money from trust funds, money from mummy, money from Americans, farming money, serious money, funny money, old money, new money, money that's all tied up and has nowhere to go.

And spent money, thus: Volvos, Range-Rovers, first-class seasons from Moreton-in-Marsh to Paddington, refurbished country seats and weekend cottages, membership of the Heythrop Hunt, good butchers, tidy lawns.

It might seem odd, then, that one of the chief concerns of the Cotswold District Council is a topic known to sociologists – and increasingly to politicians who seek the country vote – as rural deprivation. Who is being deprived and of what? The short answers are (a) the poorer sections of the native population, and (b) houses, mobility, schools, telephone boxes, shops. Technology and money are to blame. For every hundred men who worked the Cotswold land at the turn of the century, five may now be employed. Families quit their tied houses, which were bought as retirement homes or weekend retreats. The incomers had cars and telephones and shopped elsewhere. Buses grew emptier, trade fell away at the coin-box and the local store. Many incomers did not have children. Desks at the local school went unoccupied.

For a time none of this seemed to matter too much. And, then, in the Seventies, came the balancing of the books. The Department of Education decided that a school with fewer than twenty pupils was not a viable proposition. Transport authorities looked with alarm at a bus which took two women, six miles, twice a day. The GPO decided that a telephone kiosk that collected under £145 a year did not pay for itself in maintenance costs. The storekeeper became despondent at a weekly turnover of fifteen Mars Bars and six small tins of Spaghetti Hoops. Schools and stores closed, buses vanished, telephone kiosks stayed vandalised.

Meanwhile – and quite perversely – the prices of humble village houses reached heights which put them well outside the buying power of the people who needed to live there. Today the Cotswolds' population is actually rising, but the simple statistic (62,000 people ten years ago, 68,000 now) disguises an important social change. The poor are moving out and the rich are moving in.

'Rich' and 'poor' are of course relative terms. It may surprise you to know (it certainly surprised me) that Eric Teague, whom we left singing lustily in his almshouse, considered that he had made 'a lot of money' in his time. He started as a boy labouring in the fields for thirty shillings a week. That was in 1931. He ended up in 1975 earning £10 a day picking Brussels sprouts. That was before his hip went wrong. 'A lot of money, *fifty pounds* a week,' said Mr Teague.

Today, when he wants to visit his many relations who live a few miles over the hills, he hitchhikes. Buses no longer run. He doesn't complain. 'People have always been very, very, very kind to me, sir, very kind indeed.'

I went to Stow-on-the-Wold and took tea in a tea shop, and learned there that people from Birmingham like to have butter with their cream teas, which for the proprietor, a Devon man, was heresy. Stow-on-the-Wold has gone crazy with antique shops. There are twenty-six of them. They have taken over the Square. And in none of them would Mr Teague's weekly wage – even during the sprout-picking season – go very far. Nonetheless they fill up at the weekends with visitors from the Midlands and London, the people who go 'antiquing'.

It is always a danger in these places to look at anything too long, even by mistake. The risk of being tortured by a stream of fey drivel is too great. 'Yes, now that is an unusual piece isn't it? Plain wooden boxes from the 1840s are actually surprisingly hard to come by,' and so forth.

Feyness, however, cannot disguise the fact that antiques have become a shrewdly-operated and prosperous industry which no longer depends – has not depended for decades – on the casual buyer who would like something nice for the sitting-room. The drivel is really a kind of sideline. Four years ago the 200 antique shops in the Cotswolds turned over at least eleven million pounds, and the figure must be greater now. Most of the sales went to dealers from North America and Europe. It is said that from Heathrow a dealer can reach Stow in less time than central London.

You might assume, therefore, that Britain's stock of antiques was running out. But on every hand I was assured not. 'You must remember,' said Duncan Baggott, a dealer in Stow, 'that Britain raped and pillaged the world for the best part of three hundred years. The depth and range of old objects in this country is still tremendous.'

I moved south to the village of Cold Aston, to a meeting of the Heythrop Hunt. There I hoped to meet some of the descendants of our more successful world rapists and pillagers, having been assured by another dealer in Stow – who hunted himself – that they were 'quite incredibly and hopelessly thick'. This may be so. All I can say is that it is difficult to estimate a man's intelligence when he is seated on a horse and that absolutely nothing surprising happened at the Heythrop meet. In fact the only surprising thing about the English rural upper-class is that they talk – wa-wa-wa-wa, from one saddle to another – and behave precisely as we expect them to, impervious to a century of popular mockery. Time and again in the Cotswolds this point was hammered into the ear, and by the time I reached Cirencester I was no longer capable of amazement when, in the hotel's dining-room, I heard:

'I say, I hear Piglet's gorn and got married.'

'Super.'

'Shall we celebrate with a noggin in the bar?'

But other parts of English society have changed quite

dramatically since Priestley's day. The drunk, for example. Priestley went to Swindon and met a drunk. He was hanging on to a lamp post and singing *Old Soldiers Never Die*. I also went to Swindon and met a drunk, good going considering that I only spent ten minutes in the town at the bus station.

Drunks no longer hang on to lamp posts and sing. Instead they sit on benches with a cider bottle and hope to catch the eye of the passer-by. Then they make the approach to landing. 'I see you're on the road like meself. No doubt you'll be on your way to some fine job somewhere and I'm sorry to be bothering you like this and I'm hoping you don't mind, but would it be a terrible thing to ask you . . . (undercarriage extended) . . . to ask you for the bus fare?' I gave him twenty-five pence. Touchdown. 'Now I hope you don't mind me asking again, but would you care to make it fifty?' Take-off.

Neither do drunks haunt hotel bars as they did in Priestley's time. He met many, tomato-faced gentlemen in check suits, who bored him rigid in the residents lounge. Today it is no longer necessary for travellers to bore each other over brandy. There are other diversions. They tend to go to their rooms and bore themselves quietly with television.

I walked through the Rissingtons (the Rissingtons, the Bartons, the Slaughters, the Bourtons; surely these are middle-aged couples rather than villages?) and then down the Wind-rush valley to Burford. Thence by bus to Swindon and Cirencester. Thence on foot again to Malmesbury. I was making, circuitously, for the village of Slad and the home of Laurie Lee, whom I hoped would end the journey as it had begun, on a literary note. *Cider with Rosie*, after all, must be the most famous book the Cotswolds have produced.

This was a bad plan. Mr Lee certainly still keeps a house in Slad, but he spends most of his time in a flat in Chelsea. We met in a pub in the King's Road.

He asked how the journey had been. I told him about Mr Teague. He remembered a woman called Florin Florrie who would do it for two bob under the railway arches in Stroud. I asked why he, the great poet of the Cotswolds, should be living in London when all kinds of metropolitan writers were making for the country.

The village had too much 'going on', he said. There would be too much interference. He would have to play the tape – which he says he has made – of a great writer at work: the clacking of a typewriter, punctuated by the pacing of feet, groans. This would be the only way to keep people away. In any case, Chelsea had been his real village since 1940.

'I don't believe in this getting-away-from-it-all stuff,' he said. 'The way to really get away from it all would be to leave the northern hemisphere.' He said this on the grounds that, because he often typed *blub* when he meant to type *bulb*, there would surely be someone equally incompetent in the cogs of the world's nuclear missile systems. Some of these things had three warheads. He was quite sure that one of them would be aimed at the town on the edge of the Cotswolds which keeps Britain's secrets so badly: Cheltenham. And bang would go the rural retreat.

3. THE HEBRIDES, WINTER, 1982

The young men who took me for an evening's drinking in the village of Ness, the most northerly human settlement in the Outer Hebrides, said that, *per capita*, the men of their village bought more inflatable plastic women than anywhere else in the world. I don't think this was meant to be believed; indeed it's doubtful if even one man in Ness has cut out the coupon from his Sunday newspaper (delivered on a Monday) and sent it off with a postal order to the Exotica Mail Order Co, Leytonstone. But I could see what they meant. Single women, for single men, are a problem in Ness. They come across each other so rarely. None of the three young men – all in their early twenties – had a girlfriend. Therefore at the weekends –

and the weekend in the northern Hebrides means a Friday rather than a Saturday night, Saturday butting on perilously to the Sabbath – they got ruminatively drunk. In drink, they spoke of sexual fantasy: to have enough money to buy a car, which would enable them to drive to Stornoway, the nearest town, where they might meet a nice girl whom they might court and marry and bring to live in Ness.

Perhaps W. H. Auden was right. 'One goes North,' he told Louis MacNeice as MacNeice set off to discover the Hebrides forty-five years ago, 'in order to escape from sex.'

Another friend, the aesthete (later traitor) Anthony Blunt, wondered why MacNeice should suffer Hebridean discomfort when there were 'no *objects* to be seen for it'. Nature is all very well, said Blunt, but is a bore when taken neat.

MacNeice ignored the metropolitan chaff and set off with his kitbag. As a young anglicised Ulsterman with a growing reputation as a poet (regarded today as perhaps the best of his generation after Auden), he'd been given money by a publisher to write a book on the Hebrides. There he hoped to find 'the loneliness which is attractive like melancholy music'; and that the Celt in him 'would be drawn to the surface by the magnetism of his fellows'.

It was, he discovered, 'a sentimental and a futile hope'. He knew no Gaelic and therefore could not 'become intimate with the lives of the people'. He was 'disappointed and tantalised' by the islands themselves. In consequence, he wrote, his book was a tripper's book. He regarded it as a failure and tried to forget it – as the rest of the world successfully did.

Last December, retracing the poet's steps down the 130-mile island chain of the Outer Hebrides, I found few people who had heard of MacNeice ('Would that be the Mr Mac-Neish who was here from the *National Geographic* magazine?') and none who had heard of his book, rather vaingloriously titled *I Crossed The Minch*, as though the stretch of sea that separates the islands from mainland Scotland were the Timor or Sargasso. And yet MacNeice may have written a better book than he thought, unusually clear-eyed for its time and genre in its view of the Celtic Fringe, wary of the triple pitfalls of feyness, facetiousness and condescension which trap so many writers once they find themselves among peat fires, the Good Book, bad weather and strong drink. MacNeice wrote up his journey plainly: 'Why I went to North Uist I don't know. We sat in a hotel and drank double whiskies from eleven till three.'

He found Hebridean faces 'raw and imperfect, like most Scots'. He complained that the handsomeness of Hebridean women was spoiled by their over-long chins. He wished, quite a lot of the time, to be somewhere else. The islands, he found, were in decline, their culture and society threatened by the shoddy commerce of the British mainland. He wrote: 'We expect in an island to meet with insular vices. What is shocking is to find an island invaded by the vices of the mainland.'

Today, nearly fifty years on, we might expect the decay of Hebridean life and language to be complete, its individuality crushed under the weight of three television channels (Channel Four has yet to arrive), frozen food, consumerism, car-ferries and the good work of Alcoholics Anonymous. And certainly many of these have made an impact, though not necessarily the ones we might expect. *Coronation Street* has largely replaced the ceilidh; and it is strange to enter a croft, its walls battered by an Atlantic gale, to find the crofter and his family encirling the television and commenting on the Rover's Return in Gaelic. Fundamentalist Christianity, on the other hand, is fighting a (so far) remarkably successful rearguard action against the Godlessness which has made the rest of the United Kingdom, in terms of church attendance, the most heathen country in the Western World. The Outer Hebrides may be the last place in Britain – with the possible exception of Northern Ireland – where the Christian church tries to dictate the population's pattern of life. The Scottish Sabbath may be a fading memory on the mainland, but in Lewis it is no joke; and neither, for that matter, is the idea of eternal punishment in Hell.

I began my journey, like MacNeice, at the topmost tip of the island of Lewis in the parish of Ness. My landlady lit a peat fire in an upper room and plundered the deep freeze to feed me. The deep freeze and the Raeburn stove are now the trademarks of the Hebridean kitchen. Some say the deep freeze has changed the islands' way of life more than television watching, and that it is likely to contain haunch of venison and fresh salmon instead of the pigmy, processed stuff of your mainland fridge-freezer. This may be so, but in my limited experience it is equally likely to contain chunks of tasteless chicken, frozen peas and long-life milk.

Downstairs in the bar were the three young men, Roddie, Murdo and Duncan, who told me about the inflatable woman solution. They suggested I accompanied them to the only other licensed premises in Ness, the Ness Social Club. There we found a 'folk group' singing hearty songs learned from gramophone records with pictures of men in woolly jerseys on the sleeve.

> *I've been a wild rover for many a year*
> *And I've spent all my money on whisky and beer*

And so on. They had come up from Glasgow and were politely applauded.

'If you're a journalist,' said Murdo, 'no doubt you've come here to see a *bohan*.' I said I thought *bohans* were extinct. 'No, we still have a few,' said Murdo.

'But we can't be showing you them,' said Roddie, 'you being a man from the Press and all that.'

'On the other hand,' said Duncan, 'we could certainly show you a *bohag*. Now a *bohag* is certainly a possibility.'

A *bohan*, I knew, was an illicit drinking den, though that phrase over-romanticises what for generations of Hebridean men was simply a sensible substitute for a pub, in the days when liquor licences were not widespread (though they are far from widespread even now). A group of men would get together, buy whisky and beer, and then set up shop in an abandoned croft or old hut and occasionally get raided by the police. A *bohag*, however, was something new.

Roddie won a half-bottle of whisky in the social club's raffle and Murdo bought six cans of export and, at one in the morning, we went out to the car and drove gingerly down a dirt road until the headlights shone on a white-washed croft with a caved-in roof. 'There's the *bohag*,' said Murdo.

Fascinating. But what differentiated it from a *bohan*? 'Not a great deal,' Duncan explained, 'it's the same kind of place only used less frequently – for parties at the New Year and that kind of occasion.'

Roddie said that it was a great pity it was dark, otherwise they could show me the beauties of the Ness landscape. But were there, I asked, remembering Anthony Blunt, no *objects* to be seen? 'Oh yes,' said Roddie, 'a very fine object indeed.' We drove, again gingerly, along the cliff tops and against a gale that had hurled itself straight from Labrador. Eventually we came to the Butt of Lewis lighthouse; a grand object, we all agreed at two in the morning, with a powerful beam that swept across an empty, dark Atlantic. Duncan wanted to persuade the lighthouse keeper to take us to the top of his tower; Murdo wanted to return to the *bohag* and split Roddie's half-bottle; Roddie and I wanted to go to our beds. Later that morning, I explained, I had an appointment with the Reverend Angus Smith. 'For goodness sake,' said Roddie, a member of his congregation, 'do not tell him you have spent the night drinking with me.'

'Ah,' said Murdo, 'an appointment with the Ayatollah of the Isles.'

The name is unfair. Indeed a more fitting title for the Reverend Angus Smith might be the Gandhi of the Isles; for although he is famed for his strictures against sin – thundered in Gaelic every Sunday from the pulpit of Ness's Free Church of Scotland – a greater fame derives from an unusual act of passive resistance he made seventeen years ago on the island of Skye.

The ferry company had announced plans to run ferries from the mainland on a Sunday. On the first Sunday of operations, Mr Smith lay down on the slipway in his clerical black to block the passage of the first Sabbath-breaking cars – vainly, as it turned out, because police removed him and the cars rolled off the ferry and into Skye, as they have done on Sundays ever since. Thereafter Mr Smith moved west across the sea to Lewis, where very little moves at all on a Sunday and certainly not car-ferries from the mainland.

We met in his manse and sat beside a Magicoal fire. He has the manner of a stern teacher of woodwork, disappointed by generations of clumsy boys. But he is not unpopular in Ness. Every Sunday, at two services and three prayer meetings, he preaches to about 500 people – a huge number given that the population of his parish can only number two or three thousand and that there are other churches besides. He said he was extremely reluctant to see me because Saturday was his day for 'preparation'. Moreover the last journalist to call had invented the Ayatollah title, which Mr Smith felt was below the belt.

Why was the Sabbath so important? 'Because we believe the Bible is the word of God,' said Mr Smith, adding that less certain brands – the Churches of England and Scotland, for example – pecked about in the Bible, deciding which were God's words and which weren't.

Did he believe in Hell? 'Certainly. If you accept the Bible, you must accept Hell. It carries the same authority for Hell as for Heaven. Jesus Christ talks in the most scarifying terms about Hell.'

He said that in many ways life in the Hebrides had improved since MacNeice made his journey. Tuberculosis, once a great blight, had disappeared. The Hebridean cottage or *black house* had been replaced by decent homes, as good if not better than anything the mainland could offer ('It was some time before I realised that the Black Houses are for people to live in,' wrote MacNeice. 'They grow out of the ground among and in the same way as peatstacks and haystacks, as dank-looking and nearly as windowless.').

But not all the change had been good. 'Incomers' had not benefited the islands. 'The English language and its accompaniments' were destroying their way of life. Gaelic was in retreat and even the Sabbath was threatened. And what of other vices? Mr Smith said that drink was certainly a problem, though he wondered if it were any greater a problem than elsewhere. 'I went down to Glasgow recently and it was *full* of drunkards.' Still, he preached against it and Ness had a branch of Alcoholics Anonymous ('I'm not in it, of course'). And no doubt there also existed the sins of the flesh; or perhaps, by Roddie's account, the plastic.

The answer to all this and the way to avoid Hell, said Mr Smith, could only be found in Christ. Nobody would be saved who did not have Christ as his saviour. And what of me? What did I believe?

Feeling rather feeble – not to say threatened – in the face of Mr Smith's certainty, I said I thought the business of life and life and death was a mystery.

'Aha,' said Mr Smith, 'a pseudo-truth, the kind the savages believe.'

And then, after encouraging me to go in for investigative journalism and reveal the Roman Catholic conspiracy which controlled the BBC (' a tough one to crack, but well worth it'), he showed me out into the wind. We shook hands at the door. 'Now remember and read your Bible,' he called after me. 'You never know, we may yet meet in Christ.'

I walked down the long road to Stornoway across peat bogs the colour of bitter chocolate. To the west, the Atlantic rumbled like a train labouring in a cutting, invisible apart from the spume that came over the cliff tops. It seemed to me, then, that the Reverend Angus Smith made a refreshing change from most of the clerics one has encountered since childhood; the men who say of the Bible, well, *this* passage you have to take symbolically, and *this* passage doesn't quite mean what it seems to, and in those days people didn't have a lot to eat and a dozen loaves and fishes could feed *a lot* of people. As for Hell, you see it represents the penalty and the pain of loss, the *poena damni*, rather than the pain of the senses, the *poena sensus*. Hellfire is a metaphor for the absence of God.

Mr Smith and his fellows do not tread that new road. Hell will be hot and everlastingly painful and they have a duty to save us from it.

But as I met more Hebridean ministers, all certain, all righteous, the change became less refreshing.

At the township of Fivepenny Borve I caught the afternoon bus to Stornoway. It stopped at other townships – a township is a scattering of crofts; the Hebrides have few villages in the mainland sense – and soon filled up with ample, elderly women with empty shopping bags to be filled in the Stornoway shops. They chattered in Gaelic as we crossed Barvas Moor, a blasted heath completely free of objects, and then dropped to the east coast of Lewis and Stornoway.

Stornoway is the only town in the Hebrides, with a population of more than 5,000, one set of traffic lights, one Indian and one Chinese restaurant. A stretch of wooded parkland fringes the harbour and gives the town a soft, Lowland atmosphere. There are few trees elsewhere in the Hebrides.

Stornoway also has two Christian bookshops, where the people of Lewis may – and do – come to buy their Gaelic Bibles, or gifts for their children (*Man Overboard: the story of Jonah*), or plaques for their walls (*Christ is the head of this HOUSEHOLD/The unseen guest at every MEAL/The silent listener to every CONVERSATION*). The shops also contain a great many sermons by Charles Spurgeon, the Victorian evangelist. Spurgeon never visited the Hebrides – he had the good sense to holiday on the Riviera, where he died at Menton in 1892 – but his name lives on in these islands long after it has been forgotten at the sites of his great preachings to the people of London. Why this should be so, and why the northern Hebrides should remain so devoutly fundamentalist, is best explained by a glance at the history of the Free Church, founded 140 years ago.

In 1843 a large minority of ministers quit the Church of Scotland after a prolonged and bitter argument which bears a similarity to present divisions within the Labour Party. The row concerned the appointment of ministers to parishes (or, if you like, candidates to constituencies). Should their selection rest solely with the democratic decision of the congregation? Or should the church's establishment and the local bigwigs – the church's principal patrons – have the power to over-ride the people's will? The breakaway group, passionate democrats, favoured the former and created the Free Church in a moment of Scottish history known as The Disruption. The new church found especial favour in the Highlands and Islands where landlords, still busily clearing the land of people to make way for sheep, cut unpopular figures.

The split, therefore, was not about belief – for which Scottish ministers in the year 1843 did not believe in the Sabbath or the pain of hell? – but about the people's rights. Over the next hundred years, much of the dissenting church drifted back to its parent, but the rump, the 'Wee Frees', stood resolute in the islands and undisturbed by the changing theology of Lowland Scotland. Today it is undoubtedly still the strongest social force in the islands of Lewis, Harris and North Uist – the southern islands, South Uist and Barra, went untouched by the Reformation and are Roman Catholic. The Free Church's strength in these northern islands can be gauged from the church's published revenues: last September (to pick a random month) the eighteen congregations in Lewis and Harris subscribed more than £25,000 to church funds – more than one pound a head for every person on the islands and nearly a third of the church's total revenue from 156 congregations scattered across Scotland and North America.

'Our smallness and isolation were our salvation,' said the Moderator of the Free Church, the Reverend John MacLeod, when I called on him at his house outside Stornoway. 'It was a blessing in disguise that we stayed apart from the mainstream of theological scholarship and its capitulation to the philosophies of science.'

Mr MacLeod seemed a reasonable man who admitted to taking a glass of wine on social occasions. The Hebrides, he said, were a favourable environment for a minister. Life there was 'Biblical' and still governed by 'Biblical norms'.

If a member of his congregation took his family out in the car for a picnic on a Sunday, would he be conforming to the 'Biblical norms'? Mr MacLeod shook his head sadly. 'No,' he said, 'and I would have to advise him, pastorally, not to do it again.'

This may seem like the cliff-edge of Calvinism; impossible, you might think, to move further in a puritan direction without falling out of the world altogether. But the Hebrides contains a church smaller and fiercer yet than the Free Church. They are called the Free Presbyterians and left the Free Church in 1893, believing they were the true custodians of their parent church's constitution. I went to see their minister in Stornoway, another Reverend John MacLeod.

This Mr MacLeod did not believe in a great many things. He did not believe in dancing. He did not believe in television. He was pleased to note that the local cinema had closed shortly after showing the blasphemous *Jesus Christ Superstar*. He did not believe that the Roman Catholics of Barra should have their music festival subsidised by the Western Isles Regional Council – headquartered in Stornoway – because the Barra Festival had opened on a Sunday. He had been opposed to the Defence Ministry's plans to build a NATO base in Stornoway – until the Scottish Secretary assured him that aircraft would do their best to keep out of the air on the Sabbath, the atheistic Soviet Union permitting.

Mrs MacLeod served scones. Mr MacLeod said grace. I applied jam to the scones and ate. Mr MacLeod said that the real difference between the Free Church and the Free Presbyterian Church rested on the matter of discipline. What had he in mind?

'For example, we do not extend church privileges to Freemasons. We would take action against any woman member of our church who wore male garments or who cut their hair short, or any member who used public transport which operated in systematic disregard of the Sabbath to get to church on the Lord's Day.'

'Action' meant first a word from MacLeod and then, if that failed to restore the Biblical norm, an appearance by the transgressor before the Kirk Session. I said it seemed fantastic that Mr MacLeod would upbraid one of his own members for taking a bus so that he or she might hear Mr MacLeod preach. He admitted 'a difficulty' here, but added that the bus journey would be permissible if the driver was not paid double-time to disregard the Sabbath.

No dancing, no double-time, no women in tight jeans with cropped hair, no drink: such is Mr MacLeod's vision of a morally upright world and one which, he confessed, he was struggling to persuade his six children to accept. He was not, however, a cheerless man. He was a post-millenarian. A thousand years of blessedness were on their way and after that the Second Coming of Christ, which would mark the end of the world; pure joy for those who were saved.

Sunday fell on Stornoway like a butterfly net. The town fluttered briefly as its various congregations made their way to and from church and then lay still. I read the Gideon Bible provided by my hotel. The Song of Solomon. Stay me with flagons, comfort me with apples: for I am sick of love. I made notes:

One, the unemployment rate in the Outer Hebrides is 25.5 per cent.

Two, it has rained every day in Lewis since August 2, 136 days ago.

Three, Stornoway's public lavatories – one old, one new – are popularly known as the Old Opera House and the New Opera House. Men who have spent a Friday lunchtime in Stornoway's bars will sometimes go there out of the cold, to wait out the hours before evening opening time. Sometimes they take a bottle with them, and sing.

I perused the *Stornoway Gazette*, a fine local newspaper (though not quite so fine as its rival, the *West Highland Free Press*). Here are two passages from the page of district notes.

Of the first wedding on the island of Berneray for fourteen years:

A dance followed, at which music was supplied by the accordionist Aonghas Alig-an-T'struthain, as well as local artistes and records. Revelries continued in to the wee sma' hours. At the close of proceedings, it was generally agreed that it had been twelve hours to remember in the recent history of Berneray.

Of a recent crime on the island of Benbecula:

The theft of the plaque commemorating the opening of the new causeway between Benbecula and South Uist was not regarded by locals as a heroic act. Far from it. It was regarded as an act of cowardice. There was a time and not long ago when islanders could go to bed and sleep in peace leaving their doors unlocked. Not anymore . . .

In the evening I went to hear Mr MacLeod preach in English at the Free Presbyterian Church (his morning service is conducted in Gaelic). The congregation, a couple of hundred strong, sang psalms in the Hebridean way: without instrumental accompaniment and led by a precentor, a man with a loud voice who began each verse a bar or so ahead of the rest. The psalms rose and fell in peaks and troughs of melancholy – all of them sounding an approximation of the tune, *Amazing Grace*. Some say it can be a haunting and beautiful sound.

Then Mr MacLeod referred us to Acts, Chapter 24, and the story of Felix and Drusilla, a worthless pair of adulterers who had locked away St Paul. Felix, said MacLeod, was too much in love with the world and the things of the world. 'What a great pity Felix did not ask to be saved . . . the wages of sin is death . . . the lesson is self control . . . we are not to give our hearts things that satisfy the flesh, that is *absolutely forbidden* . . . as for strong drink, the Bible declares in no uncertain manner that there is to be no indulgence . . . he who tarries long with the wine is not wise . . . look not upon the wine when it is red . . . it biteth like a serpent.'

More psalms were sung and prayers offered. I returned to my hotel and, in despair, sought drink. The landlord and a friend, both Lowlanders, occupied a large and gloomy and otherwise empty bar. The landlord said he could open on Sunday – he had a seven-day licence – but if he did he knew that 'not one man in Stornoway' would dare cross his threshold on the Monday.

But perhaps the Hebridean counterpoint between alcohol and the Bible should not be exaggerated. True, many people fall out of the arms of one into the other. There is even a Gaelic word for those who have abandoned sin and found religion. They are said to have undergone the *curam*, a word which means carefulness or circumspection, when they become, in the words of the Reverend Angus Smith, 'Christocentric'. (A

Catholic priest in Barra had another definition: 'The word means *angst*'.) True, also, that people from the northern, Calvinist islands are popularly supposed to suffer a high rate of depression, sometimes known as the Lewis Depression.

Statistically, however, the ideas of unusually heavy drinking and deep depression can't easily be sustained. The islands may be no more drunken and depressed than anywhere else, if one believes (for example) the work of Professor George Brown, of Bedford College, London, who found that housewives in North Uist were no more liable to depression than women in South London; or the work of the Medical Research Council Unit of Medical Sociology, Aberdeen, which found that alcohol abuse in the Western Isles was no worse than elsewhere in Britain. The Unit's report, published last year, blamed the 'myth' of particularly heavy drinking (a) on outsiders 'who mistook the special habits of celebration and hospitality for normal drinking' and (b) on the islanders themselves. The survey showed that a majority of men – though not women – certainly drank 'but at the same time a majority expressed attitudes which were strongly against drink . . . Thus it is not surprising if there is a great deal of guilt associated with the subject.'

Ah, guilt. One of Calvinism's great gifts to the world, too often attacked by people who do not understand its uses. At the hotel in Rodel, Harris, I was to meet a man nourished, once a fortnight, by its sweet and secret pleasures.

I went south to Harris by bus. Harris is much grander – and much emptier than Lewis; mountains rather than moorland, sporting estates rather than crofting townships, many of which were cleared in the nineteenth century. Today fewer than 3,000 people live there, with a forty per cent drop in the school roll predicted over the ten years, 1976 to 1986. In 1911, Harris supported about 5,500 people and the Outer Hebrides as a whole more than 45,000. But those were boom times, when herring filled the Minch, ready to be netted and salted and exported as delicacies to central and eastern Europe. The herring and their markets never returned in such profusion and over the next sixty years the population dwindled to 30,000, where it has recently steadied – for several reasons. For one, the Hebrides are now much more comfortable places to live. For another, North America is no longer such an attractive, or possible, destination. For a third, jobs on the mainland or in the Merchant Navy or even on a North Sea rig are today as rare as trees in Harris. At least in the Hebrides you can supplement your social security by keeping a few sheep on your croft (very few crofters are full-time; it's impossible to make a living out of eighteen sheep and a dozen hens). 'If you're unemployed,' says common wisdom, 'it's much better to be unemployed here than on the mainland.'

Naturally, there are drawbacks. In the bar of the Rodel Hotel I was treated to a litany of Hebridean complaint. The daft uses that the local authority put their money to: 'If you had a heart attack here and now, it might easily take four hours to get you to the Stornoway hospital by ambulance. And yet they're spending all this money on street lights.' (True: many villages in the Hebrides now blaze away with ugly yellow lamps, as though muggers – non-existent – needed to be put to flight.) Air fares: it cost £51 to fly from Stornoway to Glasgow. The cost that transport charges added to goods: a gallon of petrol was £1.97, a loaf of bread forty-five pence.

Mind you, said a man in the corner, they had fuel, 'fuel for the taking', only some people were too lazy to work the peat.

The Rodel Hotel and the complaints cannot have changed much since MacNeice's day. The hotel stands, a grey building in the Scottish Baronial style, next to a harbour bereft of boats but full of seaweed. Like Leverburgh, just along the coast, Rodel has an air of abandonment. Leverburgh was abandoned after Lord Leverhulme died in the Twenties and his executors decided that the Lancashire soap-king's grandiose plans for Hebridean development were a useless drain on the resources of Port Sunlight. Rodel was abandoned in the Sixties when MacBrayne's, the steamship company, ceased to send steamers to its harbour.

No signs advertise the hotel, which has catered for the serious English fisherman for the past sixty years. The porch has scales where men in gumboots can weigh their catch. Elsewhere – the bar, the numerous outbuildings with tin roofs – there is an air of charming decrepitude of the kind one expects to find in the Hebrides but which, these days, is actually rather rare.

Rodel has nothing much else to look at apart from the church; 'the one considerable architectural monument in the Hebrides' according to the pamphlet provided by the Ministry of Works, and as such the only item on the journey likely to excite Anthony Blunt. The key to the church is kept by the Rodel Hotel. I borrowed it and walked up the hill and through a sodden graveyard to find a plain building with a tower, said to date from 1500 and restored by the Countess of Dunmore, the wife of the then landlord of Harris, in 1873. The nave contains a fine old carved tomb to a member of the MacLeod family. And that, I thought, was that.

What a mistake! Only later did I discover in an erudite guide book information that would have interested Mr Blunt and surprised Mr Auden. The south wall of Rodel Church bears 'a rarity, a *sheela-na-gig*, or roughly hewn small man holding his erect penis'. Rodel's is the only extant example in Scotland, though it was damaged and modified in the nineteenth century by the Countess of Dunmore, who ordered her gillie to fire his gun at it. Another in Iona has disappeared entirely.

None of this information was imparted in the Ministry of Works pamphlet or by the helpful manager of the Rodel Hotel, where on my return with the key around lunchtime I found a man in the bar drinking whisky and beer, alone with a resolve that would have caused alarm in Aberdeen's unit of Medical Sociology. He was in his fifties and powerfully built and lived in a croft with his mother. It was explained quietly that he was a perfectly good and intelligent man who went on a bender once a fortnight.

To begin with he was silent. Then he began to interrupt other speakers with the words: 'Aye, you'd make a good politician, so you would,' any vague tendency to loquacity being a mark hereabouts of politicians, Englishmen, comic-singers and others who gab on meaninglessly. Then he began to talk.

'You know,' he said to me, 'I am seriously committed to the proposition of heavy drinking. Drink makes you altogether a nicer person.' World statesmen should drink heavily. This would have them continually falling on one another's necks, singing *Auld Lang Syne* and diminishing the prospect of war. The United Nations should drink heavily. This would ensure that wars, if they got started, would speedily end in drunken peace treaties, handshakes, songs etc. Mrs Thatcher in particular would benefit from a few large ones.

But what of the morning after? No bother at all, he said, you felt good and guilty. 'You cannot remember a thing you've said or a thing you've done and you have to go about the place and be terribly pleasant to everybody.' Guilt was a fine thing because it made you meek. And the meek – was this very fact not in the Good Book? – would inherit the earth.

When closing time came at two o'clock he bought a bottle of Lang's Supreme and six cans to see him through the afternoon. The barman, meanwhile, took me back to his parents' croft where his mother fed me cheese and scones and his father asked what I made of Mr Andropov.

Later, waiting in twilight and drizzle for the boat to North Uist, I came upon the man from the Rodel bar. He sat in the back of an old van, clutching his bottle and looking drunker now and grimmer, as though he might very well start a war himself.

The ferry from Harris to North Uist goes two or three times a week, via Berneray. Only about 120 people live on that island. It was a puzzle, therefore, that the cargo for Berneray that night included 1,200 bottles of lemonade as well as the usual long-life milk and John West Apple Slices. The lemonade, said the skipper, would last out the Christmas and New Year season; the beer and spirits had travelled separately. The lemonade – ten bottles for every man, woman and child on the island – was presumably for the meek and the teetotal.

A builder's van took me across North Uist and down into Benbecula, an island blighted and/or prospering under the aegis of the Ministry of Defence. Barracks and married quarters there house the men who man the rocket range, actually sited across the causeway in South Uist. The army gives employment but seems to be tolerated rather than welcomed. 'Before the Falklands episode,' I was told, 'they'd only fire their rockets in good weather. Now they seem to have decided that they have to try them in rain and wind as well.'

A fisherman and his wife gave me a bed for the night and a supper of sliced white bread and tomatoes (the Milanda bread van makes the 200-mile trip from Glasgow three times a week). The fisherman complained not of Danes, but of fellow Scottish fishermen from the East Coast, whose trawlers – 'over-capitalised and under-employed' – were sweeping the Minch clean of mackerel and prawns.

Their croft had crucifixes and pictures of Our Lady on the walls. Benbecula is border country between Calvinists and Catholics. Southwards lay the believers in the Papal Anti-Christ, the great Whore (I am only quoting Stornoway views) of Babylon. Southwards, also, lay the vexed question of the red-necked phalarope.

You will have noticed that so far there has not been much about the cadences of the Gaelic language in this piece: is it dying? Is its death inevitable? What can be done to stop it? And so on. The short answers to these questions is yes, probably, and nothing very much outside a wholesale conversion to the language of another five million people (at present about 100,000 people are thought to speak it). Or this, at least, was the view of almost every Hebridean I spoke to. 'It's English you hear in the school playground now,' they would say significantly, remembering the recent past when English was a kind of Sunday-best language confined to the classroom and the MacBrayne's steamer office.

But by the time I reached Benbecula I decided that my knowledge of the Gaelic question was still extremely sketchy. Therefore I took a bus across the causeway to South Uist and walked several miles off the main road and into an Atlantic gale to the township of Penunerine, to the croft of Mr Donald John MacDonald, the Gaelic author and poet whose book, *In the Shadow of the Swastika*, is said to have sold more copies than any other Gaelic book in recent times outside the Bible.

Mr MacDonald said that if things went on going the way they were, there would be nobody speaking Gaelic at all in fifty years. But Gaelic, at that moment, was not what really concerned him; which was the red-necked phalarope. Or not so much the red-necked phalarope as the corncrake as Mr MacDonald's drain.

He and his fellow crofters in Penunerine wanted to deepen the ditch that drained their grazing land, where sheep were presently up to their ankles in water and troubled with the liver fluke. They had applied to something called the Integrated Development Programme for a grant for the work, which had referred it to the Ministry of Agriculture, which had referred it to the Nature Conservancy Board, which had expressed opposition and concern.

Penunerine has been designated a 'Site of Special Scientific Interest' because its marshland in summer is haunted by migrant birds, especially by the phalarope and corncrake. Drier land might drive away the birds. That very day, said Mr MacDonald, two Englishmen from the Nature Board had flown all the way from Inverness at great expense and were at that very moment walking along in the drain in green wellingtons and anoraks to see just how much deeper it could safely be dug. We left the croft where Mr MacDonald has lived all the sixty-four years of his life, apart from five years in a prisoner-of-war camp (hence *In the Shadow of the Swastika*), and went to meet them.

They explained the position to an assembly of crofters. No doubt it seemed rather bizarre to people who had lived there all their lives, they said, but the fact was the Penunerine was really rather special. Corncrakes, phalarope, etc. High-technology farming was the great enemy of wildlife. High-technology farming was possible in South Uist. Indeed it was possible to grow *bananas* in South Uist. Laughter. If the crofters left their drain alone, they might be paid compensation. Silence.

'Is that a fact?' said one man, who knew it was fact, having read in that week's issue of the *West Highland Free Press* that Lord Thurso had been paid £100,000 *not* to plant trees on a stretch of scientifically-interesting Caithness bog. The expenditure of public money is often a mystery.

The crofters tried to convince the naturalists that they were not about to turn South Uist into a banana plantation, and eventually the men in green wellingtons retreated to their hire car and the plane to Inverness. 'How do you think we did?' asked Mr MacDonald. I said I thought they would get the money to dredge the drain. Mr MacDonald smiled over his pipe and said he thought so too.

The next day snow fell on South Uist. It was time to go and see some priests, and in particular Father John Archie MacMillan who looks after 200 souls on the island of Eriskay. Father MacMillan now threatens the Reverend Angus Smith's reputation as the most famous man of God in the Outer Hebrides. Father MacMillan has water-skied and played the bagpipes *at the same time.* (The Free Church could only demonstrate superiority, as the columnist Aimsir Eachainn remarked in the *Free Press*, if they could organise a successful sponsored walk from Stornoway to the mainland.)

A rubber dinghy ferried me across the Sound of Eriskay. It was unbelievably cold and I was glad to see a coal fire in Father MacMillan's living-room. The coal comes by coaster twice a year from Glasgow. Unlike peat, it makes wonderful flames.

Did he believe in Hell? 'Well now, I don't know,' said Father MacMillan, who was trained in Aberdeen and Valladolid. Was he agin contraception. 'Not so much as my congregation suspects.'

'You'll no doubt have heard about my water-skiing. Would you like to see a video?' Father MacMillan fiddled with his hand-held control panel and suddenly there he was on the television screen, whizzing across the Sound of Eriskay and blowing hard on the pipes. Two tunes – *Morag of Dunvegan* and *Pipe Major Gray's Farewell* to the City of Glasgow Police – could be heard quite clearly. The feat had raised more than £2,000 towards the construction of a community hall for the island.

'Now do you fancy seeing last night's Scotland–Belgium game?' I did. 'Wasn't that just a splendid goal by Dalglish?' said the priest. It was.

That evening on Eriskay I got lost in the snow but eventually found the croft where, I'd been assured, a crofter would tell me all about 'the old days'. He did, but his wife refused to switch off the television, so that memories of the ceilidhs and the Sunday visiting and the cloth you had to tie over the bucket when you brought water from the well otherwise the water would simply blow away – all this was punctuated by *Falcon Crest* and then *Tenko* and then some other stuff about people being married in Los Angeles and not enjoying it very much.

At daybreak the next morning I took the mail launch to Barra. It was one of those odd, beautiful Highland days when everything seems the wrong tone: yellowing hills flecked with white, surrounded by a light green sea, both overshadowed by a sky which came black and boiling from the west. Cormorants flew low across the water.

Father Colin MacInnes met me outside his church in the north of the island. He proved to be the only man in the Hebrides who had heard of MacNeice's journey forty-five years before. 'Louis MacNeice,' he said, 'the scoundrel who wrote of the people of Barra *sit on your arse for fifty years and hang your hat on a pension.*'

That's the man. The line comes from what is probably MacNeice's most famous poem, 'Bagpipe Music', which first appeared in his Hebridean book. Like many poems of the Thirties, it is fiercely pessimistic:

It's no go the gossip column, it's no go the Ceilidh
All we want is a mother's help and a sugar stick for the baby

And:

It's no go the Herring Board, it's no go the Bible
All we want is a packet of fags when our hands are idle

And finally:

It's no go my honey love, it's no go my poppet;
Work your hands from day to day, the winds will blow the profit.
The glass is falling hour by hour, the glass will fall for ever,
But if you break the bloody glass you won't hold up the weather.

Indeed the glass was falling as Father MacInnes spoke, which threatened that day's flight to Glasgow. But the light plane came through the clouds and landed on the beach that serves as Barra's airfield, and was soon off again south and east towards the mainland. The Hebrides slipped below the wing, white islands in a black sea.

Have they, in the time between, fulfilled MacNeice's gloom? In 1937 he wrote: 'Some day it may be a good thing that the Hebrideans should lose their language and be in every way assimilated with the rest of Scotland or ... with all the English-speaking races of the world. But that day is not yet.'

Neither is it yet. For although the culture of Gaelic and the ceilidh is undoubtedly slipping away, new differences have arisen to separate Hebrideans from the people of mainland Britain. The islands are remarkably free of crime. The islanders are remarkably uninsular, much less parochial than (say) the natives of an English provincial town. True, many people in Lewis have never been south to Barra and vice versa; inter-island communication is difficult and expensive. Neither would a majority have seen Oxford or Birmingham or Leeds. On the other hand, they are quite likely to have visited relatives in Toronto or New Jersey, or travelled as seamen to Buenos Aires, Galveston, Calcutta.

There are other surprises. Calvinism is still Calvinism in the north, but in the south the Catholic priesthood have changed their role and are now often in the vanguard of local campaigns, to establish fish-processing factories and folk festivals.

And what would MacNeice have made of the sixty Pakistanis who live in Stornoway? Some of them speak Gaelic, others a species of the Lowland tongue (I went to see an old Punjabi man in Stornoway who had come to the Hebrides in the Thirties after a conversation with a memsahib on Jullundur golf course, where he had been employed as a native caddy. 'She told me I should come to her country because it was very, very rich. I came and discovered it was very, very f...ing poor and very, very f...ing cold').

The Hebrides, in fact, have not become what some of the rest of us may have wanted. They have not become a human game reserve.

4. LONDON, SPRING, 1983

From the geyser ventilators
Autumn winds are blowing down
On a thousand business women
Having baths in Camden Town.

Waste pipes chuckle into runnels,
Steam's escaping here and there,
Morning trains through Camden cutting
Shake the Crescent and the Square.

Early nip of changeful autumn,
Dahlias glimpsed through garden doors,
At the back precarious bathrooms
Jutting out from upper-floors;

And behind their frail partitions
Business women lie and soak,
Seeing through the draughty skylight
Flying clouds and railway smoke.

Rest you there, poor unbelov'd ones,
Lap your loneliness in heat.
All too soon the tiny breakfast,
Trolley-bus and windy street!

– 'Business Girls', John Betjeman

It is a cliché, but living alone in London can be a melancholy experience. That much at least I knew, first-hand, having lived during my early days in the city in a bedsitter above a hairdresser's shop in Islington. Hanks of hair strewed the passageway. Every Sunday I would rise late and take a long bath in the basement, the water quivering to the passage of trains on the Victoria Line which ran underneath. Here I planned the day's events: the Sunday papers, a chicken biriani, an expedition by tube to see a foreign film, a sweet-and-sour pork, and then home again, through the hair and past the payphone at the top of the stairs and into bed. My neighbour was a scene-shifter for an opera company. The sounds of homosexual congress came grunting through the hardboard wall. London, on such a day, seemed a good place not to be.

But for most of us this kind of life does not last. A mortgage replaces the rent, friends are made, husbands and wives appear. Soon one forgets which are the best days to consult the *Standard's* flat-share columns. The re-appearance of *Battleship Potemkin* at the Hampstead Everyman no longer causes the spirits to rise and the body to descend to the Northern Line. Bedsit days are transmuted into wry anecdotes; personally I've always liked the detail about the hair.

Meanwhile rivers of the young continue to flow into London, spilling out from the railway terminals, littered with the jetsam of the old carrier bags and brand new *A to Z*s. How does the female portion live now, the successors to Betjeman's business girls? Do the baths of loneliness still claim them? Or have feminism, liberalism and communal living in the shared flat changed all that?

Naturally I didn't expect to find unreconstructed Betjeman business girls – girls (one supposes) who were called Miss Frost at the office, who treated themselves in Lyons Corner Houses, and who returned at weekends to Tonbridge, where they had a crush on the vicar. Nor did I expect to find them in Camden Town, which has become gentrified and expensive.

On the other hand, it seemed unlikely that something called The London Supper Club could represent the general direction in which business girls had moved. According to its advertisements, the club offers 'gay professional businesswomen' the chance to meet in 'exclusive small social groups ... dining together in private elegant up-market surroundings'. In any event, such a club would not be easily penetrated by a male journalist. I set out instead for the remoter parts of west and north London – Baron's Court, Hornsey, Palmer's Green – in the partially attractive search for single girls and loneliness.

The journey was haunted by that week's developments in Muswell Hill and Cricklewood. *Mass Murder in Bedsit Land.* I first learned of the story from the *Standard*, bought at Baron's Court tube: *Human remains found in the sewer outlet at a house in north London were probably from three bodies of white people, a pathologist reported today.*

The corpses had been discovered by a plumber, called to unblock a drain. Neighbours said the house had been divided into flats 'let out by an accommodation agency on behalf of the owner, an Indian woman who lived elsewhere'. Now I stood outside such a house. I pressed one of six bells and talked into a box. Fiona told me to come on up.

'Hi.'

'Hi.'

'Hi.'

'Hi.'

There were four of them. Fiona and Nicki, Claire and Annabel. They'd all attended the same boarding school on the south coast, and then, after periods spent in various cramming and secretarial institutions, had joined up again in London. They each paid £22 a week to share two bedrooms, a small sitting-room which included a cooker and sink, and a bathroom without windows. Fiona worked as a waitress in a restaurant, *Quel Dommage*, said to be fashionable and frequented by the Princess of Wales. She got no wages but the tips could amount to £30 a night. Really, she wanted to be in the film business. Claire and Annabel worked for an advertising agency.

Or rather they did not work 'for' but 'in'. That is one of the golden rules of the well-reared business girl. One is in publishing, or in the Beeb, or in advertising, or in the City. The word avoids the suggestion of humble employment. Of course, one could hardly work 'in' Universal Sprockets, but then one wouldn't want to go near Universal Sprockets in the first place. Universal Sprockets was a favoured term of abuse with these girls; the firm – and we should hope it still exists and continues to manufacture useful items for export – is no doubt staffed by efficient women from the comprehensives.

And what of Nicki, what did she do?

'Oh, I'm in fine art.'

Where was this?

'Oh, ――'s,' naming a famous London saleroom.

And what was the nature of her business there?

'Oh, I'm in the eighteenth century picture department.'

And how did she spend her day?

'Oh, I assist Douglas Featherstone-Banks, who's our English painting specialist.'

But what was the precise nature of the job?

'Oh, I type his letters.'

Nicki laughed. One thing to be said in favour of these girls is that in some ways they do not take themselves seriously. They are ironists. They talk within quotation marks. They adopt the Funny Voice; sometimes it is the Cockney of lager commercials (' 'Ello John, squire'), at others a parody of themselves ('Yes, we live in a jolly nice hice in Haslemere'). But then the whole country is at the Funny Voice game; a comedy of manners, a triumph of form over content, as though the whole of British life was potentially ludicrous, an audience laughing at itself. Also, it means one need never run the risk of being thought straightforward, serious and therefore boring.

It was a risk I had to run, fearing that on my leaving, I would be described as 'a wally' or 'a wimp'. What kind of life did they see themselves leading in ten years' time? All envisaged a nice house in London and a place in the country. How would this be achieved on a secretarial wage of £5,500 a year? They would inherit some money and they would marry well. Some men made a lot of money; less than £20,000 a year would not be considered adequate.

At this point prospective young men began to toil up the stairs from the street. They were fresh-faced and wore corduroys and roll-neck sweaters. Jamie and Hugh, Simon and Mark. The girls were having a dinner party.

'Hi.'

'Hi.'

'Hi.'

'Hi.'

Wine was sloshed down as though it were Vimto. This kind of girl has an awesome capacity for drink. Sometimes you can spot them in offices the next morning, trembling over their little beakers of takeaway coffee. Annabel said that most people in her agency got drunk, or *wazzocked*, all the time. One man was frequently so wazzocked by four-thirty in the afternoon that on the evening train home to Winchester, he would fall into a happy slumber and be carried on to Southampton, sometimes Bournemouth.

It came as a surprise, therefore, when the girls began to talk of advertising as a highly-pressurised business. Accounts were mentioned. The Universal Sprockets account, the Central Gas Board account, the *New Statesman* account (the *New Statesman* account? Yes, the Voice of the Left pays an agency and helps in the general wazzocking).

'That wally Michael made me rewrite my copy twice the other day,' said Annabel.

'Ah, you've moved on to writing at last,' said Jamie.

Annabel looked at Claire and hesitated. 'Well, retyped actually.'

Sometimes there was so much pressure that the girls were asked to work late. This was a good thing. It got you involved, made you committed, you got to know the men in the agency, few of whom were happily married because their wives didn't understand the immense and peculiar pressures of the advertising world. Flirtation could not be ruled out.

'My boss only hired me because he fancied me,' said Annabel. Wasn't there then a great danger of sexual harrassment, a game in which Britain (according to an EEC poll) follows closely on France at the top of the European league?

The girls smiled and said they could deal with it; to take serious objection would be a mistake, career-wise. 'You have to be prepared,' said Claire, 'to be thrown against the filing cabinet and told to take your pants down. It's their way of ripping the piss out of you. So you rip the piss out of them as well.'

My memory of later conversation is imperfect. I remember Mark telling Hugh that it would be wise of him to maintain his bank account with his country branch, because overdrafts were easier there than in town. I remember thinking that Mark looked all of nineteen. I remember asking Claire if she ever encountered members of the working-class (oh, what a wimp I was!). I remember Claire's answer: 'Not really, but I did sociology to A-level so I've got a fair idea about how they live.' This was not a joke.

But chiefly I remember thinking that everybody there faced safe and very sociable futures. What kind of woman would Annabel like to be when she reached forty? 'If I was like mummy, I'd be very happy.'

Loneliness lay elsewhere. The next morning, trembling over my little beaker of takeaway coffee, I scanned the classified columns of *Time Out* magazine. Here were Lonely Hearts; sensitive people, often attractive or at least cuddly, sometimes sexy, usually equipped with a sense of humour or sincerity. Some were particular in their desires:

o *GAY ROCK MUSICIAN (24) seeks non-camp, maybe working-class type (21+) lad for sincere relationship.*
o *GAY BIKER, 34, seeks same (21+) also non-biker mate (21+). Write with photo.*
o *WHALE-SAVING, whole-food eating, Shakespeare-worshipping, pub-crawling, music-loving, poetry-reading, theatre-going male, 31, seeks similar sincere female. Must be non-smoker. Fun relationship.*

Others sought more general qualities – more general but perhaps more difficult to find; and once found, more difficult to keep.

○ *I MISS sharing the good experiences of life. Travelling, going out together or staying in, making decisions together, sharing friends, loving and being loved, sleeping close. I have a creative job and a flat in NW London. I am very attractive, lively, gentle and affectionate. Looking for successful, educated, sincere man to share my life, who is fun to be with and who still believes in love . . .*

The quest for love in London can lead to evening classes. That is one traditional route. Over the past ten years, however, several organisations have grown up which abolish the alibi, the need to pretend that you are learning art for art's sake when the true objects of desire are fellow students. These new organisations charge a fee and go straight to the matter of the heart. They cater for people who feel they need friends, or more friends, or different friends. They also advertise in *Time Out*, but their advertisements never mention loneliness: who wants to meet people who feel lonely? After all, there must be something wrong with them. Instead they emphasise the gaiety and smartness of the present membership: 'Super people . . . single professional people who are well-mannered, friendly and smartly-dressed, aged 25–45 . . . the way to meet the people you want to meet . . . the number one club for single, sophisticated Londoners . . . super new friends . . . how to improve your social life . . . would you like to make 100 new friends in a week?'

That seemed a large amount, but why not? I bought a *Standard* (*Dig For 13 Bodies*) at Lancaster Gate tube and sought out one club's venue in the basement bar of a Bayswater hotel. It requires some courage to join a group of people who have come together because they want friends. This was an introductory meeting for potential members. Most looked nervous, one or two slightly ashamed. The group comprised two Iranian men, two Australian girls, one magnificently shaped German woman in an angora sweater, Jill from West

Norwood, Salim from Karachi, Mike from Walthamstow – and Paul, who wore a blazer. First names were flourished at an alarming speed. Smoking was heavy.

Paul offered Jill a cigarette. Jill jumped. 'I hope you don't think I'm trying to pick you up,' said Paul. Jill looked miserable. Paul then took Jill's clenched hands and laid them on the table. 'Now, now, we mustn't be so tense,' said Paul, who looked very tense indeed.

Tenseness spread. The word should never have been mentioned. Lips were licked, the ceiling examined, questions pushed out like frail paper boats into a silent pond. The girl next to me, an Australian, clutched a paperback novel with the imprint of a feminist publishing house. I asked about it – any paper boat in a storm – and found myself almost adding: 'I hope you don't think I'm trying to pick you up.'

John, the club's proprietor, outlined the wonderful social life which lay in store for us once we had paid the £30 membership fee: scuba-diving, London walks, discotheques, wine bar evenings. The club had 1,500 members. It was possible to give it a two-week trial by post-dating a banker's order – forms available – which could later be cancelled if the social life did not live up to expectations. I filled in a form. Mike from Walthamstow paid in cash.

I met Mike some days later (*Murder Dig – Bones Found*) at a wine bar evening in Muswell Hill. We reminisced sadly about the German woman in the angora sweater, who hadn't joined and might never be seen again.

Only four other club members were present in the Muswell Hill wine bar; three men and a woman, all in their thirties. The men left early, one saying: 'Sorry to be unsociable but there's something I want to watch on the telly.'

That left Pam and Mike and me. Pam, who was a friendly woman, said she still lay in hope of finding Mr Right. Mike had joined because he shared a house with three male snooker enthusiasts. 'That's all they do. Go to the pub and play snooker. Stay at home and watch snooker on television. There has to be more to life than that.'

Mike and Pam agreed that they wouldn't reveal their

membership of such a club to friends. It would stigmatise them; stupid, but there it was. We talked in a desultory way about the Muswell Hill horrors, just around the corner.

'You know,' said Pam, 'it's the poor plumber I feel sorry for.'

Betjeman might write his poem differently now. Loneliness – the real stuff – does not lie in the baths of business girls or even, perhaps, in the application forms for clubs which promise super new friends. It lies among people who can vanish without anyone noticing. It lies deep – at a level which only at the very end is plumbable.

> *From young Vicki's tarnished plughole*
> *Lukewarm water oozes still,*
> *With its hint of awful blockage*
> *To the girls of Muswell Hill.*
>
> *Waste pipes blurt the message upwards;*
> *No escape at all this end,*
> *Summon help from costly plumbers,*
> *Yellow Pages be your friend.*
>
> *Come and please be quick! cries Vicki,*
> *Hugh is due at eight-fifteen.*
> *Hair unwashed, I cannot see him*
> *(Hugh is wimpish, but he's lean).*
>
> *Mummy hears the jolly story;*
> *Plumbers – really! What a clown!*
> *'Queer,' says man from Yellow Pages,*
> *'Trouble must lie farther down.'*
>
> *Rest you there, poor unbelov'd ones,*
> *Lap your loneliness in heat.*
> *All too late the probing pick-axe,*
> *Flashing bulb and plastic sheet.*

BRING ON THE EMPTY ELEPHANTS!

India, Spring, 1984

Between the cities of Mysore and Bangalore a striking range of hills stands up from the South Indian plateau. They look not so much like hills as a spectacular litter of giant rocks, some pebble-smooth, some jagged, some turreted as though warriors had built them; all ancient. They are among the oldest rocks on earth. Long before the birth of all that's thought of as 'eternal' in India – the Himalayas, the Ganges – these rocks existed. Once they formed part of the vanished continent of Gondwana, until it cracked and split and went its various ways to emerge as Australasia and Africa and isolated pinnacles in the Indian Ocean. Their granite is at least two billion years old; the famous 'Closepet' granite, which takes its name from Mr Barry Close who was once the British advisor to the princess of Mysore state.

No quarries have pitted them, few tourists have trodden over them. Their permanence has been challenged only by millions of monsoons.

Scramble to the top of these hills, look down and you can see the ribbon of dusty road that cuts through coconut groves and paddy fields on its way from Mysore to Bangalore. Along this road one morning comes a white Mercedes, with Swiss numberplates, containing David Lean, the distinguished and veteran British film director, seeking locations for his adapta-

189

tion of E. M. Forster's last and greatest novel, *A Passage to India*.

Lean looks about him and is enthralled. These huge and naked rocks, he decides, will be the Marabar Hills. Here Miss Adela Quested, fresh out from the Home Counties by P & O, will enter the Marabar Caves and emerge a changed woman. Perhaps she has been sexually assaulted. Perhaps by her Indian companion, Dr Aziz. Perhaps she has imagined it. Perhaps she has been shocked into trance by knowing, for the first time, the unknowability of the universe. Perhaps she has been changed by some of these together, or by all of them. As Forster himself didn't know, there is little point in our guessing. The consequences of the mystery, however, are enormous. Aziz is accused, friends fall out, Indians riot, the Empire briefly shakes and the English Literature syllabus is changed for ever.

This then is the big scene, the centre of the novel and the film. Imagine the hours, the days, the weeks, the years of struggle and planning which have brought Lean and his men this far. Imagine E. M. Forster refusing to yield the film rights up until his death in 1970. Imagine the long negotiations with his literary executors. Imagine the search for money in Britain and America: 'Give us an explicit rape scene in those darned caves and we'll back you,' says one mogul across the Atlantic. Imagine the eighteen months that Lean takes to produce his script. Imagine (oh dear me, yes) the permissions to be sought in India. Imagine Roger of Catering shipping out his 300 small jars of Shippam's Paste (both meat and fish) and his comparable quantities of tinned beans and salmon, his bottles of brown sauce (both HP and Daddie's), his two mobile kitchens from Finsbury Park. Imagine the castings, the hirings, the firings, the rows with the art director, the costumes that must be scrapped, the sets that don't look quite right. Imagine the logistics of shuttling 250 people back and forth across India.

And then imagine the scene at the hills. The actors have been cast and the money, $17m of it, has been found. The Shippam's Paste is en route by sea. But wait! *There are no caves.* Krishna, in all his power and multiplied forms, has neglected to put caves in this particular part of his dominion. Brahma has created the hills, Vishnu has preserved them, Shiva has not yet destroyed them. But the gods have failed entirely in the matter of caves.

Lean decides to make caves where none exist. The Conservator of Forests, who administers the region, refuses permission. Lean appeals to higher – and political rather than geological or ecological – authorities in Bangalore and Delhi. Permission is granted. Lean blasts several holes in the ancient and previously untroubled granite and scars and pits the smooth rock-face with scaffolding.

Technicians, cameras and props bounce up the track from the main road – and plasterers, because one or two of the cave entrances are a little *too* jagged. The tinned kippers arrive. Containers filled with boiled water, coffee, tea and soft drinks are arranged on tables. The rocks ring to the artisan voices of Shepperton and Borehamwood.

'Up a bit, Chunky.'

'Got a snout, Ken?'

'Right you are, Mel.'

'Hoi, Raghu!'

'What's that bugger Marcus up to?'

These people are all real. Then the fictionals come up: Dame Peggy Ashcroft who is Mrs Moore – troubled, mystic and not long for this world; Victor Bannerjee who plays Dr Aziz – mercurial, sentimental and soon to find himself in jail; Judy Davies who is Miss Quested – prettier than the novel has her and rather more aware of sex; James Fox who plays Fielding – decent, liberal and trying hard to understand.

They wait, act, wait and act again. A line here, a gesture there. Then the line modified but the gesture the same. Then vice versa. Then back to the original. Each night everyone bounces back to the hotel in Bangalore. Several days pass in this way, until Lean announces his satisfaction.

Finally, the car doors slam for good on this particular location. Back down the hill go the soft drinks containers, the cameras, the make-up women and the sound men.

Presently their convoy is heard honking at bullock-carts on the main road below. Presently, too, the sun goes down. Smoke from village cow-dung fires seeps across the plain. Dogs bark. A steam locomotive whistles distantly. The moon rises on abandoned scaffolding and new caves made in the cause of fiction. Silence.

The silence lasts for quite some time. For a month, in fact, until the day in early January when Dr Chiranjeev Singh opens his copy of his daily newspaper, the *Deccan Herald* from Bangalore, and reads an obtuse reference to Lean's cave-making activities. As the Director of Mines and Geology for the state of Karnataka – the province in which Lean's caves lie – Dr Singh is naturally intrigued. He drives immediately to the scene; is horrified; takes photographs; returns to write a very angry letter to the Government.

Dr Singh, a noble-looking young Sikh with a long black beard, feels almost as insulted in real life as Dr Aziz does in fiction. Foreigners have come to his country and abused its hospitality. His precious rocks have been violated, just as he was planning to have them declared an area of 'outstanding geological and aesthetic importance'. He sits down and prepares a fizzing press release which quotes from old imperial gazetteers: 'The decay of lofty granite masses produces some of the most picturesque features of an Indian landscape, its strange columnar piles, trees and lagging stones . . . far excel those of Dartmoor in grandeur and in the fantastic forms they assume.'

He ends, just as Dr Aziz would have done, with a stab at a joke and an accusing verse: 'David Lean's film may pass without any holes to pick, but it will leave behind a few ugly holes in the majestic rocks of Ramanagaram.' Someone has very wisely said:

> *And some behold the signs and marvel – some*
> *See nothing, being blind;*
> *Bringing no light they have no light to find,*
> *And famished pass as empty as they come . . .*

Dr Singh is still fizzing when I call on him. What would happen, he wants to know, if an Indian film director decided he would like to rearrange Stonehenge or the Cheddar Gorge? Answer: outrage. 'Precisely,' said Dr Singh, adding: 'And I used to be an admirer of Lean's work. I use the past tense because I'm shocked that a man of such alleged sensitivity could commit such vandalism.'

Moreover, says Dr Singh, it is all so unnecessary. 'If Lean had got in touch with my department, we could have shown him any number of manmade and natural caves. There are hundreds of them all over Karnataka. I am afraid what we will be seeing on the screen is neither an Indian's India nor Forster's India. This is Lean's India.' Dr Singh is right, and Miss Quested's famous demand – 'I want to see the *real* India' – is likely to remain unsatisfied in the cinema. Lean himself may not deny it. 'The style of the picture,' he has told his cast, 'is six inches off the ground.' He knows precisely how he wants to achieve this altitude and bids India provide it; and if India, never so biddable, fails him, then Lean will gladly resort to models, fakes and dynamite. Hence the new caves, hence the construction of elaborate outdoor sets, hence model trains crossing model plains into real sunsets, before real temples, photographed elsewhere and superimposed.

Sometimes historical or social truth in the shape of the art or costume department pokes its head nervously above the parapet and complains: 'I don't think we can have it quite like that, David . . .'

'Well fuck it,' says Lean, 'that's how it's going to be.'

Whereupon historical or social truth retreats; but not always. There is, for example, the famous battle of the monkey-men. Lean wanted Hindus dressed as Hanuman, the monkey god, to caper joyfully around an equally joyful Muslim crown when the news comes that Dr Aziz, a Muslim, has been acquitted of Miss Quested's assault. This sight is about as improbable as Dr Paisley stooping to kiss the papal ring, and there were considerable objections from the Indians on the set. They won the day, but only after a long fight. Lean isn't easily moved from his vision or his script – and however broad or blurred the former, the latter is marvellously exact:

> LONG SHOT: The TRAIN is crossing a STEEL BRIDGE spanning a great palm-fringed RIVER. On SOUND the CROAK of frogs mingles with the CLATTER of the train and the warning whoops of the engine's SIREN.

The people who serve up the visionary with many of his visions occupy a jumble of offices in the garden of their Bangalore hotel. This is the art department, bent over its drawing-boards, busy with its sketches, models and photographs, and led by John Box, the film's production designer. Box and Lean are an old partnership – Box won two of his four Oscars for *Dr Zhivago* and *Lawrence* – but relations between them haven't always been smooth. They had a serious rupture in Tahiti when Lean was trying to get his ill-fated *Mutiny on the Bounty* off the rocks (the film was never made), and storms have again blown up in India. Lean chose all his locations and Box has had to work within that choice. Still, the results are remarkable: so much skill, so much industry, to provide Lean with an India-within-India.

Consider the workshops. Here craftsmen have been drawn from the studios of Britain and Bombay to turn out beautiful replicas of intricate stone tracery, entwined erotic sculpture, statues of Queen Victoria, old pillar-boxes, portable anthills. Consider the sets, a mile further off in the grounds of a former Mysore Maharajah's many palaces. Bungalows with homesick names – Lochard, Fairholms, Gairloch – form the rigid geometry of the British quarter. The Indian bazaar, a long street with a temple at one end and a fortified arch at the other, needs only the filth to make it a perfect copy of the bazaar you passed in the car fifteen minutes ago, or of most bazaars in most Indian towns (and even the filth will be provided when Box drives in the cattle and lines the roofs of the bazaar with garbage to attract the crows). Consider Dr Aziz's bungalow, all picturesque clutter and window-panes and warped wood, which looks as no house in India has ever looked. Here on Dr Aziz's desk is Dr Aziz's prescription pad – each page printed with a fictional *King Edward Hospital, Chandrapore* in gothic script. Consider the portable anthill, waiting outside to take its perfect position within the frame.

No other foreign film-maker has come to India to re-create the country so fastidiously or so theatrically. Indians shake their heads in bemusement. Some mention arrogance. John Box says: 'I wish Forster were here. I wonder what he would have made of it all?'

We'll have to guess. First, Forster might be perplexed that his novel, so firmly set in the 'hopeless melancholy' of the north Indian plain, has been moved 1,000 miles to the more cheerful south, and that Kashmir and the Himalayas also elbow their way in to the script. He might point out, justifiably, that so much lovely nature has stood the tone of the book on its head; for Forster wasn't Kipling and caught the listlessness of the subcontinent rather than its *National Geographic* side. The visitor to the caves, he writes, 'returns uncertain whether he has had an interesting experience or a dull one or any experience at all'.

He might not be too miffed about this, understanding that listlessness is not a selling proposition. Changes to plot and character might disturb him more. Lean has largely de-politicised the novel. In the film, time and distance rather than imperialism become the final barrier to friendship between Aziz and Fielding. Richard Goodwin, who is co-producing the film with Lord Brabourne, justifies the change. He says the novel's ending is 'well over the top . . . there are many more obstacles to friendship between Indians and English than politics. Personally I feel that though we like one another we can never be friends. Both races are too proud for that.'

This may be, but Forster felt that individuals could escape such generalities, and spent a good deal of his time trying to prove his point, penetrating – sometimes very literally – the barriers of race and class to establish intimacies with consorts ranging from tram-conductors in Egypt and barbers in India to policemen in Hammersmith.

Lean and Goodwin also feel that Forster gave the British a raw deal. Again, maybe so; many old India hands have complained similarly since the book first appeared in 1924. But Forster knew his own feelings on the subject. Over the British in India, he wrote: 'I have to stretch and bust myself blue. I loathe them and should have been more honest to say so. Honesty and fairness are so different.' Lean has given Forster's unwilling fairness a large shove. The racial arrogance of the bungalow folk – the Turtons, the McBrydes and the Callendars – may be much reduced. 'The British,' says Goodwin, 'will be made to seem worthy but unwise.'

Meanwhile the Indians will be six inches off the ground. Sir Alec Guinness as Professor Godbole, the Brahmin, will appear comic, sinister and unfathomably wise, and will also dance and chant a little. Victor Bannerjee as Dr Aziz will combine anxiety and vanity, pathos and bravery. Above all, he will be lovable; rather – Lean's word – 'a goose'.

Bannerjee is an actor with a growing reputation in India, particularly in the Bengali cinema, but this is his first foreign film. He might well have caught Forster's fancy. He nicely combines his character's vanity and anxiety and is, as the novel describes Aziz, 'an athletic little man, daintily put together, but really very strong.' Forster, too, might have liked his determination to stick up for himself and his country. As the film's leading Indian character – and one of its few Indian actors not to be imported from Britain – he is trying hard to preserve his own idea of Aziz, not without opposition from the director. Words have been exchanged. During an early row, Bannerjee told Lean that he wasn't the greatest director in the world, and that he, Bannerjee, had worked with greater. (He first appeared on the screen in a film by Satyajit Ray and has just finished work in Ray's latest film, *Home and the World*, based on a Tagore novel.)

Mannerisms and accent are the trouble. Lean and Bannerjee have different ideas about how an educated Indian like Aziz would behave. Lean wants a little more of what might be called crudely, the Peter Sellers input. 'Playing one Englishman's idea of another Englishman's idea of an Indian isn't my scene,' says Bannerjee, and observes, interestingly, that the Indian players who have come from England are more skilled in Uncle Tom-foolery. Lean has smoothed the Bengali's feathers and may even have conceded his point – though the argument could still reach its climax in the dubbing studios.

None of this may matter in the end given that, in Goodwin's words, *Passage* remains a 'terrifically powerful story with wonderful characters'. He and Lean envisage after-dinner arguments from the intrigued audience in Putney and Pittsburgh. What really went on or came off inside the caves?

The author himself didn't know and used the caves merely as a symbol of muddle – a device he later regretted – so argument would seem unprofitable. But here Lean has bent the plot slightly to imply that Aziz *might* have done it; a possibility Forster never allowed.

'The caves? Easy,' says a senior technician, a man pining for England and a decent pork pie. 'Either he screwed her or he should have done.'

So much for the unknowability of the universe.

Now scramble again to the top of those strange hills that straddle the road between Mysore and Bangalore. More than a month has passed. Dr Singh, the geologist, has come here curious and returned angry. And the film crew is on the move again from Bangalore. Look down and you can see them moving in a large convoy that drives westwards towards higher and greener hills, the Nilgiris, where the British established hill-stations and retreated from the summer heat.

Under the instructions of a long memorandum titled *Movement Order Number Five*, the crew and cast are travelling 200 miles to install themselves for a few days in the hotels and clubs which the ancestral race left behind. A railway scene is to be filmed on the little mountain railway.

About 200 people have obeyed *Movement Order Number Five*. Led by Lean in his white Mercedes, they are travelling in twenty cars, a dozen mini-buses, several coaches and two Land-Rovers. They are taking – in sixteen trucks – electric generators, cameras, carpenters, servants, large amounts of day and evening dress, half a gross small jars Shippam's Paste (both meat and fish), and comparable quantities of tinned beans and bottled brown sauce (both HP and Daddie's). Neither have the sausages and Branston Pickle been forgotten, nor the means of their easy digestion and exit. See! There are the two mobile kitchens from Finsbury Park, and the old bus which is the mobile lavatory.

No viceroy, transferring himself and his staff from Delhi to hot-weather quarters in Simla, could have laid better or more elaborate plans. And Lean suits the role of viceroy rather well: silver-haired, curtly polite, slightly military – a man who has been known to remark, when the hotel's hot-water system has failed again, that the Turtons and McBrydes of the novel may have been right about your Indian after all. Lovable chaps, but they can drive you mad sometimes.

Over the past forty years Lean has turned great literature into successful films. *Oliver Twist* and *Great Expectations* from Dickens, *Zhivago* from Pasternak, *Lawrence* from T. E. Lawrence. Then in 1970 came *Ryan's Daughter*, which nobody wants to talk about, followed soon after by the aborted *Bounty* and a reputation clouded by anecdotes – unfair, say the people who work with him – about his painstaking and expensive slowness. Now, aged seventy-six and after a long gap, can he pull off his old trick and sell Forster?

A certain nervousness ripples through the viceregal court. This film, say various dignitaries, will have to be good, 'bloody good . . . the definitive Indian film'. Of course David is marvellous and the script is wonderful – many say they prefer it to the book – and the actors are darlings. But the market, my love, what about the *market*? Let's face it (sweetheart), we've had *Gandhi* and *Heat and Dust* and *Kim* and all that M. M. Kaye and Paul Scott oozing its way into British living-rooms. How many more sitars, elephants and ceiling-fans can the audience take?

The Western appetite for the glamorised imperial experience may prove to be insatiable. Nevertheless it will be Lean's stamp that sells the film rather than the novel's reputation – the stamp that asks Dr Aziz (for example) to frolic dangerously along the running board of a train as it hurries across a mountain ravine.

I watch the scene on the mountain railway. The train crosses the same ravine several times, and each time Dr Aziz capers along the carriage side to shout to Mrs Moore and Miss Quested in their ladies' compartment: 'Look, I am Douglas Fairbanks,' a line which in the script read: 'Look, we are all monkeys.'

Does it matter that the train in the book was an ordinary little thing that shuffled across a dull plain? That Dr Aziz did nothing more dangerous than poke his head out of the window? That a small-town Indian doctor in 1920 would not have heard of Douglas Fairbanks? 'Well, fuck it,' Lean would say, and the audience might agree.

And Forster? 'Most of life is so dull,' he wrote in *A Passage to India*, 'that there is nothing to be said about it, and the books and the talk that would describe it as interesting are obliged to exaggerate in the hope of justifying their own existence . . . a perfectly-adjusted organism would be silent.'

David Lean is far from the perfectly-adjusted organism. Bring on the empty elephants!

THE REPACKAGING OF GLASGOW

Glasgow, Autumn, 1984

Journalists from London who go north to write about
Glasgow have, for most of this century, run the severe risk of
the distressed reader's letter. There you are, safe home again
behind the burglar-locked windows of Islington or Hampstead, inserting a few harmless jokes about Glaswegian
drunkenness or Glaswegian crime into copy which somehow
seems to call for it. There *they* are, the Glaswegian readers,
picking up the paper the next day only to set it down again
with extreme exasperation.

Thunderclaps break over the breakfast tables of the
Glasgow suburbs. Pens are taken up. Fine italic script of the
kind taught in Scottish high schools twenty years ago (and
perhaps still) rushes across the writing pad, bouncing occasionally into capitals that shout with frustration, sometimes in a
different colour of ink. Two days later, in London, the
letters start to arrive.

*Sir, I am disgusted that a newspaper of your standing should
once again seek to perpetuate the image of Glasgow as a Hellish
mixture of poverty, drink and violence . . .*

*Sir, Glasgow has the best collection of art in Britain outside
London . . . the largest civic-owned library in Europe . . . more
than 70 public parks . . . an architectural heritage commended
by Betjeman and Pevsner . . .*

*Sir, I have lived in Glasgow for 85 years and never once been
assaulted on the street. I am also a lifelong teetotaller . . .*

200

Sir, I moved to Glasgow from Bradford-on-Avon and have never regretted it. Does your ignorant and prejudiced reporter not realise that the 'bonny, bonny banks' of Loch Lomond are only FIFTEEN MINUTES away by car, 'Haud yer wheesht', as we say in these parts . . . (This, of course, is from an English correspondent.)

You reply. You acknowledge the facts about the parks and museums and the propinquity of Loch Lomond; but you also point out politely that the available statistics do suggest Glasgow to be one of the most socially and economically deprived cities in Western Europe – more plainly, a Hellish mixture of poverty, drink and violence. Moreover, you add that you yourself have witnessed distressing scenes ('like something out of Hogarth') in Argyle Street at closing time on a Friday night. Why, on your last trip a man on the same bus threw up – in the traditionally unabashed, self-satisfied way of the Scottish drunk – to deposit at your feet a commendably multi-ethnic mixture of export ale and chicken kashmiri (the one with the pineapple chunks . . . but there you go again with your little jokes).

At one time that would have been a reasonable defence. Today it will no longer serve, quite. Over the past few years – since the end of that most dreadful Glasgow decade, the Seventies – some marvellous and intriguing things have been happening to the city. Epidemics of stone-cleaning and tree-planting have transformed its former blackness into chequer-works of salmon pink, yellow and green. Old buildings have been burnished and refitted. Museums, delicatessens and wine bars have opened, and thrive. New theatres occupy old churches. There are business centres, sports centres, heritage centres, arts centres. There are film-makers. There is even a nationally acknowledged novelist or two.

Much of this would seem commonplace in one of those British cities (Edinburgh, say, or Norwich) which had the good luck to escape the rise and fall of the first industrial revolution; but in Glasgow, the Victorian boom-town to cap them all (and later the slump-town ditto), it can look like a revolution in social and civic behaviour. Many Glaswegians now see their city differently. Optimists among them say that Glasgow could become Britain's first major post-industrial success; a city that has weathered the recessionary gale to emerge into the sunlight – microchips and macrobottles of the house white – which has been swept along behind. People who describe themselves as realists say there is still some way to go. Pessimists insist that all it amounts to is a grandiose exercise in self-delusion, a *placebo* which offers no cure for a terminally-ruined economy and the wretchedness of mass unemployment.

Few in any category, however, doubt that the city's appearance has been fundamentally improved and its psychology fundamentally altered, or that these days there are far worse places to live in Britain. Cities to the south – Birmingham, Manchester, Liverpool – are said to be envious. Some of them have dispatched bands of municipal pilgrims to the north, to inspect the methods of Glasgow's achievement. A fresh evaluation is overdue.

'Look son, Ah've been tae these places. Nice, Cannes, the Costa del Sol, Italy. Ah've seen them. And the truth about them is . . . take away the sunshine and you're left wi' fuck-all.'

A Glaswegian speaking, and not just any old Glaswegian (the taxi-driver on the way to the airport), but the Glaswegian appointed to speak for Glasgow. Harry Diamond is the city's public-relations manager, the Glasgow-born son of Lithuanian Jewish parents who migrated to the Gorbals before the First World War. He started work as a reporter on a Glasgow newspaper forty years ago and has rarely deserted the city since. Crime was his original speciality. *The Great Blackhill Hooch Tragedy, Seven Dead*: Harry was there. *Bridgeton Gang Terror*: Harry was there. He shot out of the office whenever Glasgow's poor and dirty face erupted in one of its vivid boils of violent or accidental death: razor-slashings, chip-pan blazes, boy (6) in tenement plunge.

He was, he confessed, one of the people who 'helped destroy

this city's reputation' by presenting it to the world as a 'grimy, poverty-ridden, drunken f . . . . n' dump'. Today he is a reformed character who sits in an office decorated, like many offices of the senior executives of Glasgow District Council, with handsome Victorian paintings borrowed from the city's art collections. A word-processor occupies one corner of the room. Here Diamond taps out the corrective to his previous career in the form of press releases which stress culture, hotel accommodation and a dynamic past.

The city, he said, had produced some great people. 'Lord Kelvin. He laid the first trans-Atlantic cable. Joseph Lister. He gave the world antiseptics. Marvellous guys. Then there was James Watt. He was taking a walk on Glasgow Green one day and he thought up the steam condenser. Right there on Glasgow Green. Aye, he thought: *Christ that's a good idea.*'

But that was 200 years ago. What of the present, I asked him, what were you left with when you took away the sunshine from Glasgow, which God's miserable direction of the westerly depressions did for most of the time? A lot? 'Oh Jesus aye,' said Diamond. 'There's so much happening in this city that it's absolutely impossible to keep track of it all.' He attempted a list: two symphony orchestras and many smaller musical groups, Scottish Opera, the largest civic-owned library in Europe, at least half a dozen theatres, the new Scottish Exhibition Centre which opens next year, new buildings for the Royal Scottish Academy of Music and Drama, the headquarters of the British Oil Corporation, the Kelvingrove galleries, the Hunterian museum, the third largest marathon in the world, the Burrell Collection which opened last year and won the British Tourist Authority award for the most outstanding tourist development of 1983.

All of this has been accompanied by an extraordinary outburst of civic pride. Glaswegian chauvinism, always a formidable if sometimes ill-founded kind of subnationalism (though Glaswegians would demur at the sub), is flowering now as it has not flowered since the years when Glasgow ranked high among the industrial capitals of the world, when the Grand Duke Alexis of Russia, attending the launch of his steam yacht, could call the city 'the centre of the intelligence of England' and get it nearly right. Those were the years of the city's great prosperity, when the Clyde launched more than twenty-five per cent of the world's ships (the figure for last year was 0.85 per cent) and when Glasgow advertised itself by its utilitarian wares. The advertisements still exist in the parts of the world which are strapped for money, in the countries which make do with the old technology, and travellers to Calcutta or Buenos Aires or Zimbabwe may inspect them with an archaeologist's interest. They take the shape of manufacturers' plates screwed to the boilers of steam locomotives, to crane-legs, to lathes, to the faces of the engine-room telegraphs whose hands spin like a daft clock's – half-ahead, full-ahead, half-astern, full-astern, stop; and there at the centre of the face, the maker: *Mechans of Scotscoun, Glasgow.*

I saw that one myself last year on a Ganges ferry. 'Tell me something amusing about your country,' said the Indian I stood beside. 'The place that built this ship has vanished,' I said. 'Nothing there but weeds. Glasgow doesn't build ships and Manchester doesn't make cotton and we import a lot of cars from Japan.' He sucked his teeth in commiseration. 'Interesting but not amusing,' he said. 'What do the people do?'

The question is pertinent to the whole of Britain, but it has a special force when asked of Glasgow. Employment in the old industries has declined spectacularly. Since 1971 more than forty per cent of jobs in the shipbuilding and marine engineering industries have disappeared. The figure for jobs in metal manufacturing is eighty per cent; for printing and publishing forty per cent; for mechanical engineering fifty-five per cent; for electrical engineering forty-eight per cent; in transport thirty-one per cent; in vehicle manufacture thirty-one per cent. The only categories of work which now employ more people are the professions, public administration, general services, and insurance and banking. More than twice as many people now work in banks, insurance companies and stockbrokers' officers as do in shipyards (the plural is still applicable, just) and engine-shops. And many more, about 60,000 of them, do not work at all.

At first Glasgow tried to resist this destruction which was raining down on it from West Germany and Japan. I trained as a journalist in Glasgow twenty years ago, and one of my first reporting jobs was to see off a delegation of shipworkers on the night sleeper to London. They were attempting to save Fairfields yard from closure; one of the first of many similar delegations and the beginning of a headline era in which the words 'save' and 'jobs' figured prominently. In the event, Fairfields was saved and, thanks to frequent injections of public funds, survives still. But other companies did not: North British Locomotive (an early casualty), Barclay Curle, Blythswood Shipbuilding, Connell's, Harland and Wolff, Stephen's, Simons Lobnitz. The names mean little now; the sites are willow-herb and Portakabins.

Sometimes closure threats prompted 'work-ins', but even the most celebrated of these, at Upper Clyde Shipbuilders, did not much more than postpone the evil Friday of the final pay-packet. And yet throughout the Seventies the city continued to imagine it had some kind of industrial future, unable to fence off a patch of its history and call it the past. When Mrs Thatcher's recession began to shut down even those factories which had been designed, twenty years before, to replace Glasgow's traditional industries, the city concluded that the jig was up. It decided to invent a future for itself.

Futures, unlike steam condensers, do not perform to any known law of thermodynamics. Inventing them was not a traditional Glasgow skill. The city looked abroad and found the USA and the slogan with the heart which proclaims *I love New York*. Advertising men and public-relations consultants were hired. Glasgow has always had a strong amateur tradition in the latter field: 'See this city son, best people in the world. Aye you could go a long way and meet worse.' (Taxi-driver on the way from airport.) Now it beefed it up with professionals. The *Glasgow's Miles Better* campaign was born at a cost of £500,000. Today the city advertises itself to the world as a 'centre'; a business and conference centre, an educational centre, a cultural centre, a tourist centre. The manufacturer's plates have been replaced by a comic figure (Mr Happy, on loan from Roger Hargreaves and his *Mr Men* books) and a stick-on slogan that can mean everything or nothing.

Than where or what is Glasgow miles better? Than Edinburgh? Than Paris? The ambiguity is deliberate, but the slogan does have a foundation of truth. Glasgow, in several respects, is miles better than it used to be; while the rest of Britain, in similar respects, is miles worse.

Consider crime, for example. Until the Seventies Glasgow had a near British monopoly in football hooliganism and gang warfare. England has easily eclipsed Glasgow in the former – West Ham v. Chelsea has overhauled Celtic v Rangers – while the Glasgow gang has almost completely and mysteriously vanished. Privatised, perhaps, or deadened by heroin. Nor are Glaswegians more likely to be the subject of violent attacks. According to the official statistics of the British Crime Survey, the victim rate for violent crime in Glasgow is roughly the same as the United Kingdom average. In the particular categories of common, serious and sexual assault, the Glasgow figures are actually much below those for England. On the other hand, Glasgow follows the rest of the country in escalating rates of burglary and motor car theft. It would seem that Glasgow is switching from the idea of crime as entertainment, violence for fun, to the more sensible philosophy of crime for personal gain.

Or consider drink. The Glasgow drunk was another brand leader. Which of us who have seen him can forget the man in the gutter singing *The Yellow Rose of Texas* and swigging from a bottle of British fortified wine? Today almost every large British city has imitations of him. The reasons aren't obscure. Alcoholism and heavy drinking often accompany a sense of abandonment and lives which lack hope or purpose. Many Glaswegians have felt these things keenly for years. Now the rest of the country is getting them in the neck and Glasgow can afford a slight smugness. Not that drunkenness has diminished in the west of Scotland – it remains a huge social problem, unaffected by the hopes of the liberalisers who reformed Scotland's drinking laws ten years ago (reforms which have left England with some of the most restrictive drinking hours in Europe). But the new laws have made drunkenness less obvious; the mad ten o'clock rush has disappeared and public vomiting reduced. Now increasing numbers of Glasgow men and women get argumentative and sentimental over wine and cocktails in palatial saloons with names – Nico's, Lautrec's, Zhivago's – which suggest their owners were once on nodding terms with Gertrude Stein.

But perhaps Glasgow has changed most significantly in its attitude to housing. More than sixty per cent of Scotland's houses are rented from the local authority, a much larger proportion than in England (where the figure is thirty per cent) and a larger public-to-private ratio even than that of several countries in Eastern Europe. Victorian industrialism gave Lowland Scotland a large bequest of rotten houses, and local authorities were usually the only agencies which had enough power and will to provide a better alternative. 'Progress' and 'rehousing' became synonymous terms, and the prospect of more and more council houses became one of the chief vote-gatherers of the Scottish Labour movement.

Glasgow's particularly squalid legacy was boiled down in the public mind to one word: tenements. Many Labour councillors, who had grown up in tenements, quite understandably loathed them. For the poor they meant grim four-storey blocks split into one or two-room apartments with shared lavatories, no baths and grubby back-courts. Not all tenements were like that, and even those that were often had other virtues – solidity, neighbourliness – but the word soon came to have the same meaning as slum, or absence of progress. Glasgow embarked on large 'slum-clearance' projects, a phrase which fulfilled itself because respectable localities, once designated as slums, quickly became slum-like. About 200,000 people were 'decanted' (the official word, still in use) into remote housing estates. A later enthusiasm for motorways and high-rise flats, stimulated by homage to Los Angeles and

the great Le Corbusier, made the city into the most com-
prehensively redeveloped in Europe outside those which had
been bombed flat during the Second World War.

The consequences of this story have been told often enough
– alienation and waste land – and today the city's officials
look back on it as a sad but forgivable mistake; forgivable
because Glasgow needed to tackle its housing problem quickly
and cheaply and was, after all, only following the planning
fashion of the day.

The fashion changed in the mid-Seventies, prompted by
sounds of pain from below and throat-clearing from above.
People who still lived in tenements shrank, by this stage, from
the prospect of decantation into a tower block or a damp
terrace. At the same time two Acts of Parliament – the Housing (Scotland) Acts of 1969 and 1974 – substituted the idea of
'housing treatment areas' for slum-clearance. Houses could
be improved rather than demolished, and money was forth-
coming from the central government in the shape of the Housing Corporation. Communities were encouraged to form
Housing Associations – a new and radical idea in paternalism
of the city fathers. Today the city has 22 housing associations,
and they have spent about £185 million in the renovation of
10,000 tenement homes. The results, sparkling sandstone outside and large and lofty rooms within, stand as a reprimand
to the city's years of heavy petting with Le Corbusier and Sir
Basil Spence.

More radicalism followed. Glasgow Council freed land for
private housing development. Last year 1,500 private houses
were built inside the city boundaries. Ten years ago the figure
was below ten. Today the council is even planning to sell
whole areas of its housing estates to housing co-operatives,
which would constitute, as a senior council official remarked,
'a great big jump in policy and dogma' for a Labour city
which has never been slow to invoke its central position in the
history of British socialism. The truth, however, is that
Glasgow's Labour council has become surprisingly pragmatic.
Representatives from the Chamber of Commerce have been
co-opted to its committees. The Confederation of British Indus-

try is not perceived as an enemy. Meanwhile other cities and other people, who discovered socialism rather later in the day than Glasgow, have pinched the clothes of Keir Hardie; Ken Livingstone's London, Derek Hatton's Liverpool, the plain people's Edinburgh (Edinburgh! Where they used to wear gloves to eat fish suppers).

I asked the city's Lord Provost, Robert Gray, about the new agreeableness. Gray, formerly a joiner in John Brown's shipyard, replied: 'There's no point in creating a city of starving Socialists. That means we've got to get our citizens working. It's really as simple as that.'

So is Glasgow benefiting from deep draughts of free enterprise, drunk at the wells of Nigel Lawson? Not quite. It is old-fashioned public money and a new-fashioned planning agency which have come to Glasgow's rescue; money from the EEC's social and regional funds, from the local authority, from the Manpower Services Commission, from central government via the Scottish Office, much of it spent imaginatively (though some say unwisely) under the direction of the Scottish Development Agency. The agency, a branch of the Scottish Office, devotes most of its energy trying to attract investment from abroad – principally from the United States, where it has four offices quite separate from the British embassy and consulates. It was pushed into Glasgow to 'knock a few heads together', in the words of a Scottish Office official. Initially it met a good deal of resistance from civic leaders who saw the implication – that the city couldn't be trusted to improve itself – but today most people speak well of it, with only the occasional snide reference to its magnificent piles of glossy literature.

The Glasgow Eastern Renewal Project (GEAR) is its especial pride: 'Probably the most comprehensive and advanced urban renaissance scheme in Western Europe,' says the booklet, which blossoms with pictures of girls on swings, smiling old people and new factory units. Ten years ago this, the city's East End, was how south Britain imagined all of Glasgow. Television companies sent film crews here. It made a beautiful location for films on urban deprivation; few European cities contained nastier views or more appalling human predicaments. Today it isn't Bath, exactly, but a budget of £212 million spent over the past eight years have transformed it from a rotting eight square miles of kaput industrialism into a place where people striving for decency might want to live. Growing numbers of them do. More than 800 owner-occupier houses have been built in the East End recently – the first private homes to be built there for fifty years – and a further 2,000 are planned. People in Glasgow speak of this with amazement. Imagine! A Barratt's house in the Gallowgate! The folk must be daft! But there speaks the unpurged memory of people who remember the Gallowgate as one of the longest and roughest streets in Glasgow; pawnbrokers, bars, dancehalls, rickets. In fact the Gallowgate now is *rus in urbe*, fringed with grasslands (more than 200 sites have been landscaped), its old form memorialised by one or two shining tenements (more than 3,000 tenement flats have been done up), its pavements thinned of people (100,000 of them, two-thirds of the East End's population, were decanted elsewhere years ago).

You can stand in the middle of the Gallowgate and watch the sunlight dash across the Campsie Hills. The west wind comes fresh and absolutely unpolluted (for where are the factories?) from the Firth of Clyde. James Watt might never have had his happy thought about the steam condenser just over the street in Glasgow Green and close to what is now the Templeton Business Centre.

Actually, it used to be Templeton's carpet factory, a splendidly weird building even by the standards of a city that invented Charles Rennie Mackintosh. It was built in 1889 in a style which the architectural handbooks record as 'Paduan Gothic with Guelfic battlements' with a façade in glazed and multi-coloured brick. A Victorian, Templeton had resolved, in the interests of both workers and citizens, 'to erect instead of the ordinary and common factory something of permanent architectural interest and beauty'. Twenty years ago Glasgow might easily have demolished it. Now the Scottish Development Agency has guaranteed the building's future by subdividing it into offices and small workshops, the manufacture of carpets having moved outside the city.

I caught a whiff of Templeton's Victorian idealism from Edward Cunningham, the Scottish Development Agency's director of projects and planning. Cunningham did not put his views as crudely as 'art for the workers', but he did stress the word 'vision' quite a lot, rather as William Morris or Martin Luther King might have done. His agency's role in Glasgow, he said, was to promote 'a vision of the city' which would build pride in its inhabitants and confidence in the investor.

Sometimes the vision on offer can look as much like Disneyland as Templeton's Disney Castle; a series of fun-factories for that part of the population that still has money to spend, built over the sites that once gave Glasgow its true function.

The Scottish Exhibition Centre, which opens next year, occupies what was once Queen's Dock. The dock's pump house will be turned into a wine bar. An old rotunda, marking the end of a disused tunnel, might become a planetarium. Someone has suggested that a large crane, standing nearby, would make a wonderful restaurant. Princes Dock, over the river, is a likely location for the next National Garden Exhibition; some of it is already a marina. Old railway warehouses are being turned into flats. The old banana auction room will house a theatre. Much of the old fruit market is already boutiques, and the same destiny awaits the fish market. With luck Sainsbury's and British Home Stores will take over the many acres of waste land vacated by the Parkhead Forge, once the largest manufactory of armour-plate in Europe.

And recently the Scottish Development Agency unveiled an even more ambitious idea, another part of the vision, when it suggested that one of the city's finest Victorian churches, now rotting south of the Clyde, might be carefully demolished and moved stone by stone a mile north of the river to a site at the top of one of the city's principal thoroughfares, Buchanan Street, so that the view from the bottom might be improved. McKinsey and Company (Inc), hired by the Scottish

Development Agency to investigate Glasgow's 'image problems', had decided that the city centre was 'amorphous and lacking in memorable features'. McKinsey's report also suggested that Glasgow might like an 'exploratorium' and Europe's first aquarium of international (ie American) class. Sites are being investigated.

'Marvellous,' I said, but at the same time thought: wouldn't it be even more marvellous if the fish market still sold fish and the fruit market fruit; if the banana auction room still auctioned bananas; if the forge made steel; if the docks had ships, the church a congregation. A hopeless thought; one might as well go to Venice and expect to find quinqueremes on the Grand Canal.

Nor did the thought, once expressed, get much change out of the agency's planners. It wasn't an option. Gone, all gone and never to return. An American kind of futurism runs strongly in these men, a fitting influence because Glasgow and North America have shared strong affinities ever since the eighteenth century, when the city made its first fortune from the Virginia tobacco trade.

Once Glaswegians and Glasgow capital migrated across the Atlantic. Now the flow is reversed. Scotland imports chunks of the micro-chip business from California, while Glasgow imports American ideas of how cities can be saved and hopes that American tourists will come to look at the result (the North British Hotel, recently privatised from British Transport into Egyptian hands, is to be rechristened the Harry Hopkins in honour of the Roosevelt aide who, nobody realised, had stayed there briefly in 1940). Many of the agency's planners have been on free trips out West. To Baltimore to inspect the harbour project, to Detroit to see the Renaissance Center, to San Francisco to walk down Pier 39. They return with a new vocabulary. I sat with two of them one afternoon watching a video which expounded schemes to establish a Scottish Trade Centre ('a superbly arcaded environment . . . electronic mail-box facilities') and brighten up the old business quarter, now known as the Merchant City. Suddenly two new phrases fell into the conversation.

'This will be a festival retail development with food-courts,' said the first planner.

A what with which?

'You know, festival shopping,' said the planner. 'You shop and you're entertained at the same time.'

Did he mean that one was besieged by RADA-trained harlequins while pondering one's choice of wok, a Covent Garden kind of thing?

'That's right,' said the planner, 'that and the café-theatre concept.'

I left the café-theatre concept alone. But food-courts?

'A food-court is a landscaped area with tables and chairs. This one will have from ten to fourteen food outlets.'

'No greasy hamburger joints, no rubbishy fast-food places,' said the second planner, who was American.

Then what? Hot croissants, brie, Chablis?

'Yeah,' said the second planner, 'stuff like that.'

I wondered about the relevance of this to a city with 60,000 people on the dole, where jobs are still destroyed faster than they can be created. Where would the festival shoppers come from? Where was the money for the Chablis and the brie? The planners said it was around, market research had shown demand, potential shop-keepers were queuing up. Moreover, the shops would provide work for the young and unskilled who lived in the peripheral housing estates; a quota system, still under discussion, would ensure that employers took a certain percentage of their workers from those areas of high social deprivation. No, not many jobs, they agreed, but better than a slap in the face with a warm croissant. Nobody in the present economic climate could think of anything better.

Ewan Marwick, secretary to the Glasgow Chamber of Commerce, confirmed their argument in a more careful way. People in decently-paid employment, he said, found it easy to raise money for consumption purposes. The financial institutions in Scotland were 'awash' with money, money looking for a return on investment but wary of risking itself in the traditional fields of venture capital. New ideas were scarce. But Glasgow firms, in terms of profits and cash-flow, were emerging from the recession. Glasgow was proving that economic recovery and rising levels of unemployment were not incompatible. A branch of Burberry's had opened recently in Buchanan Street. Had I noticed how well-dressed the young working people looked in Glasgow these days? (I had; Glasgow contains some of the most carefully-arranged young women in Britain.) 'There's a reversion to the classical style, an attempt to get back to business-like values,' said Marwick. 'Those in work try to look good. Those out of work can only distinguish themselves by looking different.'

It is the best of times, it is the worst of times, and there are two Glasgows. Perhaps the Burrell Collection exemplifies the city at its best; a fine and genuinely popular modern building, set among woods and parkland, which attracted a million visitors within the first ten months of its opening. It cost £20 million to build but entrance is absolutely free. Here the people worship art, or merely gawp at the results of one man's gobbling hunger for rare and precious artefacts. Sir William Burrell made his fortune by the simple expedient of ordering ships cheap during slumps and selling them dear during booms. The profits went into salerooms. A great man for a bargain, Sir William would buy almost anything, from any period, from any culture, if the price was right. Glaswegians are celebrating a belated monument to the city's old wealth and self-confidence.

Glasgow at its worst can be found in the housing estates, the famous 'peripheral estates' which have changed in twenty years from a solution to a problem without any solution in sight. Unemployment rates in the estates can rise as high as fifty or sixty per cent. Many of the houses are damp; Glasgow council received more than 17,000 complaints of dampness last year and spent more than £8 million trying to dry out its tenants' homes. According to a recent medical report, children who grow up there are nine times more likely to be hospitalised for diseases such as whooping cough and gastroenteritis than children born in the more privileged parts of the city. Heroin-taking increases by the week. Large numbers of people want to get out.

I took a taxi to Possilpark, a pre-war estate built on a hill above the derelict wharves of the Forth and Clyde canal and only a mile or so from the city centre. Here, quite coincidentally, Sir William Burrell owned the boatbuilding yard which laid the foundations of the Burrell fortune in the middle of the last century.

'Possilpark,' said the driver, 'that's a helluva place to get into. It's a maze, no joke. They've built all these barriers across the roads to try and stop the boys pinching cars. Not, mind you, that it stops them.'

We passed abandoned factories and then began to rumble up and down streets full of wild dogs and wild children. Many houses had hardboard nailed over the windows.

'Christ knows what the folk do in a place like this,' said the driver. 'I think they must stay inside and just screw the arse off one another.'

I got out and walked through the children ('Hey look, there's a funny man in a taxi') and called on Mrs Betty Collins to ask her if Glasgow has improved. 'Oh aye,' she said, 'miles better if you don't have to live in the damned place.' The Burrell Collection, the Citizens Theatre, Scottish Opera; to Mrs Collins they seemed hopeless fripperies, possibly located on Mars. She helps run a local tenants' group. The majority of tenants, she said, were 'decent people trying to do their best' in the face of formidable problems which people who didn't live in a place like Possilpark could never hope to understand. Take the woman who lived across the street. She was a 'wee bit simple', not quite right in the head poor girl, and frequently taken advantage of. She's been raped once. Then children had broken into her house and painted it blue – with hands not brushes, blue paint daubed on every wall. The woman came home and was delighted. 'Come and see ma blue hoose,' she'd told Mrs Collins, who didn't know whether to laugh or cry.

Housing estates, as a Glasgow councillor remarked, live in a 'peculiar psychological isolation'. Mrs Collins defined it as frustration bred from lack of hope and solved, temporarily, by alcohol, vandalism, theft and heroin. Kids, she said, were beginning to take junk (heroin spliced with Vim or sugar) at the age of twelve. Dirty needles had given the boy next door three separate doses of hepatitis. You could recognise heroin-users by the fact that they went into pubs and sat there clueless, without a drink. And yet once Possilpark had been a nice place. Mrs Collins remembered that as a teenager in the Fifties she'd had a choice of dancehalls, cafés, cinemas. Now there was nothing but pubs and bookies' shops. Nearly every local factory had closed and gangs of teenagers wandered aimlessly about the streets.

I got out of Possilpark by mini-cab. The driver was another heroin expert as a lot of his time was spent ferrying pushers and users to and from shoplifting expeditions in the city centre. 'They buy the junk in £5 bags. It's an expensive habit, the drugs: it can cost them up to £30 a day and you can't afford that on the Social Security.' He told horror stories as we drove down the hill and into the genteel zone which surrounds the University and the BBC, where the people have woks and nice wee prints of old Glasgow trams on the walls.

What has happened in Glasgow, as in the rest of Britain, is that the class system has been startlingly simplified. Ewan Marwick put it like this: 'There are the people who aspire and the people who can't or won't aspire.' The political opposition often pretend to a different social division based on the geography of North versus South. But they haven't got it quite right. Glasgow contains both groups, aspirers and non-aspirers, the rich and the poor, the upward and the down-wardly mobile – who live within minutes of each other and yet hardly seem to be touched by compassion, on the one hand, or envy on the other.

Within ten minutes of leaving Mrs Collins I was sitting in a restaurant and inspecting a menu which advertised not only food but also the manner of its recent capture. Oban-landed monkfish, creel-caught langoustines. All around happy diners talked about interesting personal developments.

'I hear Andrew's bought a wee weekend place on Loch Fyne.'

'I hear he's off the drink.'

'Heard that one before though.'

Here is an interesting change. Glasgow restaurants, unlike their London counterparts, were once filled with whispering customers who deferred both to the waiters and the food; an abnormal treat, eating expensive food, and an experience clearly devised for the luxury races to the south. But now people eat, drink and talk with unabashed enjoyment, as though, indeed, their custom made the owner's profits.

We ordered food. The Wild East Coast Salmon was especially recommended. My friends, none of them rich but all of them doing all right, discussed the peripheral estates. They had heard – heard perhaps too often – about the unemployment, the damp and the heroin. But what was to be done? 'I mean, let's face it, the Clyde is never going to build Cunarders again . . . and it's difficult to see how the bears will ever work again.' ('Bears' is a Glasgow word for yobs or *lumpens*.)

In future, then, the Glaswegian will come in two types. Here is a day's timetable for each:

The Aspirer

7.30 Rise; muesli and orange juice.

8.00 Jog.

9.30 Office; work on new software deal.

13.00 Meet Roddy, Fergus and Diarmid in Gertrude's wine bar. Discuss scheme to open print shop in disused railway signal cabin.

15.00 More work on software deal.

17.00 Festival shopping with the wife. Shiver while eating hot croissant and watching imitation of Marcel Marceau.

19.30 To see Scottish Opera's new production of *Rigoletto*, updated to the Gorbals of 1935.

22.30 Supper with lawyer friends at the Café de Paris. Oban-landed monkfish off.

23.50 Home; remember to adjust burglar alarm.

The Non-Aspirer

11.00 Rise; Wonderloaf and PG Tips.

12.00 Dress.

13.00 Watch *Pebble Mill at One*.

15.00 Watch *Willy Wonka and the Chocolate Factory* for the fourth time.
18.00 Meet pusher, buy £5 bag.
22.00 Wonder what has happened during the past three hours.
24.00 Steal car for purposes of burglary elsewhere, to finance purchase of more £5 bags.

The division exaggerates, but the evidence tends in that direction. When I called to see Kay Carmichael, a social worker and social scientist who has spent a lifetime in the city, she pointed to the destruction of the habits and culture of what was once called the artisan class. 'They're either jumping into the class above or falling into the class below.' The people earning a good wage were better off than they had ever been, and the new middle-class had a growing confidence in their city, but the gap between them and the poor was growing. The inequality was no more blatant than in any other British city, but it was made more intractable by the particular Scottish difficulty of meekness in the face of authority. 'People accept second-class citizenship as their lot. They find it difficult to experience a sense of outrage. There's very little anger about.'

There was, she said, another troubling result. Glasgow had always been enthusiastic about *ideas*. She thought it important that the city held on 'to the idea that ideas are worth discussing.' But 'lifestyle' was displacing ideas; people wanted objects, good food and drink, homes with original features, and had turned away from worrying about problems which seemed without solutions.

Not a uniquely Glasgow phenomenon, of course, but that it should have happened in Glasgow at all is a symptom of how severely it must have gripped the rest of the country. Sixty years ago an English writer, William Bolitho, could come to Glasgow and remark on the educated working man's 'positive contempt' for the 'artistic and intellectual poverty' of the middle-class:

... the brilliant son of the skilled artisan in Scotland seldom quits his class, but remains to salt it. Why should he leave the order in which he was born, where the pay in good times is sufficient; the interest of work at least as lively in a shipyard for the skilled engineer as his ledgers to an insurance clerk; where his security of employment in normal times, owing to invincible and aggressive unions, is many times as established. He lives well content in what has been credibly boasted the 'most intellectually alive milieu in the Islands'.

Today the shipyards and the skilled engineers have gone the same way as the invincible unions, and with them the old argumentative, class-conscious voice of Glasgow. Or has it quite? On my last evening in the city I went to see Harry McShane in his bed at the Southern General Hospital, just behind where Stephen's shipyard used to be. McShane is a legend in Glasgow, a man who has spent his life in marine engineering and Marxist politics and one of the last links with the 'intellectually alive milieu' of a period that has since been romanticised as the Red Clyde. John MacLean was the great figure of the day. The Bolsheviks appointed MacLean as the first native Soviet consul in Britain, and McShane at that time was his helper; an energetic young man who marched on and off public platforms and in and out of jail to speed the coming of the Workers' Republic.

Today he is ninety-four, but a vigorous man even in convalescence after an operation. He said Glasgow had changed all right. Once twenty-three shipyards had lined the river, steel and rivets everywhere, and now ... But did he think it had improved? Well, yes and no. The buildings, those that were left standing, had got cleaner and the green space had increased, but the condition and number of the unemployed were as bad as they had ever been. So was he pessimistic, a long life of egalitarian struggle having led up a cul-de-sac with a croissant shop at the top?

'No, I'm optimistic. You have to be optimistic. That woman [Mrs Thatcher] thinks she's Adam Smith. Every man his own capitalist. But it's daft stuff, son, daft stuff. No, Burns and Marx were right. Mind what Burns said: *It's coming yet for a'that.*'

Glasgow deserves McShane's optimism, and the different

brands of it purveyed by the PR men and the planning agencies. The city has survived a good many bangs on the nose. So, full employment, computers for all, necking in the parlours and dancing in the streets? Nobody, perhaps, expects so much. But if it fails to happen in Glasgow then it looks a much less likely future for those cities, lacking Glasgow's chauvinism and homogeneity, which lie to the south.

Meanwhile, the most considered judgment on the new Glasgow comes from Alasdair Gray. For thirty years Gray painted Glasgow and its people without making a fortune doing so. Then, three years ago, he published his first novel, *Lanark*, which attracted notice and praise from London and even further afield. Many remarked on its length, ambition and anarchic brilliance.

I asked Gray the old question. Had Glasgow improved? He didn't rush into the answer.

'Och, ha, hum, quack-quack,' said Gray, who often turns a mysterious phrase. 'Well, if you're middle-class, like I am, and if you're middle-aged, like I am, and if you work in a luxury trade, like I do, and if you've had a bit of luck recently, like I have, then yes, Glasgow is a better place.'

LIFE ON THE SCRAP HEAP
Birkenhead, Spring, 1985

The sight of miners and miners' children scrambling for coal over a colliery waste-heap is probably the most striking visual metaphor for poverty and desperation that Britain has produced in the twentieth century. Documentary film-makers, the pioneers of their craft, first filmed it in South Wales in the Thirties, and it received fresh life last year at the height of the pit strike in television pictures from the coalfields of Yorkshire and the North-East.

We may now forget it. We can wipe it from the tape and consign it to folk history, together with the poor matchgirl and Mr Bumble's wretched establishment for orphans. Proceed instead, fast-forward, to the metropolitan county of Merseyside and a rubbish tip on the outskirts of Birkenhead in the spring of 1985. Here unemployed men – and sometimes their womenfolk and children – are snatching a living of a sort by scavenging among the thousands of tons of waste matter which Merseyside council dumps every week in twenty-three acres of barren ground surrounded by a railway line, an old dock and a steelworks and known as Bidston Moss.

'Waste matter' is the careful and correct phrase. These are not people who go out at dead of night to retrieve pine chests from skips in gentrifying zones. These are people up to their shins every day in old tea-bags, cat-food tins and onion skins, sliding and falling on slopes of polythene bags and bacon rind, scrambling to get to the copper wire before the next

man, seizing a pair of discarded shoes, triumphantly unearth-
ing a bicycle pump, shouting warnings when the municipal
bulldozer bursts forward again and threatens to bury half a
dozen of them in a grave of discarded nylon stockings and
fish-finger cartons. A visitor to Bidston Moss has some
difficulty in believing what he is seeing. Later, on the train
back to London, he is not sure whether he has witnessed
scenes in Birkenhead, England, or in the nastier slums of
Bombay.

But no, it must have been Birkenhead. Untouchables in
Bombay do not scramble as energetically or dangerously as
these men. Instead they squat on their haunches and sift
patiently through the filth: old newsprint in this pile, cardboard in the next, tin cans in a third. Everything is recyclable
in India. In Birkenhead, so far, they are more selective.

Rubbish tips, of course, have always attracted totters – the
professional scrap gatherers – and in the Seventies Bidston
Moss had one or two of those. But over the past few years an
entirely new kind of scavenger has crossed the railway line
and slipped through the high wire fence. The unemployment
rate in Birkenhead now runs – officially – at twenty per cent.
In the council estates which lie near the tip, however, it is
much higher; according to Frank Field, the local MP, nearly
one person in every two cannot find work. Quite crudely,
unemployment is creating a new scavenging class. Every week
Bidston Moss gathers new recruits. Old hands at the tip
borrow the National Coal Board's terminology for strike-
breakers and refer to them, with no detectable irony, as 'new
faces'.

At Bidston Moss I talked to a man, formerly a labourer
with a decorating firm, who was burning the plastic sheathing
from a few rolls of copper wire which, if he collected a
hundred-weight, would fetch him thirty pounds. He said he
had been coming to the tip most days for the past two years.
In front of us a dozen men were slithering around on the tip
trying to take up strategic positions behind a waste lorry
which had just arrived. The lorry's back reared up, rubbish
spewed out and blew into the wind, while the men beneath,
rubbish cascading onto them, went poking into the plastic

bags. Fresh lorries arrived every few minutes. Always there was the same scramble.

'I couldn't believe it when I came here at first,' said the man with the wire. 'For the first two weeks I just stood here and looked at them. Well, I'd never been out of work before and never seen anything like it. But there's not much else you can do, you know what I mean? Just now the kids' bedroom needs redecorating. I could never afford the paper and paint on social security. This way you earn a bit extra, but I still can't stand the shit and the dogs. You get about half a dozen dead dogs up here every day. And cats. People just put them into plastic bags. Even now if I come across shit or a dead dog, that's it. I just walk down the road and go home for the day.'

In fact, the tip does not smell too badly. Anyone who has had their head stuck in their own dustbin for an hour or two, the result of some unfortunate prank, could tolerate Bidston Moss quite well. Many of its scavengers say theirs is a fine and healthy life. The wind, they say, comes straight off the Irish Sea.

Only a few cuts have turned septic, and the most serious accident in the living memory of Bidston Moss has been only the matter of a few fingers. A youth lost them recently when his over-eager hand got caught in the machinery which was still cranking a skip to the ground. His friends, eyes sharpened by months of peering into waste, found his fingers easily enough and quickly bagged them; but it was too late for surgical repairs.

Some scavengers at Bidston Moss go further. They say that the tip has saved them from madness, divorce, crime, alcoholism and heroin. Mick, who was once a chargehand at Cammell Laird's shipyard, said that coming to the tip every day had saved his marriage. Max insisted that it had helped him recover from a nervous breakdown. Several said that the tip and the money they made from it was a better alternative to 'mugging old ladies in Wallasey'. One man said: 'It keeps me outa jail.' Another: 'You come every day and meet your mates. It's like a proper job. It's so boring being unemployed.' And another: 'I eat, breathe and sleep tip. I'd still come if I won the pools. It's part of life, getting your hands dirty, isn't it?'

The day I went in March, about fifty men were picking their way over the tip, searching for anything sellable, repairable, wearable, or even eatable, provided it was safely sealed inside a tin. According to Merseyside council the same phenomenon can be observed at others tips in the county, though on a smaller scale. The scavengers themselves said they thought it was happening not just over the county but throughout the country. 'Or it will be soon,' said Gerry, unscrewing a brass door-fitting.

The weekend is the most rewarding time. 'That's when the poshies come,' Gerry explained. 'They drive up from Hoylake and New Brighton in their Mercs and Granadas and they dump some lovely stuff.' To cater for this influx, the scavengers at Bidston employ their wives and children as extra hands. They bring flasks and sandwiches and make a day of it. Gerry said that with hard graft he could make £80 or £90 a week. Add that to his social security and the money his officially unemployed wife made 'on the fiddle' and his family were approaching a decent weekly wage. Most men, however, do not do nearly so well; perhaps enough, on average, to get decently drunk twice a week. One man commented, stretching and yawning: 'Oh, a great life. I go home, I have a shower, I sit down and I watch the video.'

As we talked, the scavengers displayed that day's catch: old bicycle handlebars, books, vintage postcards, a television set that could be easily made to work, a new pair of ladies' shoes from Taiwan, an old pair of men's shoes that were still wearable. 'It's disgusting what people throw away,' said Max, and presented me with a Durabeam torch, still in its manufacturer's packet. Max was wearing stuff he'd found on the tip: good boots but of different sizes and a plastic baseball cap. From behind us he kept up a sombre political counterpoint, the Greek chorus of Bidston Moss. This being Merseyside, everybody talked vividly, knowledgeably, and at once.

Jim: 'These postcards are that old I bet Fox-Talbot took them. You can get threepence each for these in Liverpool . . .'

Max: 'She's a murderess, that woman. People on the dole are killing themselves and it's going to get worse . . .'
Frank: 'Sometimes you get tinned food. When somebody passes away, dies like, they clear out their kitchens and dump it all. Nothing wrong with it like . . .'
Max: 'The rich get richer and the poor get poorer . . .'
Mick: 'A fella got married in a suit he found on this tip. A proper pinstripe. Imagine, married in his tip suit . . .'
Max: 'The next time it won't be riots, that namby-pamby Toxteth stuff. The next time it'll be bloody revolution. Belfast'll be nothing in comparison . . .'
Old man in woollen hat: 'These shoes'd cost me eighteen quid in a shop.'
Max: 'She's a murderess, a murderess, a murderess . . .'
Jim: 'Who's that Max?'
Max: 'Her, she's a murderess . . .'
Jim: 'Oh her. Right, right.'

Times have changed. Twenty-odd years ago Samuel Beckett placed two of his characters in dustbins and filled their dialogue with incoherent melancholy and anger, and audiences in Paris and London applauded the result as a piece of *outré* (if profound) symbolism. Today, should the same play be staged in Bidston, it would pass merely as a humdrum work of documentary realism. An irrelevant and pretentious thought to have on Bidston Moss, but it struck me all the same, listening to men who had so quickly learned to rationalise what they did to make money and who had adjusted to such radically altered circumstances. Frank said that he knew scavenging was 'the lowest form of life', and in the next breath added: 'But I'm proud to work here on the tip. I mean we're giving work to scrapyards and putting antiques back into the system, aren't we?'

Anger is mainly confined to the new-comers. One man, trembling with a violent rage, threatened to give Peter Marlow, the photographer, a 'proper doing-over' if he ever saw him and his bloody cameras on the tip again. But it was explained to us that he was a 'new face', fresh that month. A year or two ago you might have asked for his picture in the shipyard and he would have posed quite happily beside the launch-chains. Older hands at Bidston Moss have already featured in a film made for Granada Television's current affairs programme, *World in Action*, and talk about it a lot. They complain that the film made their work harder because it popularised the tip as a source of income, increased the labour force and lowered individual profit. They do not complain that the film intruded into areas of private shame; they have long since stopped worrying about how other people see them.

'I've got it on video,' said Frank. 'Come home and watch it.' He hoisted a back-pack, heavy with bric-à-brac, over his shoulders and climbed on to his motorbike. We followed him over the level-crossing and into council estate Britain, where it is dangerous to leave a car unattended for half an hour because of the price of heroin. Frank carried the motorbike upstairs to his flat and kept watch on our car through the window.

The flat was immaculate: well carpeted and well furnished, with trophies from the tip hung on the walls. Two Victorian watercolour prints. A photograph of the Blue Funnel freighter *SS Nestor* at the Liverpool landing stage around 1920. Shelves beneath contained a salvaged set of Arthur Mee's *Children's Encyclopedia* and *The Oxford Companion to The Law*. 'Yes,' said Frank, 'the tip has been good to us.'

He added, however, that he and his family intended to move out quite soon. 'We want to get somewhere decent,' he said. A pair of heroin dealers lived upstairs; there were recurrent visits from the police, interminable rows and outbreaks of drugged madness. He has saved enough from the tip to put down the deposit on a house and trusts the social security to look after the mortgage repayments. Samuel Smiles and his present apostles of the gospel of self-help should be proud of Frank. They might remember that George Stephenson, the great Smilesian hero, began his working life as a 'picker' on a coal tip and ended up as a country gentleman who grew prize pineapples, having perfected steam locomotion in between.

Of course, the social security agents could find out about Frank's income from the tip and cut his benefit. The police could also prosecute Frank for trespassing on the railway line. Merseyside council could even get him for disturbing rubbish and endangering health (his own, in this case) under Section 28 of the Control of Pollution Act, 1974. But officialdom in Merseyside, one senses, has been visited by shame and impotence as well as realism. There are both moral and practical difficulties in taking legal action against hard-pressed men who are merely removing goods which someone else has thrown away.

And so Bidston Moss will probably outlive Cammell Laird's shipyard as a source of local employment, though even Bidston Moss will not survive for ever. By the Nineties it should have reached its planned growth height of one hundred feet, when it will be nicely contoured, covered with topsoil and planted with grass and saplings. By that time, too, North Sea oil should be running out and we shall have the opportunity to find out if, as the more pessimistic futurologists insist, Britain will finally slide into the Third World.

The only question about that prognosis, after a visit to Bidston Moss, concerns the use of the future tense.

FOOTBALL RIOT: 38 DEAD

Summer, 1985

An interesting thing happened to the English language last week. For some time it had been straining at the leash of sympathy and sociological neutrality. Now, with one bound and thirty-eight dead, it was free. A writer in the *Guardian* described the lethal mobs in Brussels as 'boozed-up cretins'. Anthony Burgess, writing in the *Daily Mail*, wondered what had happened to England's 'lower orders'.

Their way had been signposted. Two weeks ago the *Sunday Times*, suggested – perhaps provocatively – that many football supporters were 'slum people' who watched 'a slum sport' in 'slum stadiums'. Five years ago it is likely that the *Sunday Times* and the *Guardian*, if not the *Daily Mail*, would have been talking about 'a hooligan minority from socially disadvantaged communities'.

Mass death does have a way of colouring vocabulary, but the fact is that the hesitant, polytechnic terminology, newly unfashionable, was never as current in Britain as the polite readers of the better newspapers might have assumed. Eight days ago the Scottish and English soccer sides met in Glasgow, Mrs Thatcher having switched the game from London to avoid Scottish vomit in the front gardens of Wembley. England fielded two black players, Anderson and Barnes. Whenever either of them touched the ball, a loud simian grunting erupted from the terraces: *Hoo-hoo-hoo-hoo.* When Anderson stepped forward to take a free kick, the chant changed and grew: *Sambo-sambo-sambo-sambo.*

Not much sociological – or anthropological – neutrality here, but the television commentator let it pass. Such chants are the everyday currency of English football grounds, whence they appear to have spread to Scotland; and, after all, what could he say? The game was played five days too early for the invective which has been released by Brussels. For the past decade television has sanitised the awful reality of football.

Now, at least linguistically, we are all on the same side. Some youths get drunk, fight, shout *Sambo!* Other people, watching them, can describe it as cretinous. But does this mean that we all feel responsible? Britain's Chief Rabbi, Immanuel Jakobovits, writing in *The Times*, suggests that it does. The one consoling afterthought from Brussels, he said, was that the British people as a whole were 'all united in feeling collectively guilty and disgraced'; a refreshing contrast, he went on, to the callous indifference shown by many German citizens towards a much greater calamity.

Certainly, there is evidence for collective shame. Manifestations of collective guilt are more difficult to find. Collective puzzlement – how many times did Jimmy Hill express 'bewilderment' on Wednesday night? – and a collective distancing-operation might be nearer the mark. As one set of sociological terms has flown out of the window another set has flown in, but the basic language remains one of distance, free of moral judgment, unencumbered by intimacy. We are now talking about 'sub-cultures' and 'under-classes'. The popular revival of that old Marxist favourite, the lumpen proletariat, is upon us.

Does such a drunken, violent and almost psychopathically amoral under-class exist in Britain? That the question needs to be asked says a lot about the nature of the country, so much of which – video Britain, tinned-beans Britain, heroin Britain, council estate Britain, Britain on the dole – remains under-reported and little understood. But the answer from the people who are striving to live in it, decently, is clearly yes. They will tell you that the place is close to economic, social and moral collapse.

In some respects, this under-class is a revival from Victorian Britain. The history of the football crowd is illuminating. In 1891, when Scotland played England in Blackburn, several thousand Scottish drunks spilled in to that Lancashire town and behaved, up to a point, like Liverpool supporters in Brussels. 'Sleeping townsmen,' wrote the reporter for the *Northern Daily Telegraph*, 'were alarmed by shrieking war-whoops and riotous singing, accompanied in several places with the crash of glass and the smash of door panels.' Blackburn knew about the noise and 'incipient blackguardism' of English supporters but these scenes were 'indescribable'.

So, the violence is not new. Nor is it peculiar to Britain. Turin has football gangs. Fights break out sporadically at American sporting events. Last month 127 Chinese fans were arrested after a match against Hong Kong in Peking. Even the Soviet Union (could there be an under-class there too?) has *fanaty*, gangs of fanatical supporters who can cause great damage. In 1982, nearly seventy people died when a crush barrier broke at Moscow Spartak's stadium and fighting broke out among drunken Muscovites. What does seem peculiar to England, however, is the singular savagery of its football-following under-class and its need to be seen to be so savage abroad.

Whole books have been written about this – good books, well-researched harbingers of doom – and we have a choice as to the possible cause. We can opt for Original Sin and off-load the collective guilt, or we can look to a difficult combination of morality and socio-economics and try to address the problem, collectively. Few people, even the 'left-wing sociologists' derided by Anthony Burgess in the *Daily Mail*, now see the equation simply as unemployment equals psychopathy equals savagery on the terraces. On the other hand, the collapse of religion and family life, and the dispossession of the working-class from work do point to the end of moral values as we have known them.

The unemployment rate in Italy and the United Kingdom is much the same, but the United Kingdom has twelve times the Italian divorce rate and three times as many illegitimate births. Italy also carries little baggage from an imperial past. A hundred years ago Britain had the best-paid workers in the world and Liverpool was the greatest seaport in Europe. Turin was an ancient capital of Sardinian kings. Watch out for brigands and swindlers, said the English guide books. Many localities are dangerous after nightfall.

Today the position is reversed. Liverpool taxi-drivers advise against trips to Toxteth. But, once so superior, the British still have names for inferior breeds. The Liverpool supporters who crashed through the barriers at the Heysel stadium were chanting, before and after: *Wops-wops-wops-wops.*

A joke, of course. Surely even Croxteth and Toxteth have a broader image of Italians than that of icecream sellers who surrendered, too promptly but sensibly, in the western desert. Or do they, or we?

During the recent royal progress through Italy the *Mirror* carried a front-page story about the Princess of Wales's dress sense: *Italian designers say FRUMPY DI! Our advice to them SHUTTA YA FACE!* Another joke, of course; a harmless line from a popular song. Robert Maxwell, the *Mirror*'s proprietor, has already opened a relief fund for the Italian victims of Brussels. Jokes do not lead to savagery. But they are, perhaps, a part of the dull-witted chauvinism that helps promote it.

LIVERPOOL V TURIN

Summer, 1985

When I asked Derek Hatton if he thought that football might perhaps matter *too much* to Liverpool, I expected a thoughtful or at least an ambiguous answer. Hatton, the deputy leader of Liverpool city council, is a member of Militant Tendency and therefore presumably something of a Marxist. And Marx, had he witnessed the fervour of what remains of the Liverpool working-class on a Saturday afternoon at Liverpool or Everton – profitable capitalist enterprises both – would surely have classed football with religion as the people's opiate. (Why, I've even heard mild old members of the Independent Labour Party accuse football of preventing a revolution in 1926.)

But Hatton's reply came back as snappy as his suit: 'That's like asking if mice care too much about cheese. Football has always been a part of the heart of this city.'

In Turin the question was redundant. Its citizens certainly take football seriously, but then they are also serious about a great deal else. Cheese, for example. Turin's shops display mounds of it: baby mozarellas swimming in their milk, varicose-veined gorgonzola, rounds of honey-coloured grana that rise above the counter like moons, smoked mozarella looped in lassos. Cheese matters in Turin, though perhaps pasta matters more. Turin's pasta shops lay out their products like souvenirs: pasta in the shape of butterflies, feathers, little hats, ears, pasta in three colours, pasta with obscure names, *spacatelle, millerighe, biogoli.* Too much pasta? Then proceed to the butcher's to inspect the baby chicken, the lamb, the pigeon and the duck, the tiny quail and the dozen varieties of long sausage. Enough meat? Step this way to the fruit and vegetable market where out of their boxes come tumbling the fresh Sicilian lemon and the Tuscan tomato, the smooth nectarine and the furry peach, dark aubergines and bright peppers, the wild mushroom and the mysterious fig.

Enough food? Come, let us find a table on the pavement in the shade. Waiter, a fresh grapefruit juice and soda, and one of those delicious little chocolates, a *giandujotto di Torino*, that your café has been making since 1858.

I sat in the shade and watched the evening crowds sauntering through the arcades of the Via Roma, past windows stuffed elegantly with biscuits and bottles of aperitif, books, oriental carpets, shiny leather shoes. I thought of Liverpool's Kwik-Save supermarket where the Giro folk queue every fortnight with their trolleys full of wrapped bread and economy-sized bottles of orange squash; and other, smaller shops meshed against vandals where the bell still pings when the door opens and the customer is confronted with the usual jumble of Embassy Tipped, Bounty Bars and tinned beans, the sustenance of lower English life. And I remembered something Fred Ridley, professor of politics at Liverpool University, had said: 'The difference between Liverpool and a European city is no longer the difference between two European countries. It's a gap between two continents. England has grown poorer than the rest of Europe. Liverpool is getting poorer than the rest of England. People here still haven't caught on to the extent to which they've been excluded from prosperity.'

They haven't. Of if they have, they have converted their hard times into a form of truculent chauvinism. Some say in Liverpool: 'If you have to be shat upon, I'd rather be shat upon here.' Some even pretend that their city still has 'greatness'. When Liverpool's civic delegation flew to Turin this summer – the famous 'peace mission' – its members worked hard to sell the idea that the two cities had comparable problems, which, in some vague way, they could together try to solve. Turin listened politely. It bore with Liverpool's Roman Catholic archbishop when, in a manner long discredited by the clerical pastiche of Alan Bennett, he told his Turin congregation of the street which joined Liverpool's two cathedrals – 'It is called Hope Street' – and then sprang from this rickety springboard to explore the theme of Hope. It heard out Tony Mulhearn, the president of the Liverpool Labour Party, when he talked of youth unemployment in Italy and England and blamed it for 'the lumpen, brutal elements' which festered in Liverpool.

Only occasionally did Turin become peevish. At a press conference an Italian reporter asked John Hamilton, the leader of Liverpool's council, about the city's distress fund for the relatives of the victims of Brussels. More than two weeks after the disaster, the appeal had raised the grand sum of £3,500. This was less then ten pence for every person in Liverpool. Was it a symptom of the city's economic condition?

Hamilton might have said: 'Yes. We come as tribunes from a poor and sometimes unruly people to beg pardon.' Instead he ducked the question and went on to talk about how much in common he saw with the people of Turin: 'We too are a great city, an industrial city, with a car factory and two great football teams. The tragedy has given us hope that the two cities can be united and that together we can face our common social and industrial problems.'

It was absurd, and anyone with respect for either the truth or Liverpool should want to cry. On an index prepared by the European Economic Community which measures the relative intensity of regional problems within the EEC, Merseyside comes near the bottom of the table with a reading of 43.8. Only Calabria, Sicily and Sardinia come lower. The European average is 100; the higher a region rises on the table, the fewer problems it has. Piedmont, the region which contains Turin, emerges at 100.7, Oxfordshire and Berkshire at 106.2. Turin, therefore, has problems like the Thames Valley has problems. Liverpool has them on a Sicilian scale.

The difference can be measured in more detailed ways. Liverpool's unemployment rate now runs at more than twenty-five per cent (and much higher in many council estates), twice the rate of Turin. There is a car for every 2.14 people in Turin, in Liverpool a car for every 6.2. Or, to put it another way, more than sixty per cent of Liverpool households lack access to a car, a figure that can rise to ninety per cent in the poorest areas, whereas nearly every Turin family has access to one. Figures such as these work their way into the EEC regional survey and help establish Liverpool as one of the poorest cities in Europe. But other figures, because they imply a moral rather than a social or economic judgment, do not. Take, for example, the illegitimacy rates. Last year out of 7,053 live births registered in Liverpool, 2,078 were to un-married parents; almost one baby in three. Last year out of 12,500 live births in Turin, only 950 were to unmarried parents; roughly one baby in thirteen. The English and Italian divorce rates show a similar disparity. Of course, Italy is a Catholic country, and the destruction of traditional family life does not necessarily mean that Liverpool children are any less loved, disciplined or perfectly reared. That would be too crude. On the other hand Tony Mulhearn's equation – youth unemployment equals 'lumpen, brutal elements' – seems equally over-simple.

Other less quantifiable factors come into play here. They include the culture of both countries, the history of both cities, and (not least) the claustrophobic prison house of English social class.

Between the wars, when Liverpool began to move its workers out along the tram tracks and into the new garden suburbs, an infamous rumour arose in Merseyside and in England. It has since become a joke. 'These people,' so the joke went, 'keep coal in the bath.' A similar myth spread in Turin in the Sixties. The city's buoyant car plants had drawn hundreds of thousands of migrants from the poor south. In one decade 300,000 people were added to the population. The Torinese looked on them as crude rustics. Overcrowding added to the

235

social strain. Advertisements for flats to let often carried the words *non ai terroni* – southerners need not apply – as a rider. Eventually Fiat and a public housing authority, the Casa Populari, came to the rescue and built high-rise estates in the suburbs. The southerners moved into their new and well-plumbed homes.

'These people,' said the native Torinese, 'grow basil in the bath.'

Basil can be grown in England, even in Liverpool, and people do grow it. But those who add the fresh green leaf to their food tread unsteady social ground. The working-class might consider it 'funny' or 'posh'; the middle-class risk precipitation into the new category of 'foodies'. Italian food recognises no such social boundaries; neither does the Italian language. Italian has no equivalent for 'foodie', no noun for 'yuppie', no verb for 'gentrify'. These are American-English concerns. In any case, the terms describe nothing more unusual than ordinary Italian behaviour and aspiration. Who in Turin does not want to eat good food, drive a decent car, do up his home?

Neither does Turin know the meaning of the phrase 'a working-class accent'. I asked several people if they could identify the social positions of other Torinese by their accents, and none could or was even interested to try. An eminent economic and local historian at the University of Turin, Professor Piero Bairati, said that at one time there were words and phrases peculiar to the working-class. He seemed amused. 'I am probably one of the few people who can even remember some of them. But they have almost completely died out.' The regional dialects of the migrants from the south do provide a linguistic division in Turin, but they give no clue to social status; doctors and computer programmers may speak that way as well as the man in the Fiat paint shop.

The situation in Liverpool is rather different, in fact almost completely reversed. For historical reasons – mainly the power of southern England – regional accents in Britain have tended to become class voices. Liverpool's working-class voice is 'scouse', a peculiarly isolated accent, a hard, fast and nasal speech which doesn't extend beyond the city boundaries, where Lancastrian takes over. Thanks to the Beatles it enjoyed a brief fashion in the Sixties. Now it has intensified. In Birkenhead I talked to a steelworker. He had quite a lot on his plate; his steelworks was closing down ('Over-capacity in the European steel industry, a simple case of too many bread-shops in the village,' said a management spokesman airily), he was facing redundancy. He had grown up in a poor and large family in a now-demolished part of Liverpool and took his fate philosophically. What baffled him was his teenage daughter. They had done their best by her, cared about her education, allowed her an adult-free party on her fourteenth birthday. The party had nearly wrecked the house. He didn't understand the violence. Moreover, she'd begun to speak in the street voice of his childhood. 'Real scouse. I can't see that there's anything clever in it.'

Since 1983, when Labour removed the Liberals from power, Liverpool city council has also spoken in this voice. Militant Tendency, though its members form only a small minority of Labour councillors, is the real source of power within the party; and not so much by conspiracy of caucus, though these are often alleged, as by the fact that it has hit on a vein of genuine populism which few dare challenge. Its policies are simple and widely understood. One, build better council houses. Two, save jobs. Three, harness local chauvinism, or 'stand up to the bitch' as Liverpool knows it. The régime has little time for values or ideas that might be construed as 'middle-class' – feminism, the black lobby, conservation, hous-ing co-operatives. St George's Hall, one of the finest classical buildings in England, may rot. The blacks in Toxteth may moan. But the council has a wider constituency to satisfy: the poor, their decaying houses, their disappearing work.

The results can be surprising. In some ways Liverpool has embraced Victorian values more firmly than Mrs Thatcher. The large number of sports 'complexes' under construction, for example, reflects an old belief in the benefits of muscular Christianity. And Liverpool's new model house is the Vic-torian terrace. New houses have a height limit of two storeys, with room in front to park the (usually non-existent) car, and front doors which always open on to real streets. Aimless patches of grass are out. Many houses built in the Fifties and Sixties do not conform to the new decree. Council workmen (more jobs) are now ruthlessly knocking them down to size, or sometimes demolishing them completely. The Victorian park has even returned to fashion. The new Everton park, sprawling across a hill above the Mersey, will cost four million pounds. Traditional features such as pointed iron railings and stone gateposts already enclose the area. Complete, it will look like parks are supposed to look, as though it had been gifted to the oppressed citizenry by a merchant philanthropist. Militant councillors in their sharp dark suits will no doubt stroll towards the bandstand on a Sunday afternoon.

But nobody should object. Any small conversation with the unlucky inhabitant of a twenty-year-old council flat will confirm the view that the Sixties were the great architectural age of shoddiness and silliness. Damp spreads down the walls, the drains collapse, the 'adventure playgrounds' stand abjectly among the weeds. The era has no greater monument than the St John's Beacon, 450 feet of concrete with an abandoned restaurant at the top.

The farther past appeals to Liverpool. No other city in Britain, and possibly in the world, has declined so steeply and absolutely in the last two decades. The docks have shrunk, factories close, wealth flees. In the past six years 50,000 manufacturing jobs, half the former total, have vanished. Liverpool faces out to old imperial trade routes and empty seas. At its back, the Lancashire textile industry has collapsed. The city undergoes a new British process; museumification.

There is a lot to museumify: thirteen miles of wharfage, fine warehouses, the great palaces of Victorian commerce built by Cunard, White Star, Blue Funnel and the Mersey Docks and Harbour Board. Some have been splendidly restored, and stand like ornate wardrobes in a junk shop. In terms of grandeur, Turin has nothing to touch them. Nor, for that matter, does it outshine Liverpool in the narrowest sense of the word culture. The British city has lively theatres, a respectable symphony orchestra, libraries and museums that can stand comparison with any provincial city in Europe.

Where Liverpool fails is in culture in the broader sense. The city seems to have seized on football as its last living totem of greatness. Football is what Liverpool is now famous for, because the real functions of Liverpool have largely disappeared. Critics of the Hatton régime – and there are many of them – say that local politicians, the media and the football clubs themselves form a nexus which perpetuates Liverpool's exclusive idea of itself as resilient, male, white and working-class. So when Derek Hatton sits in his office under a picture of Everton FC and says 'football has always been a part of the heart of this city', he is only being one of the lads. (A legend on the mirror on the opposite wall reads: *Yes Derek, you look terrific.*) Liverpool loves to sentimentalise itself into comic likeability, though this summer it has been hard for others of us to gratify the wishes of the errant child.

But the deputy leader also betrays a rather stunted sense of the city's history. Professional football took off in Liverpool only in the twentieth century; and the particular success of Liverpool FC is a phenomenon confined to the past twenty-five years. Other important elements of Liverpool life – sectarianism, the slave trade, Quakerism, the Overhead Railway – have already slipped quietly into history, and football may not last for ever.

A more enduring cultural thread is drink. For much of the last century Liverpool enjoyed a reputation as the most drunken town in England. In 1874, to take a random year, police arrested 12,000 drunks, several hundred of them aged under twelve, representing about ten per cent of the total number of drunks arrested in the whole of England and Wales. The city had more than 2,000 pubs at the time, and when they came up for sale in poor areas their locations were often advertised as *'good drinking neighbourhoods'*. P. J. Waller writes in his political history of the city * that 'altogether

---

* *Democracy and Sectarianism*, Liverpool University Press, 1981

Liverpool was a writer's byword for squalor and philistinism'. Vandalism was rife: 'Taps became scrap-metal, ashpits became fuel.' Thousands of Irish immigrants were packed into shoddy houses; the phrase 'jerry-built' is thought to have originated here. And the great debate on housing wrapped itself around the question: *'Is it the pig who makes the sty or the sty who makes the pig?'* – an argument that rumbles on, unofficially, in housing departments to this day.

On this evidence, the past seems altogether too uncomfortably connected to the present. Soon after the Brussels disaster the *Echo*, Liverpool's evening newspaper, invited readers who had attended the match to give their version of events. A great catharsis of letters followed in which the blame went in all directions but where drunkenness was the common theme. One man wrote vividly of the scene at the Brussels branch of the McDonald's hamburger chain. Outside, two Liverpudlians urinated against the front window. Inside, waitresses collapsed in tears as another drunken Liverpool man, half-naked, tried to crawl across the floor.

Liverpool must be one of the few cities in the world where in reply to the question, 'Do you ever go out in the evening?' the answer comes back: 'No, I don't drink.' That reply came from a young unemployed man in Walton. 'Ale is all they care about round here,' he said. 'They're all plonkies in this part.'

At least the Victorian moralist-politician, under no pressure from the popular vote, felt free to condemn it. But then he could also point to the virtues of work. Liverpool has many statues of men like these. They stand resolutely on their pedestals and hold books, unlike their colleagues in Turin who ride horses and wave swords and usually prove to be some or other scion of the royal family of Savoy. When they were erected Liverpool contained twice as many people as Turin, which was only just beginning to crawl from its old role as the capital of the Savoy kingdom towards an industrial future within united Italy. Today Turin has twice the population of Liverpool. Yet, curiously, this enormous growth has left the city centre unscathed by property speculation or fashions in town planning. It remains an eighteenth-century city, mile upon mile of arcaded streets and shops filled with little luxuries. On clear days you can look down one of those rich dark streets and see the whiteness of the Alps.

Liverpool owed its prosperity to the river, the Empire and engineers who invented the tide-free dock. Its money came from trade rather than industry. Socially, it divided neatly into a pyramid: a small band of merchants at the top, a larger band of clerks in the middle, and at the base a thick layer of casual labour – dockers, ship's stewards, seamen – who were hired and fired as trade suited. The richer folk in the pyramid decamped to houses across the Mersey or up the Lancashire coast. Only a small artisan class emerged – tiny compared with Glasgow or Manchester – because Liverpool did not make things. Local and national governments have been trying to broaden the city's economy since the Thirties, and for a time succeeded. Dozens of factories appeared on the outskirts. But they were branch-factories and over the past fifteen years they have closed with a frequency which has bewildered the city. A saying from the days of casual dock labour, 'There's nothing down for us', meant at one time 'no work today'. Liverpudlians use it now with a bleak finality, to describe not individual circumstance but the city as a whole, and not just for today but for an infinite future. There is nothing down for it.

The traveller from Liverpool to Turin finds that the hardest thing to adjust to is not so much wealth as optimism. Shortly before I left Liverpool, Professor Ridley had talked despairingly of the bubbling pot of discontent which South-East England and the British middle-class in general didn't realise they were sitting on. His counterparts in Turin, Professor Bairati and his colleague, Professor Luciano Gallino, one of the most distinguished sociologists in Italy, seemed by contrast almost unbelievably content. Both said: 'They could close Fiat tomorrow and Turin would survive.' Fiat, of course, will not close. Last year it made 1.5 million cars and took 13.3 per cent of the European car market (Spain excluded), a higher share than any other company, including

Ford. But it is a large statement. Fiat, to an outsider, *is* Turin.

Free trade made Liverpool. A family of Piedmontese landowners, the Agnellis, made modern Turin. They helped found the Fabbrica Italiana Automobile Torino as early as 1899 and were soon travelling to the United States to see how Henry Ford managed his first production lines. Giovanni Agnelli, grandfather of Fiat's present chairman, opened assembly lines of his own soon after the First World War in two huge buildings, each half a kilometre long and five floors high with a test track built on the roof; the Lingotto works. Corbusier called it 'one of industry's most exciting spectacles'. It stands empty now – production has moved elsewhere – but Giovanni Agnelli, the founder's grandson, is reluctant to knock it down. Celebrated architects have been asked to produce ideas for new uses. Professor Bairati thinks this is all nonsense, quite blasphemously for an economic historian. He said: 'I told the *avvocato*: "It's only a damned factory, a box of cement, tear it down!"'

All Turin knows Agnelli as the *avvocato*, the lawyer. He and his family also own Juventus, the football club, and the city's newspaper, *La Stampa*. I asked Bairati if Fiat's success could simply be put down to familial shrewdness and enterprise. 'Sure, Fiat has always been well-managed,' said Bairati, 'but it has been well-protected too.' Discreet pressure from the Agnellis led Mussolini to keep Ford out of Italy in the Twenties. He also imposed a high tariff on imported cars which stayed until 1961. Fiat prospered mightily in the Fifties, when many Italians could just afford to buy their first small cars. Fiat had a market and got it right with the 500 cc. Liverpool has never had that kind of powerful friend in a high place; nor, for a long time, that brand of shrewdness.

By the Seventies Fiat had 150,000 workers in Turin. Then it decided to robotise its assembly lines. In the early Eighties more than 50,000 people, a third of the workforce, got the sack. Gallino the sociologist said that ten years ago he would have predicted 'severe social strain' as a result. And now?

'Some problems certainly, but solvable. It's quite incredible in a way.'

But as Gallino said, it was good but it wasn't mysterious, at least for an Italian. First, many redundant workers had simply moved back to the South where they had never abandoned their houses and small-holdings (too late now for Liverpool to up sticks and head for County Mayo). Turin has lost nearly 200,000 people over the past few years and the population is now around a million.

Second, Turin was no longer just Fiat but 'a thousand other firms' making all kinds of electronic and computer gadgetry, which was exported all over the world. Third, many of the redundant still got paid ninety per cent of their wages under a complicated Italian system called *cassa integrazione*.

But there are other, less tangible reasons. One, which the Italian inland revenue department would love to be more tangible, is the *economia sommersa*, the black economy. The unemployed do not hang about in Turin; such a concentration of wealth means all kinds of part-time jobs, while the basic state benefit, the *cassa integrazione* apart, comes to only twenty-five pence a day. The state decrees that an Italian family has a duty to look after its own.

Another reason, still less tangible, is *furbi*. 'Ah,' say the Torinese, tapping their heads knowingly, '*furbi, furbi*.' It means street wisdom, sharpness, low cunning, doing the best for oneself. When we visited a worker and his family one evening in Turin, for example, the first thing he did was to ask the interpreter, a teacher, if she could wangle his son into a new school. That was *furbi*. People in Liverpool may be more witty but they are not often so wise. And also, to be fair, English institutions cannot be so easily penetrated by *furbi* because they are (still) less open to wangling and corruption. Civic-minded Italians admire this. Liverpool is still a better place to post a parcel, borrow a library book, see a policeman, lie in a hospital; or, because of its more secular nature, to receive punishments from God such as madness or bisexuality.

'England is vastly superior in so many aspects of public life,' said Gallino. 'So often here our institutions sink below the level of decency.' He had worked for a Californian university which had offered him a job. He had a fine office there, much nicer than the basement cell we were sitting in, and a secretary. What made him return?

'Italian food and Italian sociability. It may seem ridiculous but both of them are, after all, important elements of civilisation.'

And then he said perhaps the most interesting thing. Tradition still gripped Italy strongly in terms of family life and social behaviour, but it was no brake at all on economic creativity. Italy industrialised itself only in the Fifties. In England, it seemed to him, tradition had little grip on how people lived but an absolute throttlehold on how they made their money.

Altogether it adds up to a cliché known as the Italian Miracle; or, on the other side, the English Catastrophe.

On my last day in Turin we drove to see a family who lived on a 'problem' housing estate called Le Vallette. Publicly-rented accommodation is rare in Turin – only six per cent of its housing stock compared to nearly forty per cent in Liverpool – but anyone reared on an English housing estate would immediately recognise its Italian equivalent. It is because of places like these, the Torinese say, that they must remove the car radio every time they leave the car, and also why the statue of King Carlo Alberto is surrounded by English graffiti. *Mods Will Never Die, Boot Boys, Stinky Rats, Skinheads*, the King waving his sword ineffectually.

Le Vallette even has a drug-treatment centre, one of four recently established in the city. The similarities with Liverpool look promising; but they are superficial. In Le Vallette the telephone kiosks work and cars, minus their radios, can be parked safely overnight in the street. People speak of the 'problem time' in the past tense. 'In the Sixties it was filled with scum from all over Italy,' said Domenico Lopreiato. 'It was tough then but it's quiet now.'

Lopreiato himself moved north from Calabria as a child, when his father got a job as a Turin garbage collector. His wife, Elisabetta, is also Calabrese. Both left school aged thirteen. Today he earns £7,000 a year as a laboratory assistant in Fiat. She is pleased to stay at home and cook and clean. They have two children and live in a two-bedroom flat in precisely the same kind of four-storey block that Liverpool is now vigorously demolishing for social as well as structural reasons. *Is it the pig who makes the sty or the sty who makes the pig?* What had improved Le Vallette?

'A lot of the scum moved out,' said Lopreiato. Others proved that they weren't scum after all. 'People have grown up, they've matured, they've *improved*.' His wife nodded. Recently they had joined a book club. Two new novels by Italo Calvino stood on the shelves next to encyclopaedias. The television was blank and silent. 'Money spent on books is money well-spent,' said Lopreiato, speaking, as it were, to camera. Their fifteen-year-old son made a face.

'He likes only English rock music,' said the mother.

'It's so hard and violent,' said the son, approvingly.

'Ah,' said the mother, 'there'll never be another group like the Beatles.'

The name evoked Liverpool in a kinder age. Or did it? Think of little Lennon being parked with his Auntie Mimi after the disappearance of his errant father, Fred; or of the Starkeys separating soon after the birth of little Ringo; or of Mrs McCartney dying and leaving a bewildered teenage son. Perhaps unhappy families created pop like the cotton fields created blues. Perhaps some other great creative wave would come from all those Liverpool homes I had seen, where the television was never switched off, where babies lay asleep on mock-leather sofas, where unmarried fathers visited at times convenient to them but inconvenient to the agents of the Department of Health and Social Security; marriage does not pay.

These homes had many knick-knacks, just as the Lopreiatos had. The eighteenth-century figurine and its offspring are an international taste. But, unlike the Lopreiato house, several also contained representations of the Pope, sometimes pictorially and sometimes as a small figure in a glass sphere filled with water. Turn the sphere upside-down and it snows, to remind His Holiness of childish somersaults performed during the cold Polish winter. But in the city of the Holy shroud the Pope was nowhere to be seen.

The Lopreiatos laughed at the idea. 'No pictures of the Pope and certainly not *this Pope*,' said Mrs Lopreiato. She made a wet clicking sound: tut-tut. She took the church seriously; it wasn't meant for travelling showmen.

Another clicking sound came when I mentioned convenience foods. Ooooh, said Mrs Lopreiato, tut-tut: 'The only thing I buy in tins is tuna fish.' Once a year, during the Tuscan tomato season, she buys one hundred kilos of tomatoes and clears the kitchen and makes a year's supply of tomato sauce, you know the kind of thing, a little olive-oil, a little salt, a little basil. That night they would sit down to some tuna and salami, green salad and tomato salad, cheese and fruit, wine. For breakfast they'd taken biscuits and milk. For lunch, *pasta al burro*, veal cutlets, more salad, more cheese, more fruit.

The talk of food made them impatient to eat. That seemed to be the trouble with these Liverpudlians, said Domenico Lopreiato: they drank but they didn't eat. He had never met Englishmen, but he had come across other curious races such as the Germans and the Dutch. Such drinking! *Stupido*, crazy people!

Naturally, Liverpool sees itself differently. In the great council suburbs of the city, where young arsonists regularly burn down vacant houses after they have nicked the copper piping, an odd sense of libel endures. A housewife said: 'I think Maggie's making a meal out of this Brussels business, don't you?' And a young man added: 'I don't think she likes us. I think she's jealous. We've always had good teams, good comedians and good rock groups in Liverpool. I think she's got it in for us.'

He spoke in a staircase littered with the broken glass of the vandal and the smoked silver paper of the heroin user; Liverpool knows them as 'druggies' or 'smack 'eads'. Some stairs had vomit stains. 'It's them druggies,' said the young man, 'they're always puking.' The staircase had no lights and several of its flats were empty and blackened by fire-raisers; but in other flats people still lived, with fragile items such as babies and bad backs. 'The lady downstairs did her back last winter,' said the young man. 'You have to be careful in the dark. She slipped on the puke.'

Only an inmate of old Bedlam could be jealous of Liverpool. But while there is little to envy, there are still things – individuals, projects, institutions – to admire; things which are a good deal better than they ought to be, given the general Liverpool condition. One of them is the girl who lives at the top of this staircase, a single mother with a fat baby and his birth certificate framed above the mantelpiece 'so I won't lose it'. Last week someone kicked her dog to death. She blamed the druggies. She had cleared them from the stairs and they had 'got back' at her. She never left the neighbourhood, Croxteth, because they might break in; she confined herself to the local chip-shop and the corner store that drew the steel shutters after six. We met her climbing the stairs with a bag of chips, grease shining through the paper, destined for the baby, who would only eat them cold.

Mrs Lopreiato would not have approved, but decency in Liverpool perseveres by its own lights. 'There's good and bad everywhere,' said the middle-aged woman, 'even in a posh place like Manchester.' She had a husband, seven children and ten grandchildren. All the adults were on the dole and none of them really imagined they would ever work. Every week she went to the Kwik-Save and bought bread, potatoes, eggs and tinned beans. Mrs Lopreiato would not have approved of that either, but the Liverpool woman took her fate cheerfully. 'We've just made our lives the best we can. We have good neighbours and that's the important thing. If we had loads of money we'd be miserable.' She laughed at the unlikely prospect.

I left the city by one of British Rail's brave new experiments, the *Merseyside Pullman*, which began to run between London and Liverpool earlier in the summer. It's a fine train –

Atkinson's Gold Medal Eau de Cologne Toilet Soap in the lavatories – but expensive; you can buy two second-class saver returns for the price of a single ticket. The staff do not expect it to last. No trade, said the steward. 'All the industry's gone, the ships and all that.' Thirty years ago on the old express, the *Red Rose*, they would serve 200 breakfasts, 200 lunches and 200 dinners. But our Pullman car was empty, save for myself and a young public-relations woman who had come up from London that morning to announce the closure of an electronics factory and the loss of 300 jobs. The story was the splash in the Liverpool *Echo*. A management spokesperson, the young woman with whom I was drinking gin-and-tonic, was quoted: changes in technology . . . no alternative . . . hope that some staff might find jobs elsewhere in the group.

The new Pullman cars have names. Ours was the *William Roscoe*, a great Liverpudlian parliamentarian, anti-slaver, poet and scholar. According to the *Dictionary of National Biography* he helped restore the Italian Renaissance to fashion throughout northern Europe. Unfortunately, he died in 1831.

We slid slowly uphill through the green slime of Edge Hill tunnel and then gathered speed through the Liverpool outlands. At Wavertree a gang of children pelted the train with stones. They missed *William Roscoe*, but hit *John Lennon*, which was travelling behind.

Is it the pig who makes the sty or the sty who makes the pig? Soon the train clattered across the Mersey and surged through the neat pastures of Cheshire: Volvo country, basil sauce country, homes with loft conversions and ceramic hobs. And the Pullman wheels replied: *the sty, the sty, the sty.*

A SEVERED HEAD

Bradford, Autumn, 1986

This autumn in Bradford it became clear that Ray Honeyford would have to go; that at some stage, late this year or early next, he would have to clear his desk and pack his briefcase and drive his small car over the Pennines home to Manchester, never to step inside his school again.

So many people wanted him to go. His employers, Bradford education authority, wanted it. His employer's employers, Bradford metropolitan district council, wanted it (even some of the council's Tories said so privately). Many of his pupil's parents wanted it. The Council for Mosques wanted it. They all agreed that Honeyford should not, more probably could not, be kicked out (even the council's leftists had dropped their 'no pay-off for racialists' line). He might leave with 'dignity' – that is, a lump sum, an enhanced pension and a form of words which implied he had quit of his own accord – but leave he must. The arguments which started eighteen months before had largely ceased to matter. Was he a racist? Did he run a good school or a bad one? The fact was that his mere presence in Bradford, or rather some of the people who supported or opposed his presence in Bradford, had begun to pose a threat to public order. As the lord mayor of Bradford put it in a public speech: 'I cannot see the unity of our great city being destroyed by one man.'

The lord mayor, Mohammed Ajeeb, paid for that remark. He is from Pakistan and a swelling correspondence told him,

not politely, to go back there. Council officials, white Englishmen, began to censor the mail so that the more maddened
insults never reached him.

Then came the football match. Bradford City were away to
Grimsby Town, whose supporters had raised money for
families of the Bradford fire disaster victims. Lord mayor
Ajeeb stepped on to the pitch to receive the cheque. As his
shoes touched the turf a cry broke out. *Honeyford, Honeyford,
Honeyford!* The lord mayor's speech could not be heard. For
possibly the first time in British history a football crowd had
invoked a school headmaster as a hero. A remarkable sight,
according to some who were present: a thousand youths with
bad CSE results applauding an absent double graduate with an
MA in socio-linguistics and an MEd in educational psychology.

Some weeks later, in October, I asked Honeyford if he felt
worried by the fuss that now surrounded him; about being
projected, as it were, as the great white hope. He said the
letters to the lord mayor and the football chanting had horrified him and naturally he condemned them, but that Ajeeb
himself was not blameless. As a former governor of the school
he had stirred up trouble for Honeyford, and Honeyford
deeply resented his statement that he, Honeyford, somehow
threatened the city's unity.

We sat in his office in Drummond Middle School, a
century-old building of yellow Yorkshire stone set on the
slopes of one of Bradford's many hills. Inside, twenty-two
teachers taught 500 children aged from nine to thirteen, almost
all of them sons and daughters of Muslim migrants from
Pakistan. Outside stood a small picket line, a dozen young
whites and Asians, some from Bradford University, some selling the *Socialist Worker*, plus a local eccentric called Geoffrey
in a monk's habit and sandals. There were no parents present.
The anti-Honeyford parents' organisation, the Drummond
Parents' Action Group, had temporarily called off their boy-
cott to allow the council to get Honeyford out by diplomatic
means. Also, television news bulletins had shown their in-
volvement in terms of angry scenes: adults trying to stop

children attending school, arguments, some physical force. It didn't look good.

'Did you hear that lot this morning?' asked Honeyford. I had. A few shouts of *Honeyford out* and *Racist out*, with some of Honeyford's own Asian boys taking part. 'It's very disturbing when you see kiddies being taught to chant slogans of that kind,' said Honeyford, speaking (as always) quietly and carefully.

His office has coloured photographs of Mecca on the wall, a few cards from well-wishers (some of them Asian), and a drawing from one of his pupils (*Welcome back Mr Honeyford*) which he received on his return to the school in September after a five-month suspension. All of these he might have pointed out to demonstrate his racial tolerance. But he didn't. Some photographs had just arrived from an old pupil – school football and cricket teams of the Thirties, boys with stiff partings and open Yorkshire stares, who, if they survived the war, must be sixty-five by now. Like all old portraits, they touched you. 'Interesting, aren't they?' said Honeyford. A sense of tradition – cultural, scholastic, national – is one of his dearest themes.

Such traditions survive in Bradford. They survive in the few remaining chimneys and the wool exchange that once set the prices for the world's worsted trade. They survive down the hill from Honeyford's school in the fine Italianate Town Hall whose niches hold statues of every English sovereign from William the Conqueror to Queen Victoria, where the frieze in the banqueting chamber shows Yorkshiremen toiling under the inscription *Labor omnia vincit*. They survive in the person of Gordon Moore, the city's chief executive, an old Bradford hand soon to retire, but determined to solve the Honeyford problem – 'the biggest this city's had to face in my twenty years here' – before he does. This is J. B. Priestley and John Braine country. Large stretches of *Room at the Top* were filmed in the Town Hall and when Moore appears in his official dress of black tails and striped trousers he looks like a man who, were you to ask for his daughter's hand in marriage, would lunch you at the Conservative Club to sound out the brass situation. Indeed Moore has tried this kind of tactic with Honeyford, so far without success: 'He's the most stubborn chap I've ever met.'

Many Bradfordians, however, come from a different tradition. For *Labor omnia vincit* substitute *There is no God but Allah and Muhammad is his prophet.* About 62,000 of the city's 464,000 citizens are non-white, the overwhelming majority of them Muslims from the Indian subcontinent. A high birthrate (Asian women in Bradford are four times more fertile than white) and a steady trickle of secondary migrants (brides, grooms, dependent relatives) add 3,000 to that number every year, to make Bradford probably the fastest growing metropolitan district in England. In ten years' time they will number 91,000; sometime in the next century their proportion of the population is expected to level out at between twenty-five and thirty per cent. In Bradford schools today almost one pupil in four is Asian. In nineteen out of seventy-three inner-city schools more than seventy per cent of the children are Asian.

They are there because twenty-five years ago Bradford's mill-owners needed cheap labour; not, contrary to the popular view, because Bradford's mill-owners chose cheap labour as a shortsighted and typically British alternative to capital investment but because Bradford's mill-owners responded to the beginnings of foreign competition by re-equipping their mills with new machinery and then found they had to work it twenty-four hours a day to recoup their outlay. The new nightshifts found few volunteers. Labour was short, mill-work was badly paid (ten per cent below the average for manufacturing industry as a whole). The mills began to recruit 7,000 miles away in the then Commonwealth country of Pakistan.

At the time, nobody in Bradford seemed to have given much thought to this process. At first the Pakistanis were seen as a temporary phenomenon – men who had come to make money and then go home – and in fact thought of themselves in this way. They rented homes which white Bradfordians did not want to rent, hid themselves on the nightshifts, and tried to save. But they did not go home. Instead wives and children came to join them. Bradford now shifted its position. The new migrant families would be 'absorbed' into the patterns of Bradford life. Over the past 150 years the wool trade has drawn migrants from almost every quarter of Europe and Bradford is proud of its tradition of assimilation. Gordon Moore, the chief executive, says: 'I suppose we thought in our stubborn Yorkshire way that we'd coped with the Poles, the Ukrainians and the German Jews. They hadn't been a problem, so why should the Asians be any different?'

Bradford was not exceptional then in its astonishing naivety, for almost all of Liberal Britain held the same view. But the new migrants *were* different – different in their food, clothes, religion and habits of family life. Most observably, they *looked* different, with a skin colour that marked them out to reluctant landladies, prejudiced employers and ignorant shopgirls. White Bradford knew them as 'blackies', though the folk in the Town Hall had learned to call them 'Asians'. But Asia is a big place, stretching from the Bosporus to the Aleutian Islands, and although Bradford does contain a few Chinese and more substantial numbers of Sikhs, Muslims and Hindus from India and Bangladesh, the bulk of Bradford's Asians come from those parts of Punjab and Kashmir which Pakistan received when India was divided in 1947 – and principally and more exactly from the middle peasantry (poor, but not the poorest of the poor) of a district called Mirpur, which lies in the foothills of the Punjab plains and where, in the early Sixties, a great dam was built which displaced 100,000 people and gave some of them enough compensation to afford the fare to Bradford.

In the context of Pakistan, Mirpur people were thought to be poorly-educated and 'traditional'. In the context of Bradford they became, according to the sociologist Verity Saifullah Khan, 'among the most encapsulated and home-orientated Asian migrants in Britain'. Even today only about half of them can read or write in their own language (though that is not quite as it sounds: they speak Punjabi but must write in Urdu, because Punjabi in its written form is available only to Sikhs, and Urdu has become the national language of Pakistan). Female emancipation is not encouraged. Religion matters deeply and has to be lived. Bradford today has thirty mosques and a new one costing three million pounds is planned for the city centre, where its 130-foot minaret will rival the Italianate turrets of the Town Hall.

In different times, Bradford might have coped. As long as the textile mills thrived, so did the nightshifts. The Pakistanis filled undesirable jobs and undesirable houses in the inner city and kept apart from white Bradford, which also kept apart from them. 'We used to think we had good race relations,' said Gordon Moore, 'when in fact we had no race relations at all.' But then, in the late Seventies, the recession suddenly caught up with the wool business. About 36,000 jobs have been lost in the past seven years, about twenty per cent of the previous total.

At the same time the city's Asians began to make their presence felt politically. All three parties, Labour, Tory and Liberal, woke up to the fact that Islam in particular was a powerful political force. 'Ethnic politics' emerged as councillors began to send out feelers to 'community leaders' (some of whom represented very small communities indeed) who might deliver the brown vote. The council and its officers began to devise palliatives for an alienated population which, if it could not be given work, might at least be kept happy by patronage and a recognition of difference. Assimilation was about to be replaced by what a Bradford council memorandum knows as the 'cultural diversity perspective'.

And then, one morning in January, 1980, a new man arrives in the middle of all this cultural, social and economic fragility. Ray Honeyford has driven his small car over the hills on the M62 from Manchester.

Honeyford is an extremely literate man. He likes to read and, more controversially, he likes to write. His small terraced house in the Manchester suburbs contains a wallful of books beside the prints by Lowry and Seurat. Ask him about race and he will produce a metaphor which compares it to the place of English landscape in eighteenth-century poetry. 'It's all around us but somehow it can't be talked about. Alexander Pope stood inside his drawing-room with his face to the fire and his back to the window. We had to wait until Wordsworth and Coleridge came along before people sat up and took notice.'

To be fair, he does not see himself as the equivalent of Wordsworth or Coleridge on the race question. His pieces in the *Salisbury Review* were hardly the equivalent of *Lyrical Ballads*, and of the most controversial even Honeyford now says: 'When you look at it, it's not much of a bloody article really.' But he does draw a parallel between himself and another piece of English literature. That morning in his school when I asked him if he would quit for the sake of his wife, his teachers, his school, for the sake of Bradford itself, he said: 'I can't help thinking of *The Winslow Boy* . . . you know, how far should a man push a principle when the lives of other people begin to be affected.'

Terence Rattigan wrote *The Winslow Boy* in 1946 and based it on a real Edwardian drama, the Archer–Shee case, where a boy faced expulsion from his naval college after being wrongly accused of stealing a five-shilling postal order. His father hired eminent counsel to clear his name, but damaged the establishment in the process.

It's not easy to see how the analogy fits – is Honeyford the wronged boy? Are his articles the postal order? – but it is somehow typical of Honeyford that, in a week when gangs of white youths are smashing Asian shopwindows in the Bradford suburbs, he should settle on a metaphor drawn from a quarrel about reputation and honour in the palmy days of Edward VII. That, I think, reveals the single most important strand in Honeyford's thinking. Like many of us, he would like to see the future not as an extension of the awful present but as a leapfrog back to the values of a less awful past. There is a happy land, far, far away. The past served Honeyford well, though his beginnings were not auspicious.

He was born one of twelve children (seven of whom did not survive infancy) in a poor home in south Manchester in 1934.

His father – 'a fairly combative, ignorant kind of Protestant', says Honeyford – had gassed lungs from the First World War and worked only occasionally as a general labourer. His mother was a devout Roman Catholic. Honeyford still practises her faith. He failed his examinations for grammar school and, aged fifteen, took a job which led to a clerkship in a little Manchester business which dealt in fancy comestibles such as glacé cherries and desiccated coconut. Ten years later, when Britain was desperately short of teachers, he seized the chance to join a two-year teacher-training course. 'A marvellous opportunity,' says Honeyford, and speaks of it with a sincere gratitude.

At night school he went on to take an MA in sociolinguistics at Manchester University and later an MEd in educational psychology at Lancaster. He married, had two children, remarried a fellow teacher, joined the British Psychological Society, and eventually became a senior master and head of English at a fairly tough school near Manchester United's football ground (Honeyford himself supports Bury FC). So when he says that 'as a member of the lower working-class myself, I have seen the instrumental value of education', it is, as his fellow students of socio-linguistics would know it, 'a felt experience'. It has not come out of a book.

His family were passionate Labour supporters and he says that he himself was 'really a Marxist at one time'. What changed him was the classroom. Honeyford says: 'My experience in school made me question my ideas. You know, the egalitarian myth. Schools are there to educate children and the aspiring working-class have little time for "progressive" ideas. I believe that children will respond to a challenge. Too many schools have fallen into the trap of patronising and entertaining.'

These ideas were already well developed when Honeyford arrived at Drummond Middle nearly six years ago. In the same year Bradford stopped its 'bussing' policy and the proportion of Asian children in the school rose from forty-five per cent to ninety-five per cent. Assimilation was out and the 'cultural diversity perspective' was in, later to be refined to the 'equality perspective', which wished schools 'to acknowledge the central, pervasive influence of racism'. Bradford council began to produce documents, some of them prolix, setting out its new aims; and Honeyford, 'robustly' in his word, began to respond in private and in public.

He made his first mark with a letter to the *Bradford Telegraph and Argus* in July 1982. A columnist had suggested that the city was giving in to blackmail (the threat of riots) by providing £100,000 for a West Indian youth club. If so, wrote Honeyford, then some public-spirited citizen should call in the district auditor. The letter was written on school notepaper and Honeyford got a warning from his employers.

Soon the real issue was addressed. In a series of initiatives Bradford education authority began to implement 'multicultural' policies in its schools. Teachers were asked

1 to seek ways of preparing all children for life in a multicultural society;
2 to counter racism and racist attitudes;
3 to build on and develop the strengths of cultural and linguistic diversity;
4 to respond sensitively to the special needs of minority groups.

Beneath the abstract nouns lay pure pragmatism. You cannot teach the school assembly to sing *Onward Christian Soldiers* when ninety per cent of the singers are Muslim. Some Islamic groups had begun to demand separate state-aided Muslim schools – an idea opposed both outside and inside the Asian community – and Bradford was determined to show that the 'educational needs of the ethnic minority can be met . . . within the framework of a common school curriculum'.

The school meals service started to serve *halal* meat, though the decision caused uproar among animal welfare groups and cost the Tory chairman of the education committee his seat. Parents were informed of their right to withdraw children from school assemblies. Physical education classes were split into boys and girls to cater to Muslim sensibilities. Girls were allowed to wear tracksuits in the gym and pyjamas during swimming lessons to ensure that modesty was preserved. Urdu was introduced to the authority's schools as a language option.

Honeyford implemented the new directives at his school, though his employers sensed reluctance. In November 1982 he wrote in the *Times Educational Supplement* that some teachers (implying himself) regarded

> ... the whole notion of multi-racial education with scepticism and even resentment. They would argue that the responsibility for the adaptations and adjustments involved in settling in a new country lies entirely with those who have come here to settle and raise families of their own free will ... They enjoy the rights and privileges of equal citizenship including immediate and unlimited access to the welfare state. In return, they are obliged to bear the corresponding duties and responsibilities of their chosen land ... Their commitment to a British education was implicit in their decision to become British citizens. Maintenance and transmission of the mother culture has nothing to do with the English secular school. If they want their children to absorb the culture of Pakistan, India, or the Caribbean, then that is an entirely private decision to be implemented by the immigrant family and community, out of school ... This is pragmatism, not prejudice, and it is based on equality. There should be a welcome for the strangers in our midst, but no attempt by the education service to confer a privileged position on this sub-culture or that.

He went on to take several swipes at current educational theory and concludes that the theories of multi-racial education, with their emphasis on 'racism' and exploitative imperial history, could well

> ... help to generate a wholly artificial and harmful colour consciousness in our schools ... By emphasising sectional interests, the multi-racialists may well be exacerbating the very problem they claim to be trying to solve – the tendency we all have whatever our colour, to adopt a narrow and rejecting view of others.

Those paragraphs are probably the clearest expression of Honeyford's position, and ironically, they came in his first article. But Honeyford did not stop writing. Another piece appeared in the *TES* in September, 1983. Then he saw an advertisement for the *Salisbury Review*, decided he liked the sound of this magazine of the 'libertarian' or 'new' Right and sent off an unsolicited manuscript. The *Review*'s editor, Roger Scruton, liked and published it and solicited further pieces; four have appeared in all.

The *Salisbury Review*, named after the Tory prime minister, sells 1,000 copies a quarter and Honeyford might have dwelt in happy obscurity within its columns had not Michael Whitaker, an officer in Bradford's education department, spotted Honeyford's second article and talked about it to a reporter on the *Yorkshire Post*. The *Post* published a story and the *Telegraph and Argus* followed with a cut-down version of the original piece, which was entitled *Education and race – an alternative view*. Three days later, in March, 1984, the newly formed Drummond Parents' Action Group held its first major meeting and passed a vote of no confidence in the headmaster. Soon Honeyford found himself embattled against both the parents group and his employers. Inspectors were sent to the school, but could find little substantial to complain of and quite a lot to commend. It was Honeyford's attitude that seemed to be the problem. 'Very authoritarian . . . grudging . . . defensive,' wrote Bradford's education advisers. 'He has clearly stated that he does not go along with much of the authority policy in that it is based on "fashion" and is following a "bandwagon".'

The clamour grew. Honeyford was suspended by the education authority and then reinstated by the school governors. He and his union won a case in the high court which made Bradford abide by the governors' decision and then had the judgment overturned in the court of appeal. His employers refused him permission to publish further articles unless they had cleared them beforehand. Honeyford complained of censorship. In large sections of the media a picture emerged of a sincere headmaster hounded because he dared to speak against fashionable orthodoxy, the victim of a curious alliance between the radical Left and far-from-radical Islamic fundamentalism upon whom the label 'racist' had been hung to foreclose debate.

That, I must admit, is the view I took to Bradford, and the city does contain evidence to substantiate it. I stood among the pickets outside Drummond Middle School one morning and chatted to a white man with a hangover. A Church of England priest approached and went through the school gates, his black robes flapping in the wind. 'There goes a proper wally,' said the man with the hangover. 'We've had the Falklands, we've run out of imperialist wars, so here's that wally from St Chad's trying to impose imperialism on the back streets of Bradford, trying to turn Muslim kids into Christian.' The vicar walked out of the school a few minutes later. Not many conversions, I remarked, could have been made to the fluid beliefs of the Anglican church in that time. 'What a wally,' said the man with the hangover, who turned out to be a race relations advisor to Bradford council.

Or, for the Orthodox Islamic perspective, there is Liaquat Hussein of the Jamiayat Tablighul Islam, a missionary college which runs Koranic classes for Bradford's Muslim children. About 2,500 children recite and memorise the Koran in Arabic for two and a half hours every day, six days a week. Hussein doesn't fear Christianity. The struggle, as he sees it, is between Islam and godlessness, which in schools takes the form of co-education, Darwinian theory, female emancipation and 'Muslim girls running away with non-Muslim boys'. He says: 'There's no such thing as freedom in religion. You have to tame yourself to a discipline. We want our children to be good Muslims whereas this society wants children to be independent in their thinking.'

A week in Bradford, however, tells you that many (and perhaps most) Asian families are neither oppressed by the views of their *imams* in the mosque nor impressed by the 'racist-out' slogans of the left. None of them I talked to chose the word 'racist' to describe Honeyford; the word has several meanings but little currency outside council documents and pressure groups. Nor are they fervent supporters of the educational theories which Honeyford opposes. In fact, being believers in discipline and authority themselves, they would probably agree with Honeyford when he says: 'They want a good sound education for their children with a moral and spiritual content and the three Rs. They want them to pass exams and get good jobs.'

Still, they do not like Honeyford. 'I don't know if he's a racist or not, but the smell I get from him is hate,' says Chowdhury M. Khan, the president of the Council for Mosques. The issue is quite simple and the word 'racist' need never occur. The written works of Honeyford have deeply offended them. Take this example from his article in the *Times Educational Supplement* of September 2, 1983:

> A figure straight out of Kipling is bearing down on me . . . His English sounds like that of Peter Sellers' Indian doctor on an off day.

This is Honeyford describing a parent. I asked him why he had written that.

He said: 'I wanted to get an impression of my school across to fellow professionals with a certain humour and honesty. The race relations lobby is a particularly humourless lot. We've developed this phoney tradition that the ethnic minority needs to be treated especially sensitively. I don't see how it's offensive. Actually, I went on to describe this man's moral courage.'

But would he describe a white parent as 'looking like Andy Capp on an off day'?

'Why not?'

I then suggested a hypothesis. If the Mancunian Honeyford had migrated to a Scottish school and then written a piece for a posh London publication in which I would identify my (Scottish) mother as 'sounding like Harry Lauder on an off day', would he blame me for wanting to kick his shins?

Honeyford paused. 'Perhaps there is a problem with English humour.'

Humour does not come into the second example. Here is

Honeyford writing in the *Salisbury Review* for winter 1984, on the country most of his pupils' parents were born in:

> Pakistan, too, is the heroin capital of the world (a fact which is now reflected in the drug problems of English cities with Asian populations).

This suggests that Asian migrants introduced the heroin habit to Britain, which is not true.

Honeyford said: 'What you have to understand is that for several years I worked as a voluntary social worker and I saw what heroin did to people. It was against that background that the remark was made.'

But why confuse Asians with his horror of heroin? Several cities with large heroin problems – Glasgow, Dublin, Liverpool – have insignificant Asian populations. How could the two things be correlated?

'I would accept that,' said Honeyford. And added mysteriously: 'But the central point is correct.'

The third example concerns West Indian single parents. Later in the same *Salisbury Review* piece, he wrote:

> It is no more than common sense that if a school contains a disproportionate number of children for whom English is a second language (true of all Asian children, even those born here), or children from homes where educational ambition and the values to support it are conspicuously absent (ie, the vast majority of West Indian homes – a disproportionate number of which are fatherless) then academic standards are bound to suffer.

Bradford has only a small number of West Indian families and Honeyford here does not seem to be writing from direct experience. But wasn't it provocative to link fatherlessness with poor academic ability? And also to imply that single parenthood was a mainly West Indian phenomenon?

Honeyford explained: 'There are three major explanations for West Indian failure in schools. The first is generic. I reject that. The second is racism in the educational process, in teachers and in the curriculum. I also reject that, because it can't explain the difference in achievement between West Indians and Asian children. The third is environment and culture. That's what I back. Very few educational theorists would quarrel with the idea that broken families have educational consequences for the child. Nobody has ever doubted this with regard to white children, so I can't see why it should not also apply to black children.'

Put like that, it seems reasonable. Shouldn't he have written it that way?

'Perhaps,' said Honeyford. 'But I see what I've written as robust and honest rather than wishing to offend. I wanted to get away from the stilted priggishness of the race relations lobby, which inhibits dialogue across the racial boundaries. But I will concede there was a certain degree of indignation in that article. I was very angry at the time.' Roger Scruton, the *Salisbury Review*'s editor, also agrees that certain phrases were 'tactless'. But he did not cut them out. And his magazine's first issue carried a piece which called for the voluntary repatriation of immigrants, which has also shaded the debate in Bradford.

The consequences are that the city's Asians believe, with some justification, that Honeyford has portrayed them as heroin pushers who talk in funny voices; whose children have caused English educational standards to decline; and who (thanks to malign or faulty translation by Urdu pamphleteers) are often 'bastards'. Naturally, they want him to go.

And the lessons? Perhaps that headmasters, men who depend on public confidence and trust, should not try to become polemical journalists. Or that, if they do, they need to find good editors. Honeyford's journalism has made him famous. He has taken tea with Mrs Thatcher, luminaries of the Right such as Scruton and Sir Alfred Sherman have befriended him. But it seems doubtful if, as Honeyford so genuinely wanted, an educational debate has been opened up. His own unhappy (but 'robust') phraseology closed it down before it could properly get started.

1986 DIARY

I suppose I should have known it would be a funny year when the Chancellor of the Exchequer's daughter showed me her walnut-oil.

'There's a marvellous wine warehouse that stocks it just around the corner,' she said. It was a large tin, big enough for several months of salad dressing. 'They're very helpful. You just ring them up and they'll deliver your order right through the picket line.'

'Really?' I said. I like Nigella. She has big dark eyes and always looks as though she needs someone tall and strong to protect her; and it seems unjust somehow to blame her for monetarism. I took down the wine warehouse's phone number. Nigella went off to her afternoon's work on the literary pages, and I settled down in front of Rupert Murdoch's new computers at my desk next to the rubber plant in the *Sunday Times* foreign department. This was Wapping in February. Outside, the cries of the pickets rose and fell:

'Scab, scab.'

'Judas.'

We had entered what Andrew Neil, the editor, used to refer to as the 'Armageddon scenario'; a military allusion the Biblical meaning of which seemed to have been forgotten. It was, in the trench-warfare sense, accurate enough. We were besieged and had dug in for the duration behind looped barbed wire and pools of mud. But we were winning. The *Sun* got out and the walnut-oil got in, and the Chancellor of the Exchequer's daughter went on correcting the galley proofs of the book reviews which were still submitted by critics, some of whom were 'on the Left' and perhaps even members of the party whose membership had been instructed to have no dealings with the workers of Wapping.

It is, of course, unfair to pick out Nigella. There were hundreds of us. But I can't forget the walnut-oil. For me it was the first clue in a trail of evidence that sealed the case against many writers of English fiction who try, in their novels, plays and films, to describe the condition of England by heightening its reality. They are wasting valuable imaginations. The reality of England is already high enough; just getting it right in simple documentary terms should earn any writer the *Prix Goncourt*. Isn't Jeffrey Archer, after all, more interesting than any character he has managed to create?

Winter

Things fell apart. I argue for going to Wapping, vote (meaninglessly) against going to Wapping, go to Wapping, leave Wapping. Others of my colleagues argue against going to Wapping, vote against going to Wapping, go to Wapping, stay in Wapping. This is a mote-and-beam situation and nobody should cast the first stone; most journalists on the *Sunday Times*, I guess, are on the proprietor's rather than the printers' side, but few of us want to be seen as greedy and opportunistic. A few people never go to Wapping and get the sack; others go determined to make it work. These occupy the moral high ground; the rest of us below are mired in contradictions.

The Parliamentary Labour Party decides it won't speak to Murdoch journalists, while the National Graphical Association, the more militant of the two unions in the dispute, permits its members to continue setting the *Sunday Times Magazine* and the *Times* supplements.

Sogat members call me a scab every time I leave or enter the gates but cannot persuade their fellow members in the provinces to stop distributing scab products. John Mortimer, sometimes mistaken for the unhumbugged voice of literal England, is in a dither. He doesn't want to cancel his contract with the paper, but at the same time would prefer if his stuff didn't appear in it. He tells Andrew Neil he would like to 'wait and see', which Neil describes as 'a very English decision' and I can see what he means. Armageddon is a cosier place if you're knitting socks at home in Blighty.

Around this time, too, I can't help noticing that some strong anti-Murdoch sentiments voiced elsewhere come from people who weren't shy to take large lump sums of Murdoch money. But perhaps I feel bitter because such large lump sums are no longer available to me.

Enter Samantha's bazookas. Two old friends, David Blundy and Jon Swain, are making their way out towards the pickets one day when they see a reminder of their days in Belfast or Beirut growling up and down inside the barbed wire entanglements. It is an armoured personnel carrier with some Royal Marines perched on top. Surely we're not now protected by the British Army on the Rhine as well as the Metropolitan Police? 'No,' says a security guard, 'it's just brought in Samantha Fox.'

It has too. The next day the *Sun* carries a page one story – *Samantha joins the War of Wapping* – which describes her 'pointing her bazookas at the enemy lines' and inspecting 'her privates' who are loyally at work in the *Sun*'s new offices. What it omits to mention is that this spectacularly-endowed daughter of the Finsbury Park working-class sat on top of her armoured car as it drove through the picket lines *twice* on the way in; the second time to recreate the fun, as it were, of the first passage, when her old fans, the sacked members of the *Sun* machine-room, jeered and whistled.

David Hare and Howard Brenton, the authors of *Pravda*, could sit together for weeks over black coffee and still fail to produce such a stunning piece of theatre, or such a ghastly metaphor for the state (or indeed State) we're in. I'm surprised it hasn't transferred to the South Bank, where it would not be believed.

Spring

The best lack all conviction. In my resignation letter to the editor I compare him to Captain Queeg in the *Caine Mutiny*. In his hurt reply he says he had 'never interferred with anything you wanted to write, or when you wanted to write it'. This is true. Remorse sets in and I apologise for the needless insult, but I still leave because the rights and wrongs of Wapping, going round in my head like a cat with a tin can tied to its tail, are beginning to drive me barmy.

The next week, in Los Angeles on an assignment for *Vanity Fair* magazine, I meet the man who took his name from Captain Queeg's ship. Michael Caine (*né* Micklewhite) bangs on about the state of the old country for a while – *New Statesman* readers may be pleased to know that he thinks Socialism and the Labour Party mean the same thing – and concludes with a line from *Pravda*, the play, which really tickled him; when Anthony Hopkins (as the Murdoch–Maxwell–Rowland proprietor) tells his eager but confused little editor: 'the trouble with you people is that you don't know what you believe'. And that, says Caine, is precisely the trouble with the British.

Well, yes and no. The beliefs of the machine-room minders on the picket line at Wapping are absolutely unequivocal; they believe they have the right to go on earning the same large wages in the same old way. Even more unrealistically, they believe they can achieve this by massing in the cold and shouting at newspaper lorries.

Belief isn't the problem here, but thought is. On a couple of Saturdays I go down to the picket line to discover what it's like to be among the jeering rather than the jeered at. White middle-aged men with semi-detacheds in Essex mill about on the pavement, muttering about their new-found disenchantment with the police (inside Wapping the workers who have dispossessed them are young, often female and some-times black, and too young ever to have been enchanted with the police who protect them).

I meet a compositor who used to work on the *Sunday Times* literary pages. I say he must be pleased that two of the journalists he worked with, Claire Tomalin and Sean French, are among the few who refused to cross a picket line. He is, he says, and then adds wistfully of the Chancellor of the Exchequer's daughter: 'That Nigella, she's a bold one. She comes through those picket lines as calm as you like.'

He thinks for a moment: 'It must be in the breeding.'

Summer

We're househunting. We get to know estate agents, sometimes more quickly and intimately than we'd reckoned on:

'Hi Ian, it's Mick here from the Stoke Newington office.'

Mick is one of the new breed. Last month he was selling insurance, this month he's selling houses. He doesn't hold with all this crap about estate agents being a profession, like doctors or the law; he's into selling houses and these days in the North London market they move very fast. In a way, I like his attitude. Estate agents are middle men in the purest sense, unfettered by responsibility, whose skill lies in introducing buyers to sellers. Why pretend there is more to it?

One day Mick arrives at the door in his yellow jeep with the slogan *The Trendiest Estate Agent in The World* painted on its side.

'Hi Ian.'

'Hi Mick.'

He's come to give our house the once-over and trots up and down the stairs with a sound-meter gadget which measures room sizes. Then he speaks into a tape-recorder; he has more electronic equipment as a house agent than I do as a reporter.

'Cornicing in front room. Original working fireplace. Patio. Garden laid to lawn.'

We have a cup of tea. Who, I wonder, is buying all these
£80,000 flats in Stoke Newington?

'Yuppies.'

Well of course. I've seen the word in the Sunday newspapers
now for years, but the only working definition I have for
them is as consumers, with their infamous fixation on Filo-
faxes and Perrier water. Mick's definition cuts out the frills.
'They're in their early twenties, they're earning maybe twenty
to twenty-five thousand a year, they've no trouble getting a
hundred per cent mortgage equal to three times their salary,
they work in video, advertising or in the City and the media.'
He likes them; they've never bought property before and they
are 'very malleable', easy to sell to. 'Usually you only show
them two properties. Let them see the worst one first and
they'll usually take the second.'

Later in the summer, politely tapping the walls in other
people's houses, I think I begin to recognise the type. They
have very pretty homes in pastel shades, where dado rails
have been painstakingly restored and fireplaces, bought from
shops with names like Amazing Grates, put back. This and
the mortgage payments have left their owners with very little
money. Often a stereo is their most striking piece of furniture;
very rarely there are books.

Autumn

The richer the society, the fewer people smoke. In California,
smoking is now regarded as a weirdly old-fashioned activity,
on a par with medieval flagellation or electronic trams. Things
are not much better (or worse) in New York. Pathetically, I
still smoke, and when Tina Brown, the Editor of *Vanity Fair*,
invites me to lunch at the Four Seasons restaurant I am filled
with foreboding.

The Four Seasons is rather a grand place, in fact it features
as the cover story in that week's *New York Magazine* as the
true home of the power-lunch. Tobacco and power used to be
inseparable (as Stanley Baldwin used to say on the tobacco

tin: 'My thoughts grow in the aroma of Presbyterian Mixture'), but now power combines most potently with health. Not only are there no smoking lunchers at the Four Seasons, there seem to be very few drinking lunchers either. The atmosphere is Alpine in its clarity, the ashtrays merely decorative objects like spittoons. Occasionally ice tinkles in a water glass. After the fresh raspberries I allow myself one Silk Cut, feeling rather like H.M. Bateman's man who dared to throw a snowball at St Moritz.

Winter

Bradford is not a rich city, though it once was, and matches are scratched soon after most people meet one another. Here the Perrier and Filofax culture has not caught on, despite the chastisements of Mrs Edwina Currie. When she arrives to address a meeting at Hebden Bridge she is greeted by members of the local Labour Party, who, to mock her idea of the North, have dressed up in shawls and flat caps. Also, according to the *Yorkshire Post*, they hand her a pound of tripe. But I wonder if Mrs Currie is so far wrong? My nights out in Bradford are great fun but punishing: twenty cigarettes, six pints of Guinness, a prawn biryani, five poppadums, a packet of dry-roasted peanuts. A year of evenings like this and I'd be dead.

The Oldham Two are celebrating. Actually they used to be the Oldham Nine, nine people who had been arrested while trying to disrupt a National Front meeting in Oldham, but the magistrate has dismissed charges against seven of them. Now they are the Oldham Zero; that morning the court has dismissed charges against the rest. We go to a pub that doesn't close till one in the morning. It is dangerously manic, like Alan Bleasdale's pub in *The Boys From the Blackstuff*, and I expect the barman to call the Last Trump rather than last orders. Then we go for a curry, then to a club where they play soul music and I can't hear what the antifascist from the private detective agency is trying to tell me.

'There'll be civil war with the whites,' says an Asian boy. 'I don't care if I die.'

A drunk girl wants to buy a cigarette from me. 'Just have it,' I say.

'No, I want to buy it, you fucker.'

One of the Oldham Zeroes kindly offers me a lift back to the hotel. He engages first gear and drives straight into a lamp post. I walk down the hill alone, past the sites of textile factories and the Asian corner stores. Eventually, close to the hotel, I reach estate agent territory. Their office windows are still lit. I look inside and make calculations. In January this year our little house in London was worth the equivalent of 7.5 similarly terraced houses in Bradford. This month, December, it could buy ten of them.

Perhaps, in that statistic, there lies the real story of the year: and perhaps, soon, English fictionalists will take lessons from old realists such as Bennett and Galsworthy and restore property closer to the centre of the English novel. Together with Samantha's bazookas and walnut-oil, it is, after all, so very close to all our hearts.